TIBET
THE LAND
AND THE PEOPLE

Written by Tiley Chodag
Translated by W. Tailing

NEW WORLD PRESS
BEIJING, CHINA

First Edition 1988

Cover · Design by Richard J. Hentz

ISBN   7-80005-072-6

Published by
NEW WORLD PRESS
24 Baiwanzhuang Road, Beijing.

Printed by
Foreign Languages Printing House
19 West Chegongzhuang Road, Beijing.

Distributed by
China International Book Trading Corporation
(Guoji Shudian)
P.O. Box 399, Beijing, China

Printed in the People's Republic of China

TO MY READERS ᕮᓬᕮᓬᕮᓬᕮᓬᕮᓬᕮᓬ

I am not a writer but an editor by profession. Over the past twenty years, more than forty books I edited have been published. Meanwhile, I devoted my spare-time to writing articles and essays about Tibetan folk-lore and to the translations of Tibetan classics, which had aroused much interest.

However, over these years, I have been thinking of writing a book specifically introducing the land and people of Tibet. It is that I have come across a kind of misunderstanding of Tibet among friends at home and abroad. Many people think it an out-of-the-place barren land isolated from the outside world and us Tibetans savagery and barbarous. As a Tibetan myself, I cannot ignore such misunderstanding and thus the desire of writing a book about Tibet became stronger and stronger.

Nevertheless, the book is by no means produced merely on the spur of the moment but through a sustained and cumulative effort of over twenty years of material collecting and research. To complete this project, I made investigation trips all over Tibet, collecting folk tales and legends, looking into historical records and books, interviewing with many people. It is thus that the book about Tibet was formed. It includes scenery description, local environment and customs, historical research and abundant myths and legends. The book is not in the form of textual research by scholars, nor visions and imaginations conjured up by people who have poor knowledge about Tibet, but it is the Tibet in the eyes of an ordinary Tibetan who had a passion for his native land and his fellow people.

I heartily hope my readers enjoy the book. Nothing will please me more than to have my readers acquire through the book a true knowledge of this nationality both its long history and brilliant culture.

CONTENTS 𒊹𒊹𒊹𒊹𒊹𒊹𒊹𒊹𒊹

1 己Ƨ己Ƨ己Ƨ己Ƨ己Ƨ己Ƨ己Ƨ己Ƨ己Ƨ己Ƨ己

AN ENCHANTING LAND

The legend of how the sea became land

A many-faceted land
rich natural resources

A nationality with a long history

Monkey to man the legend of the origins of the
Tibetan people

The first King

The beginning of agriculture and animal husbandry

The rise and fall of the tubo dynasty

The cultural exchanges between the Han people and
the Tibetans

The Legend of How the Sea Became Land

Was the Tibetan plateau, known as "the roof of the world," once really a great boundless sea? Modern science says it was, otherwise no one would have ever believed it. However, in the Tibetan's widespread folklore there is a legend about the Himalayas which tells just such a story.

Once upon a time the land of Tibet was a great boundless sea whose foaming waves crashed onto the beach densely covered with pines, hemlocks and palms. Above the forest, mountain ranges rose one upon another, and wisps of clouds rolled over the horizon. Within the forest, exotic flowers and grasses grew in profusion, deer and antelopes galloped in herds, and rhinoceroses roamed slowly in small groups, leisurely ambling to the water's edge to drink. Cuckoos, thrushes and larks hopped to and fro on treetops, warbling harmoniously, and hares gambolled in the green meadows. Such was the charming picture of peace and tranquillity!

But one day, a giant five-headed poisonous dragon suddenly rose up from the sea. It threw the forest into confusion, stirred bottomless waves, and destroyed the flowers, plants and trees. The birds and animals dwelling in the forest thought catastrophe had befallen them. They fled to the east but the eastern forest had toppled over and the green meadows were flooded. They swarmed back to the west, but the west, too, was a world of angry waves. As the animals and birds prepared to meet their doom, suddenly over the sea there appeared a five-coloured cloud which transformed itself into the Five Sister Dakinis. Alighting on the beach, the Dakinis used their supernatural power to subdue the five-headed poisonous dragon. Once the demon was defeated, the great sea became calm again, and the deer, antelopes, monkeys, hares and birds that lived in the forest prostrated themselves before the Dakinis and expressed their gratitude to their saviours.

As the Dakinis prepared to take their leave for heaven, the animals and birds begged them to stay and favour them with their presence. Out of compassion, the Five Sister Dakinis agreed to remain and share their peaceful days with the forest dwellers. The Dakinis then ordered the sea to retreat. As a consequence, the east changed into a dense forest, the west became a boundless expanse of fertile soil, the south was transformed into a garden of flourishing flowers and grasses, and the north turned into an endless open grassland. The Five Sister Dakinis next transformed themselves into the five main peaks of the Himalayan Range: Tashi Tseringma (Auspicious Longevity Goddess), Tingki Shalsangma (Blue Joyful Goddess), Miyo Losangma (Constant Benevolent Goddess), Chopen Dinsangma (Harmonious-Voiced Goddess), and Tadkar Dosangma (Reliable Passionate Goddess) all of which stand towering at the south-west border of Tibet in defense of the happy paradise. The main peak Tingki Shalsangma is now known as Mt. Qomolangma (Mt. Everest) and is the highest peak in the world, beloved by the local people as the "Goddess Peak."

This folk legend reflects the fact that the Tibetan plateau was originally a boundless sea which later gradually changed into dry land. Recent fossil finds and geological investigations have proved beyond doubt the origins of the Tibetan plateau. In 1964 and 1966 two ichthyosaurs were discovered in the Hima-

3

layas and in Nyalam Dzong, dating back 180 million years. These ten-metre-long prehistoric fish lived at the bottom of a great sea which then covered what is now the Tibetan plateau, thus verifying the old legend.

But the change from sea to dry land did not happen overnight. Dinosaur fossils have also been unearthed in the Tamala Pass which prove that sixty or seventy million years ago the Tibetan region was a hot, humid swampy land with lush vegetation. Over the millenia, the swamps gradually dried up and the earth's crust rose bit by bit, making life impossible for the dinosaurs which eventually died out.

Even today this gradual movement of the earth's crust continues, and the Tibetan plateau is calculated to be still growing at a rate of one or two centimetres a year.

A Many-Faceted Land

Many people, when the word "Tibet" is mentioned, often conjure up the image of a world of ice and snow, a barren wilderness, a high mountainous region short of oxygen, so on and so forth. In fact, the Tibetan plateau presents a rich appearance of gorgeous colour.

Lofty mountains there are, imposing and magnificent. Tibet's southern border adjoining India, Nepal, Bhutan and Sikkim is the Himalaya Range, the highest mountain range in the world, stretching 2,400 kilometres in length. The famous Mt. Qomolangma (Mt. Everest) and Shisha Pangma are the highest peaks of this mountain range. The Himalayas and the Gangdise Range, which both have an average altitude of 6,000 metres above sea level, run parallel to one another across the south-western part of Tibet. To the north lies the Nyanchen Tanglha range which joins Qinghai and Tibet. Though it has an average altitude of "only" 4,500 metres above sea level, owing to its northerly aspect and everlasting winter, it possesses a number of majestic glaciers. To the east lie unique mountain ranges which are the only ones in the world to run north and south. Green open grassland lies to the north of the plateau. Tended by fierce-looking mounted herdsmen, millions of yaks and sheep graze on these vast pasturelands of northern Tibet, which is one of the five major pastoral areas in China.

Metok, Zayul, Lekpo and Dam, known as the "rongyul" (deep valleys) of Tibet, offer another kind of beautiful scenery. The climate in these regions is mild with clearly defined seasons, and exotic flowers and rare grasses grow everywhere.

The plateau also has the highest rivers in the world. The famous Tsangpo River (Brahmaputra), 1,787 kilometres long, winds like a giant silvery dragon from its source on the north side of the Himalayas where the altitude reaches 5,300 metres above sea level, until it empties into the Bay of Bengal. In its lower reaches, as it passes through the Metok region, it makes a famous ninety degree bend, creating a most magnificent and breathtaking scene. In the east, the Zachu River (Mekong), 4,500 kilometres in total length, roars along its narrow, rocky course through high mountains and deep valleys. In addition, the rivers Gyamo Ngulchu, Yangze, Lhasa Kyichu, Gyantse Nyangchu and Kongpo Nyangchu, are dispersed over the whole of Tibet. Their waterpower resources are the foremost in the country.

Tibet possesses lakes in plenty. Byang Namtso, Yamdok Tso, Siling Tso and Tso Mapham are the four largest lakes of the plateau. These lakes contain fish in plenty and lap up against fine pasturelands. Even those airy mountain regions covered with snow and ice all the year round possess attractions in the form of marvelous crystal palaces, ice-pillar forests and ice-mushrooms.

The grasslands of northern Tibet, deep valleys of southern Tibet, mountain ranges of the Himalayas, highlands of western Tibet and three river valleys of eastern Tibet, are Tibet's natural divisions. According to the traditional division of the past the whole of Tibet once was divided into three regions: the Upper Three Regions of Ngari, the Central Four Regions of U and Tsang and the Lower Six Plateaus of Domme (Qinghai) and Kham. These divisions still hold to this day.

Rich Natural Resources

As befits a land with such varied geographical features and landforms, Tibet is very rich in animals, plants, waterpower, geothermal and mineral resources.

Primaeval forests grow in every corner of Tibet. The forest zone of eastern Tibet joins the forests of the Yunnan-Guizhou Plateau in a single expanse, forming the major timber producing region of Tibet, while to the south, over 90 percent of the area of Zayul, Miling and Metok Counties (Dzongs) is covered with forest. Tibet is the third biggest forest zone of China with her great reserve of timber, and provides ample resources for the development of the country as a whole.

As one might expect, the forests are alive with various wild animals such as tigers, leopards, bears, gorillas, wild yaks, wild asses, apes, lynxes, antelopes, foxes, wolves, deer, musk deer, etc., while the vast stretches of prairie and rich pastureland support yaks and sheep as well as goats, "zo' (offspring of a bull and a female yak), donkeys, horses and cattle. Wild animals provide Tibet with a rich source of precious medicinal materials such as musk, pilose antlers, gall-bladders of bears, etc., whereas the pasturelands supply wool, yak hair, and raw hides in great quantities to the nation. The wide variety of wild plants which grow in the primaeval forests has not yet been fully investigated and classified, but, medicinal herbs such as Chinese caterpillar fungus, fritillary bulb (fritillaria thunbergu), Chinese angelica, rhizome of Chinese gold-thread (Coptis chinensis), rhizome of chuanxiong (Ligusticum wallichu), Rheum officinale, Vladirimia souliei, Chinese ephidra, and Mentha haplocalyx, etc., have been gathered and used for a long time.

The narrow valleys of southern Tibet and the river basins of the Yangtze, Zachu (Mekong) and Gyamo Ngulchu rivers are the major agricultural areas of Tibet. Crops include barley, wheat, beans, maize, potatoes, and rapeseed, and in Metok and Zayul, rice and peanuts are grown too. Cash crops such as tea, tobacco, walnuts and chilli are grown in many regions, while apples, peaches, oranges, bananas, pears and water melons which were introduced during the last twenty years have shown increasing yields every year. Over forty species of vegetables are grown in Lhasa, Chamdo, Lhoka and Shigatse, and many of the government headquarters and industrial enterprises are partly self-sufficient in vegetables.

According to initial investigation and exploration by the Chinese Academy of Sciences and Tibetan departments concerned with geology, Tibet is extremely rich in ferrous metals, nonferrous metals, and non-metal deposits. What is potentially the largest copper mine in Asia lies hidden under the Tibetan plateau.

Tibet also has other mines producing iron, manganese, chromium, zinc, copper, antimony, mercury, coal, oil shale, arsenic, vitriol, alkali, borax, mica, mirabilite, sulphur, rock crystal, graphite, azurite, barite, magnitite and talcum.

Tibet is also famous for its hydroelectric potential. The plateau's swarming mountain ranges and the steepness of its geographical features cause rivers to drop sharply; for example, the overall drop of the Tsangpo River (Brahmaputra) is more than 5,000 metres. Moreover, the countless mountains and lakes scattered over the plateau mean that Tibet's hydroelectric potential is one-fifth that of the whole nation.

Tibet is gifted by Nature with geothermal heat, too. The geothermal power station at Yangpachen has already reached the stage of using steam on a small scale to produce electricity. Hot springs scattered all over the plateau are another natural resource of Tibet; Ngari alone has a belt of forty-five. They provide a natural hot water supply as well as having curative properties, and can also be used for irrigation purposes.

A Nationality with a Long History

Like the other major nationalities of China, Tibetans possess a long history and a well-developed culture. Since ancient times, the industrious, courageous, intelligent and honest people of Tibet, living in compact communities on the Qinghai-Tibet Plateau, together with other nationalities, have jointly opened up this extensive land of mountains and rivers. Tibet's development has followed its own course, creating a history brilliant beyond question.

Monkey to Man: Origins of the Tibetan People

Where did the Tibetans originate? Over the years many different explanations have circulated as to the origins of the Tibetan people. Some say they came from India, and are the descendants of the Sakya race; others say they came from the Malay Peninsula, which explains why they resemble the Malays in facial appearance. Some even claim the Jang people are their ancestors; while yet others hold that before the Yellow Emperor entered the Central Plains, he established his capital at Kunlun, and in the course of his journey to the Central Plains a branch of his community was left behind, which is said to be the Tibetan people of today.

There are also people who claim the Tibetan language belongs to the Burmo-Tibetan language family, therefore it is possible that the Tibetans came from Burma. With so many conflicting hypotheses, it is hard to know which is correct. But let us first take a look at the following interesting myth taken from the Tibetan history book *A Mirror of the Genealogy of Kings*.

Avalokitesvara, the Lord of Mercy living on Mt. Potala, ordained as a disciple a monkey who was a reincarnation of a celestial being, and ordered him to travel from the South Sea to the Land of Snows to do a retreat in seclusion there.

Arriving at a cave in the Yarlung valley, the monkey concentrated his mind on the merciful nature of a Bodhisattva. While he was deep in meditation, an ogress appeared to him from the mountains and tempted him with all sorts of passions, urging him openly, "Let us be united!" At first the monkey replied, "I am still a disciple of Avalokitesvara. In obedience to his command I have come here to meditate, and I would be breaking my religious vows if we were to be united."

"If you refuse I shall have no alternative but to kill myself," said the ogress cunningly. "Condemned by the karma of my previous life, I was born an ogress. We are bound by fate, and now that I have found you, I shall make you my beloved. If you refuse to marry me, my fate will bind me to become the wife of an ogre in the future. If this comes to pass I will be the cause of thousands of deaths, and will also give birth to countless ogre children and grandchildren. Then the Land of Snows will become nothing but a world of ogres, and more lives will be lost. Thus I hope you will consent to my request."

On hearing these words, the monkey, being a Bodhisattva who had descended to the material world, murmured to himself, "If I were to be united with her, I would have to break my religious vow; but if I were to refuse her request, I would be committing a great sin." At this thought, the monkey, turned a somersault, and then made his way to Mt. Potala to ask Avalokitesvara what he should do. Avalokitesvara pondered deeply and then said, "This is the will of heaven; it is a good omen. If you unite with the ogress, mankind will multiply in the Land of Snows. This would be a deed of great virtue." Being a Boddhisattva, the monkey shouldered his responsibility bravely and married the ogress, who later gave birth to six monkey offspring. The monkey took the young ones to a forest where fruit grew in abundance and left them to live on their own.

Three years later the father monkey paid a visit to the young monkeys, and saw that they had increased to five hundred. By this time, the forest fruits were steadily dwindling and were on the verge of extinction. At the sight of their father, the young monkeys stretched out their paws with a look of misery and shouted in chorus: "What are we to eat in the future?" The father monkey, when he saw this, said to himself, "It is all because of Avalokitesvara's command that I have so many descendants. This has given me a terrific headache. I had better go once again to ask Her for further instructions." So thinking he immediately left for Mt. Potala to ask the Sage's advice.

"I will feed your descendants," Avalokitesvara assured him. At his Master's command, the monkey left for Mt. Sumeru (Mt. Rirab), and returned with five different kinds of wild grain seeds, which, when scattered on the unploughed earth, eventually yielded forth various kinds of grains. The father money then bade farewell to the young monkeys and returned to his cave.

As the young monkeys were supplied with abundant provision, their tails gradually became shorter and shorter, their tongues became accustomed to human speech, and in the end they became human beings. These were said to be the ancestors of the inhabitants of the Land of Snows.

The tale of the monkey's transformation into man is not only widespread among Tibetans but written records of it can also be found in ancient scriptures, and paintings of the ancient myth can be seen on the walls of the Potala Palace and Norbu Lingka (the Summer Palace). According to myth, the cave in which the monkeys lived is said to be on Mt. Gongpori near Tsetang. "Tsetang" which means "playground" got its name because it was where the young monkeys had played. According to the myth the first barley field was said to have been put under cultivation at a place called Zara, (present-day Zara Village), about two kilometres distance from Tsetang. Ever since then, when the sowing season comes around each year, folk visit this place and gather a handful of "sacred earth" in the hope that their ancestors will bless them with a bumper harvest.

The myth shows that man has inhabited the Yarlung valley since the earliest times. The first inhabitants were hunter-gatherers, but in time they gradually acquired the art of making implements such as bows, arrows, axes, arrow-heads, armour and shields, and grouped themselves into tribes.

The remains discovered in Nyingtri, Metok, Tingri and Karo (in Chamdo) over the last twenty years fit in with the myth. These remains tell us man had been living on the Tibetan plateau since earliest times. Later, the Jang people of Gansu and Qinghai moved southwest and mixed with the aborigines of Tibet, resulting in the "Bod" people or Tibetans. When Songtsan Gampo founded the powerful Tubo Dynasty, he and his later descendants adopted a series of measures for strengthening the country and brought the different tribes living in the border regions of Sichuan, Qinghai, Gansu and Yunnan under Tibetan control by armed force. Over the centuries, these different peoples merged and developed into one single nationality, the Tibetans.

The First King

Tibet's recorded history only goes back a mere 1,300 years, as prior to that time the Tibetans had no script. But existing records make mention of earlier history, and together with oral traditions and inscriptions from the Yin Dynasty (16th - 11th centuries BC) and Zhou Dynasty (11th century - 221 BC) provide evidence of human activity on the Tibetan plateau from a very early stage in history.

After their evolution from the monkey, the primitive people of the Land of Snows at first lived by gathering wild berries and fruit. Gradually they learned to fashion bows, arrows, knives and axes to protect themselves from wild beasts, and developed fishing and hunting skills. In other words, they were already engaged in nomadic production and by degrees a rudimentary form of agriculture was starting to emerge.

Their beliefs and social structure at that time were moulded by the extremely backward mode of production. In those days, people did not understand natural phenomena and changes such as the weather, seasons, birth and death, and so they worshipped Nature, believing all earthly things were imbued with "spirits." This state of animism is called the period of primitive Bonism by Tibetan scholars. Tribes had not yet taken shape in this society and the people lived in simple communities, fixed by their geographical environment, which had no strict organization but were led by wise elders.

How then did the first tribe come into being? This forms the subject of another interesting folk legend. The story goes that the herdsmen of the Yarlung valley one day saw a fine youth on Mt. Tsantang Goshi. When they approached him, they discovered the young man spoke a different dialect from the native inhabitants. The herdsmen did not know what should be done with the stranger, and sent messengers back to explain the situation to the rest of the community. The elders then sent twelve intelligent men to the mountain to ask the young man where he had come from. But the youth merely pointed to the sky. Believing the stranger must have descended from heaven, the twelve rejoiced and proclaimed him a "heavenly son." The leader then offered to carry the "heavenly son," and amidst rejoicing and embraces, he was brought down the mountain seated on the leader's shoulders. The community rushed forward to greet this intelligent, handsome youth from heaven and made him the chieftain of the tribe as an honour. Thus the young man became the first leader of a tribe which later became known as the Tubo tribe.

This event is historically said to have taken place in the year 237 BC. The youth was ceremoniously given the name Nyatri Tsanpo, "the chieftain seated on the throne of a neck," referring to the manner in which he was carried down the mountain, so from then on the Tibetan kings were known as "tsanpos." Ancient Bon records say that Nyatri Tsanpo, the first chieftain of the Tubo tribe, was a son of the Thirteenth Generation of the Illumined Heaven who had descended to the mortal world, and so he was recognised as king by both the clans and the adherents of Bon. Thirty-two generations after Nyatri Tsanpo, the Tubo Dynasty was founded by his descendants.

With the emergence of kings, royal palaces began to be built. In fact, the first palaces were merely ordinary houses, and to this day the ruins of a house known as the Yumbulagang can still be seen thirty kilometres from Tsetang. According to Tibetan legend, this was the first royal palace built especially for Nyatri Tsanpo the Heavenly Son. There are two different interpretation of the Yumbulagang; one goes that "Yumba" means "mother and son" while "lagang" refers to "palace." Thus Yumbulagang is the Palace of Mother and Son. Another interpretation goes because the Yumbulagang or the Red Willow Palace was built by the ancient Tubo king, Nyatri Tsanpo, on a hillside in Yarlung, Lhoka. On this slope red willows grew from which the name of the palace was derived.

Seven generations after Nyatri Tsanpo, there was a king named Drigum Tsanpo. His name, given to him by his grandmother, meant "death by a sword" and true to his name, Drigum Tsanpo met his death at the hands of one of his subjects named Lo-ngam Dazi. After murdering Drigum Tsanpo by deception, the assassin drove the queen into the mountains to tend sheep, took the princess for his wife by force, sent the three princes into exile to the Kongpo and Bomi regions, and made himself chief of the tribe. Later, Chatri, the second son of Drigum Tsanpo, recruited some troops and staged a comeback. After defeating Lo-ngam, he recaptured the throne and held a grand funeral for his father, erecting a mausoleum to his memory. Even from this time, interment began to appear in Tibet.

From the story of Drigum Tsanpo it is clear that the Tubo tribe of the Yarlung valley had already grown quite powerful by the ninth generation (after 100 AD). With the economic progress, animal husbandry was no longer the only form of production. Agriculture and handicrafts began to rise. The gradual improvement of the tools resulted in the increase of productivity. The private property had developed in such a degree that the struggle for power and property often arose. Tobu Society, in fact, had changed from a patriarchal clan system to paternalist ruling society.

The Beginning of Agriculture and Animal Husbandry

When Chatri assumed the kingship, he changed

his name to Pude Gongyal and took up residence in Chingwar Taktse (on the border of present-day Chongye Dzong) where he built his Chingwar Taktse palace. Pude Gongyal paid great attention to the development of agriculture and animal husbandry. In cultivation, the use of wooden ploughs was introduced, domestic beasts were used to reclaim the plains, while water channels were dug to irrigate the fields. Advances in animal husbandry, too, were notable, with the practice of storing fodder for cattle, mules, and "zo" (offspring of a bull and a female yak) already in evidence.

A major figure in this development was the first of the Seven Wise Men, Rulekye, Pude Gongyal's chief minister. As Tubo society developed from a tribal community to a dynasty over a period of several hundred years, outstanding men of great ability and wisdom appeared in Tibet, known as the Seven Wise Men of the Tubos. Records differ, but the account given here follows *The History of the Great Tubo* written by the great lotsava (translator) Taktsang Shirap Rinchen Gyaltsan. Rulekye taught the people how to cut grass in summertime and store it for winter fodder, and also devised methods of land reclamation. It is said that the first piece of arable land at Zara, near Tsetang was put under the plough in his time. This new leap forward in agriculture marked the change from hunting and gathering to an agricultural society. Pude Gongyal gave Rulekye a senior position, showing the importance he attached to the development of production which played a positive role in accelerating Tibet's social development.

During the time of the tenth Tsanpo, Esholek, social development took another step forward. One of his ministers, Lhabu Gokar, another of the Seven Wise

Men, was the first person to use the unit "dor" to calculate one day's ploughing by a pair of oxen as a measuring unit of area for cultivated land, thus introducing the concept of measurement. Lhabu Gokar also taught the people how to channel mountain streams into lower regions so as to create paddy fields.

The Tubo economy continued to develop apace up to the reign of the twenty-eighth Tubo Tsanpo, Lhato-Thori Nyantsan, by which time the tribe had become a well-trained, powerful army, now and then extending its territory. Growing contacts with the outside world also facilitated the development of Tubo civilization.

The Rise and Fall of the Tubo Dynasty

By the sixth century, the Tubo tribe had already developed into a slave society and was ruled by the thirty-first Tsanpo, Takri Nyansik. The Tubos had by this time amassed considerable economic and political might, and Takri Nyansik's time was spent in preparation for the establishment of a royal dynasty. The third of the Seven Wise Men, Ngornang Tsanmang, made his appearance as production developed to a higher stage. The minister of Takri Nyansik, his main contributions were teaching the people how to prepare charcoal for use in smelting metals, the introduction of silver, copper and iron smelting, the invention of bridge construction, and in agriculture, the invention of harnessing oxen with wooden yokes so as to make use of animal force. With the improvement of implements and the use of metal in weaponry along with the development of the economy, the Tubo tribe became a threat to the security of nearby tribes. In some cases, the subjects of certain tribes in fear of the Tubo's strength came to surrender in secrecy. The most well-known of these plots was the famous conquest of the Sumba people by the Sumba ministers Nyang Tseng-gu and Wa Yitsal who secretly made their way to Chingwar Taktse in the Yarlung valley and brought the Sumba tribe into an alliance with Takri Nyansik.

Takri Nyansik was succeeded by his son Namri Songtsan, the thirty-second Tsanpo, who was desirous of conquering the nearby tribes with all speed. He set out to the north with his troops to extend his territory, but while he was meeting with success in his expansion campaign, trouble arose within the Tubo tribe itself. Consequently, Namri Songtsan was poisoned by his own former nobles, and thus the weighty burden of unifying the plateau fell on the shoulders of his son, Songtsan Gampo.

Songtsan Gampo became the thirty-third Tsanpo of the Tubo tribe at the age of thirteen. A promising youth, he had some powerful ministers as advisors. His first task was to deal with internal disturbances and consolidate his royal power. He moved his capital to Lhasa, and then developed the economy, promulgated laws, systematised the army, divided the area under his control into military and administrative areas, appointed officials and sent out generals to take charge of other tribes, and established the centralised political power of the Tubo slave owners. Thus appeared the first dynasty in Tibetan history the Tubo Dynasty.

Songtsan Gampo pacified the whole of Tibet and developed agriculture and animal husbandry. Livestock numbers increased, with yaks and sheep scattered all over the open country, and cultivated land flourished, as methods for preventing drought and draining out waterlogged fields were introduced.

One of Songtsan Gampo's ministers called Thonmi

Sambhota took his place in Tubo history as the fourth of the Seven Wise Men. Together with a group of followers, he set off for India to study Sanskrit. The founder of the Tibetan script, Thonmi Sambhota created an alphabet of thirty consonants and four vowels for recording the Tibetan language. This meant that Tibetan history could be written down for the first time, and it greatly accelerated the development of culture and art. For this invaluable contribution, Thonmi Sambhota's name will never be forgotten.

The fifth of the Wise Men was a minister named Trisang Yangtonyak who appeared in 754 AD at the time of Tride Tsugtan's reign. His main contributions were the standardization of weights and measures, the introduction of exchange through money and the development of trade. In 787 AD, during Trisong Detsan's reign, Trisang Yangtonyak took charge of the construction and religious affairs of the Samye Monastery and sent seven children of wealthy families to become monks. Trisong Detsan also invited eminent monks from inland China and India to the Samye Monastery to preach Buddhist doctrine and translate Buddhist scriptures, thus facilitating the spread of Buddhism. At this time, another Wise Man, Go Trisang Yaplhak came to the fore. He was renowned for moving the people from the hills to the plains, reclaiming the barren lands that surrounded the new settlements and introducing the channelling of mountain brooks to the plains for irrigation. These measures formed the foundation of Tibet's village structure which has survived up to the present.

The seventh Wise Man was Taktsap Dongsik, a minister of Tride Songtsan in the late eighth century. He promoted the idea of making a distinction between friends and foes: enemies were to be thoroughly investigated and beaten ruthlessly, but if it was a friend who had committed a wrongdoing, advice should be given and fines imposed, but cruelty should be avoided.

Songtsan Gampo, the founder of the Tubo Dynasty, contributed to the spread of Buddhism, which explains why Buddhism managed to gain ground at such speed. During the reign of Tritsug Detsan, the Tsanpo himself not only took the lead by becoming a Buddhist, but had monasteries built in many places, and promulgated laws which required each family to provide one monk, and which laid down that every seven households should support one monk. In addition, panditas (pundits) from neighbouring countries were invited to participate in the translation of Buddhist scriptures.

The rapid rise of Buddhism and the growing power of the monastic community aroused dissatisfaction among the Tubo nobles and court officials. Tritsug Detsan was subsequently murdered by treacherous court officials and political power fell into the hands of the Tsanpo's brother, Lang Darma. Ridding himself of all those who opposed him, Lang Darma widely suppressed Buddhism and persecuted its adherents, an act which earned him the deep hatred of the Buddhists and the populace. Eventually Lang Darma was assassinated by an arrow secretly shot by a Buddhist monk. The nobles' support was divided between Lang Darma's two sons, and so the internal struggle of the ruling clique intensified. This together with the successive famines which caused large-scale uprisings among the common people and slaves under Tubo control caused the total collapse of the Tubo Dynasty. From then on, the Tibetan plateau fell into a state of internecine strife with the nobility forming a number of separate regimes each enjoying autonomy. This situation lasted for over four hundred years, marking the end of ancient Tibetan society.

In the thirteenth century, after the founding of the Sakya Dynasty, Pagpa unified Tibet once more, and with the support of the Yuan Dynasty's central government, founded the first theocracy. The Pagdu Dynasty and Karmapa Dynasty which succeeded the Sakya Dynasty maintained this system, and in the mid-seventeenth century, when the Fifth Dalai Lama Ngawong Gyaltso received his title from the Qing Emperor, the state power of the unification of state and church became further consolidated, its feudal-slave system lasting right up until the Democratic Revolution of 1959.

The Cultural Exchanges Between the Hans and the Tibetans

From ancient times, the inhabitants of the Qinghai-Tibet Plateau have exchanged visits with the people of the Central Plains. Excavations in Karo (Chamdo) started in 1978 have revealed primitive villages, and archaeological finds such as stones axes, adzes, spades, hoes and knives very much akin to those unearthed at neolithic settlements in the Yellow River valley. Ethnologists and archaeologists agree that the remains excavated in Karo prove that the aborigines of Tibet and the Han nationality of the Yellow River valley had contacts prior to four thousand years ago, which have continued up to the present.

Relations between the Tibetans and China's various nationalities, particularly the Han, became closer and closer, especially from the start of the Tang Dynasty (618 AD).

In 641, the Tang Emperor Taizong gave the hand of Princess Wencheng of the Tang court in marriage to the Tsanpo of the Tubo Dynasty, Songtsan Gampo. This policy of alliance by the Tang Dynasty played a positive role in promoting unity, expanding exchanges and enhancing understanding and friendship between nationalities, as well as serving to improve the relationship between the Tang Dynasty and the Tubos. The "marriage alliance" meant that Songtsan Gampo and his successors all acknowledged that their relationship with the Tang Emperors was that of nephew and uncle.

Emperor Taizong died in 649 and was succeeded by Emperor Gaozong who conferred on Songtsan Gampo the titles "Fuma Duwei*" and "Prince of the Western Region." In return, Songtsan Gampo sent an envoy with condolences and a memorial expressing loyalty to the Tang Dynasty. Emperor Gaozong then offered him the additional title of "Precious King" and had a stone statue carved for him. Later, in 710, Emperor Zhongzong gave the hand of his adopted daughter Princess Jincheng in marriage to the Tubo Tsanpo Tride Tsugtan.

Princess Jincheng was a lover of literature and art, and brought with her to Tibet many ancient books and records of the arts and crafts, as well as musicians and acrobats. The Tubo Tsanpo cleared the way for her journey, and built a palace in Lhasa to receive her. Princess Jincheng's marriage to the Tibetan king was another great contribution to the development of friendship between the Hans and Tibetans. As a consequence, friendly visits between the Tangs and Tubos increased from then on, and the civilisation of

---

* "Fuma" means the son-in-law of the Emperor. "Duwei" was an ancient administrative title.

the Central Plains became widely known in Tibet.

When the Tang Emperor Muzong came to the throne in 831, the Tubos sent an envoy to ask for an alliance to which the Tang court expressed assent. In 822, the imperial court sent Liu Wending to Lhasa to establish an alliance with the Tubos, and in the following year the "Tang-Tubo Alliance Tablet' was erected. Expressing hopes for everlasting friendship between the two peoples, this tablet is preserved to this day at the front gate of the Jokhang Temple.

Two hundred years elapsed from the "marriage alliance" with Songtsan Gampo in the reign of the Tang Emperor Taizong up to the time of the Tang Emperor Xuanzong when, in 851, internal disruption marked the decline of the Tubo Dynasty. Over these two centuries, Tang envoys paid over fifty visits to the Tubo Tsanpos, while Tubo envoys made more than ninety trips to the Tang court. The highest-ranking envoys sent by both sides were of ministerial level, and the purpose of the visits included the maintenance of friendly relations, marriages, funerals, memorial ceremonies, the establishment of alliances, greetings on successes, requests for craftsmen, escorts for monks, and so on. The escorts sent for the Princesses Wencheng and Jincheng were composed of several hundred to a thousand men, but generally parties consisted of ten to fifty men at least.

The Tangs and Tubos exchanged visits with the astonishing frequency of a visit almost once every year. Considering the poor communications of the times, this represents an astounding fact, and remains etched in the minds of both the Hans and Tibetans.

In the mid-thirteenth century, the Yuan Dynasty unified the whole of China and pacified Tibetan internal strife, bringing Tibet under its control. With the consent of local rulers, the Yuan Dynasty exercised its central authority over the Tibetan-occupied areas throughout China; such was the development of relations between the two nationalities the Tibetans and Hans, the direct historical result of earlier Tang alliances.

During the Ming and Qing Dynasties, the local chieftains of Tibet formally received titles from the emperors, and the Tibetan local government frequently sent envoys to Peking either to pay tribute or to receive titles. At the invitation of the Qing Emperor Shunzhi, the Fifth Dalai Lama, whose rank was formally acknowledged by the central government, visited Peking and was given a grand welcome. At the beginning of the eighteenth century, the Qing court began stationing Ambans* in Tibet to supervise the appointment or removal of Tibetan local officials and to direct recognition of the incarnations of the Dalai Lama, Panchen Lama and other high ranking lamas or their ordination to the religious throne.

After the founding of the People's Republic of China, the Agreement on Measures for the Peaceful Liberation of Tibet, commonly referred to as the 17-Point Agreement, was signed between the representatives of the Central People's Government and the local government of Tibet (the Kashak) in May 1951. In 1956, the State Council approved the founding of the Preparatory Committee for the Tibet Autonomous Region, and in 1965 the Tibet Autonomous Region was formally founded and regional national autonomy was put into practice.

---

* A Manchu term, the title of the resident imperial minister in Lhasa

2

BONISM AND BUDDHISM IN THE LAND OF SNOWS

Bonism

Buddhism

The Four Major Sects of Tibetan Buddhism

Tsongkapa's Religious Reform and the Emergence of the Gelugpa Sect as a Political Power

The Impact of Buddhism on Tibetan Culture

The "Pure Land" in Chinese religious mythology refers to the land where Buddha and the Bodhisattvas originated. It is identified as today's India, where in the past Buddhism flourished. Tibet, regarded as second only to India, was crowned with the title of "Second Pure Land," a name well befitting a country where Buddhism has long permeated every aspect of its life and culture.

Lhasa, without exaggeration, may well be called a Mecca of Buddhism. Even today the surging crowds of prostrators inside and outside the Jokhang Temple day and night seem as large as ever, clouds of incense still rise in the Potala Palace, while fervent believers supporting the elderly and clutching children by the hand still visit the monasteries of Drepung and Sera. Among these people, many have come over a thousand miles from Sichuan, Qinghai and Gansu. They are prepared to stand in long queues waiting to add butter to the butter lamps, burn incense and pray for happiness in the "next life."

Buddhist influence in the Land of Snows is all-pervasive. Monasteries, for example, are truly Tibet's most magnificent buildings, to which even the mansions of the nobility seem far inferior in comparison. Moreover there are an astonishing number of monasteries in Tibet. According to a report made by the Tibetan Local Government to the Administrative Council of the Qing court in 1737, there were 3,477 Gelug-pa monasteries harbouring 300,000 monks alone. Today, over twenty famous monasteries still remain, all well known to the people. For anyone travelling on the Tibetan plateau, whether in mountain wildernesses or in narrow valleys, amidst the vast, rolling grasslands or deep within virgin forests, ancient temples may be glimpsed or the sound of a hand bell may be heard. In preliberation days, besides the great number of professional monks, almost every household had a member renouncing his home and taking religious vows. Buddhism really is rooted deep within the life of every Tibetan household.

Also familiar to every household and every person in Tibet is the doctrine of Buddhism. Indeed, the Tibetan script was initially created expressly for the purpose of translating the Buddhist sutras. Tibet's traditional block prints are of religious texts first and foremost, and paintings mostly depict the Buddha's birth or nirvana and reincarnations. The contents of the stories of popular Tibetan operas too are usually in praise of Buddhist teachings or of enlightenment. Carvings, without exception, depict the Buddha or Bodhisattvas, and as for architecture, there are buildings like the Potala Palace which, towering into the clouds, its golden roofs glistening in the sun, appears like a hovering ethereal dakini. Monasteries such as Drepung, Sera, Tashilhunpo, Sakya and Samye present a different picture. Built against a backdrop of mountains with buildings clustered one upon another, supreme halls towering above others, incense smoke curling up into the air, and a labyrinth of winding corridors, quiet and serene, these monasteries are like one might imagine the jewelled palaces of celestial realms. Buddhism is everywhere, and everything has something to do with Buddhism, too; the prayerbeads in people's hands, the prayer flags hoisted on rooftops, the auspicious "   " signs painted on doors, the "prayer walls" erected amidst fields or on roadsides, the folksongs people hum under their breath, and the widespread folk stories.

Bonism

To trace the origins of the Tibetan people's belief in Buddhism we need to go back 1,300 years into the past. Buddhism has not always existed on the Tibetan plateau. Prior to the advent of Buddhism, the native religion of the Land of Snows which flourished more than 1,300 years ago was Bonism, founded by Shenrab Miboche, born in Tsanda Dzong of present-day Ngari Prefecture. It is traditionally said that not long after Sakyamuni had passed into Nirvana, there lived a young boy named Shen who was kidnapped by a demon at the age of thirteen and was not released for another thirteen years. When the boy returned at the age of twenty-six, he was found to have miraculous abilities with the powers of prophecy and exorcism. People named him Shenrab (Great Teacher) and respected him as an immortal. This Shenrab, the founder of Bon, brought with him neither scripture nor doctrine, but simply taught the people to worship gods, to pray, to drive out ghosts, to subdue demons and so on.

Primitive Bon religion shared similarities with animist religions still in existence in some regions of the world. In those days because of man's lack of understanding of natural phenomena such as the movement of the sun, moon and stars, the peculiar shapes of the mountains and rivers, and various climatic phenomena, in the minds of the people these things became invested with divinity, resulting in the worship of the sun, moon and stars, and even animals such as cattle and sheep. Such beliefs gradually took form as the beginnings of Bonism. The Bon religion divided the universe into three worlds: Heaven, Earth and the Underworld. In order to ward off harm from the spirits, people commonly smeared red dye on their faces, and in dealing with any sort of mystery, rituals were performed such as "avoiding misfortune by praying," the consultation of oracles, and exorcism. This primitive stage of Bon is known to historians as Dolbon.

A second wave of Bon exponents came from the west when after the assassination of the eighth Tubo Tsanpo, Drigum Tsanpo, his descendants invited some Bon followers from Kashmir, Drusha and Shangshung, with the aim of avenging Drigum's murder. Later, a Bon scholar named Pandita Shamthab Ngonpo introduced the doctrines of the six different philosophic schools, also known as the doctrines of the Six Non-Buddhist Masters (contemporaries of Sakyamuni), and combined them with the native Bon religion to form the complete Bon doctrine of the Tubos, known as the Kyarbon.

In the latter half of the eighth century, the Tubo Tsanpo, Trisung Detsan, was himself a Buddhist and widely spread the dharma. Gyalwa Changchub, a Bon scholar, was very much opposed to this, and translated Buddhist scriptures claiming them as Bonism's own. For this crime, Trisung Detsan sentenced Gyalwa Changchub to death and ordered the Bon followers to change their belief from Bonism to Buddhism. Following the Tubo Tsanpo Lang Darma's persecution of Buddhism, a man named Shegur Luga and several others from the Upper Nyang valley in the Tsang region continued the translation and reform of the Buddhist scriptures and enriched the Bon doctrine. Historians call this the Gyurbon or the "Translated Bon."

From the time of Trisung Detsan, the Bon religion became divided into three sects known as the White Bon which sided with Buddhism, the Black Bon which retained its independent primitive form, and the Striped Bon which was a mixture of both Bonism and Buddhism.

As the Bon religion took shape, both its scriptures and doctrine absorbed the way of Buddhism, but it can be said that the Bon religion was a major influence on the development of Tibetan Buddhism.

Buddhism

Buddhism first penetrated Tibet when Songtsan Gampo's ancestor Lhato-Thori Nyantsan was at the age of sixty, around the fifth century AD. It was then that a sacred text, a stupa, and a ritual object were said to have descended from heaven onto the roof of the Yumbulagang in Lhoka. But without a writing system the scriptures remained unrevealed, and at first Buddhism spread extremely slowly.

From another angle, the social production of the Tubos took on a new prosperity from the sixty century. The relationship between the various tribes headed by the Yarlung tribe was consolidated and strengthened, and close political, economic and cultural contacts arose between the Tubos and the Tuguhan and Dangxiang tribes living to the west of the Tang Dynasty and the nations of Nepal and the Pure Land (India). Buddhism thus entered Tibet mainly because of the needs of the internal social transformation of the Tubos and through the development of external contacts.

In the seventh century, the two brides of Songtsan Gampo, Princess Wencheng of the Tang Dynasty and Princess Bhrikuti Devi of Nepal, each brought an image of Sakyamuni, one from the east and one from the west. It was from this time on that Buddhism actually started to take shape in Tibet, and not long after, the earliest temples such as the Tradrug, the Jokhang and the Ramoche were built in the Land of Snows. During Songtsan Gampo's reign the Tibetan script was created and with the translation of the Buddhist canons, the real spread of Buddhism in Tibet began in earnest. A century later, the thirty-eighth Tubo Tsanpo Trisung Detsan sent special invitations to the Buddhist scholar Shantirakshita and the saint Padmasambhava, built the Samye Monastery at Samye in the Lhoka region, and selected children of wealthy families to enter this first community of monks. He also invited two Buddhist monks from the Han regions to translate Buddhist scriptures and preach Buddhist doctrine, and consequently Buddhism spread far and wide.

At the beginning of the ninth century when the Tubo Tsanpo Tritsug Detsan came to the throne, a great number of Indian and Tibetan lotsavas (translators of sacred texts) were gathered to translate not only volumes of Buddhist canons but also check the previous translations of scriptures. The amounts of translation were so great that they exceeded the number of volumes translated in the Han regions for over a thousand years. Under Tritsug Detsan's patronage Buddhism prospered, and the king himself set an example of devotion. Parting his hair to the left and right, he tied it with silken bands and then spread it on the floor and asked monks and priests to sit on it as a token of his respect for Buddhism. People gave him the name "Ralpachen" meaning "one with long plainted hair." This Tibetan king established the historically famous monastery of Wushangdo on the southern bank of the middle reaches of the Kyichu River, where he commanded monks to go into meditation and recite scriptures. He also issued a decree commanding every seven households to contribute to the upkeep of one monk, and if anybody committed offences against Buddhists, the Tsanpo punished them severely. However this state of affairs did not last for long. Several former nobles, disgusted with Tritsug Detsan's devotion to Buddhism, schemed to put an end to his two principal advisers, Tritsug Detsan's elder brother who had become a monk and his tutor, and staged a palace coup by murdering him while he was drunk. The two-century-long period from Songtsan Gampo to Tritsug Detsan when Buddhism was at its zenith is known as the "Former Prosperity of Buddhism." Buddhist followers call Tritsug Detsan, Songtsan Gampo and Trisung Detsan the "Three Ancestral Forefathers."

The death of Tritsug Detsan began a disaster for Buddhists in Tibet. In 838 Tritsug Detsan's elder brother, Lang Darma, succeeded to the Tsanpo's throne. He was a leading exponent of the Bon religion, and no sooner had he ascended the throne than he began to carry out his policy of persecuting Buddhism. He ordered the Jokhang Temple in Lhasa and the Samye Monastery in Lhoka to be closed, and went so far as to turn the Ramoche Temple into a cowshed, while Buddhist frescoes in the monasteries were erased and pictures of monks seeking for luxury painted in their stead. Lang Darma furthermore issued orders for the images of the Buddha to be thrown into rivers or for blood-dripping animal hides to be hung over them, and he forced monks to go hunting and butcher animals. He even destroyed monasteries, slaughtered monks, sealed off religious thrones, and forced monks to resume secular life. This period is known in Tibetan history as the "Persecution of Buddhism." Lang Darma's enmity against Buddhism was not by any means because he was an atheist, but represented the victory of the restoration of the old Bon religion over the dominant position of Buddhism.

While Buddhism was suffering defeat, a Buddhist monk named Lhalung Paldor, wearing a black cloak with a white lining, riding a white horse painted black, and consealing a bow and arrow in his broad sleeves, shot Lang Darma while the latter was out for a stroll. Then the successful assassin rode his horse through the river to wash off the black paint and turned his cloak inside out so that it too appeared white, and fled to the mountains until he came to the Kham region where he undertook the arduous task of restoring Buddhism. The power of the Lhasa Bon regime did not extend as far as Kham, and so it was in this region that the dying embers of Buddhism were fanned into flame once more. The major figure in this restoration was a one-time shepherd named Lachen Gongpa Rabsal. Slowly he built up a following and revived the doctrine which had been weakened by Bon proponents headed by Shegur Luga who had claimed the Buddhist sutras as their own.

When the Lhasa Bon regime finally collapsed, Tibet fell into chaos unknown hitherto. Politically decentralised, separate principalities arose, one of which was the Kingdom of Guge in Ngari to the west. The monk-king Lha Lama Changchub Od, unable to bear the thought of Buddhism's extinction, sent a group led by Nagtse Lotsava Tsultrim Gyalwa to Bengal to invite the great Indian pundit Atisa to come to Tibet to spread the teachings of Buddhism. His arrival marked the beginning of the "Latter Prosperity of Buddhism." After Atisa's demise, one of his disciples Domtonpa Gyalwa Jungne took over his master's philosophical teachings and in 1056 founded the Rating Monastery which became the base of the Kadampa sect. The embers of Buddhism finally burst into flame when in the mid-eleventh century the four major sects of Buddhism developed.

The Four Major Sects of Tibetan Buddhism

There are many religious sects in Tibet, but the four described below are considered the major groupings. The earliest established sect, the Nyingmapa Sect, mainly teaches the ancient tantric mysticism, and so it is known as the Ancient Mystic Order. It is also called the Red Sect because the monks of this school wear red hats and *kasavas* (an outer vestment worn by Buddhist monks). It was formed by a combination of Indian mystic teaching and native Bon religion by Padmasambhava in the eighth century. The Nyingmapa Sect, because of its lonely teaching of mystics, in its early stage had neither monasteries or communities of monks, nor a complete set doctrine. After the eleventh century, the Nyingmapa set up its own monasteries and gradually arranged its sutras, and only then did it become a real religious sect paying homage to Padmasambhava as its Master.

The Sakyapa Sect, or White Earth Order, is also called the "Striped Sect" because of its three stripes of red, white and black on its monastery walls, representing Lord Manjusri (Lord of Wisdom), Lord Avolokitesvara (Lord of Mercy) and Vajrapani respectively. The mother monastery of this sect is the Sakya Monastery, built in the Sakya region, from where the sect gets its name. The Sakyapa Sect was originally founded in the eleventh century by Khon Konchog Gyalpo of the Khon clan in Sakya. In his boyhood he studied ancient tantric Buddhism with his father, and then later went to Nyugulung where he studied new tantric Buddhism, taking as his master Drogmi Sakya Yeshe, a great scholar and translator who had studied in India. In 1073 he established a monastery in the valley of the Drongchu River, Sakya, to teach the doctrine he had developed, and so the Sakyapa Sect took shape.

From the beginning, Khon Kunchog Gyalpo stuck to the idea of inherited religious power so as to centralise both religious and political power in the hands of one family. Sakya had five great abbots called the "Five Forefathers of Sakya."

The Kagyupa Sect, or the Order of Oral Transmission, is so called because all instruction is passed on orally from Master to disciple, with the idea that words are transmitted to the ear and the meaning absorbed by the heart. Kagyupa lays stress on tantric Buddhism and does not consider philosophy of importance. The founders of this sect such as Marpa, Milarepa and others, used to wear white robes when meditating which is how it got its name of White Sect. The Kagyupa Sect came into existence in the mid-eleventh century, and has a complex array of sub-sects. From the very beginning two major sub-sects emerged: the Shangpa Kagyupa and the Dhagpo Kagyupa. The Shangpa Kagyupa vanished from the scene in the fourteenth and fifteenth centuries, while the Dhagpo Kagyupa has continued up to this day. Today when we speak of the Kagyupa it is none other that the Dhagpo Kagyupa. The founder of the Dhagpo Kagyupa was Khagpolhaje Sonamrinchen. He was born in the Nyal district of Lhuntse Dzong in Tibet, and was a renowned Buddhist scholar at the time of the Song Dynasty (960-1279). He studied medicine in his youth, and then became a monk at the age of twenty-six, specialising in studies of tantricism and philosophy in which he attained achievements. Later he took Milarepa, Marpa's disciple, as his Master. After completing his studies of tantricism, he took up residence in the Dhaglha Kampo Monastery and taught many followers and gradually formed the Dhagpo Kagyupa Sect. Four of his most notable disciples established monasteries and taught disciples in U and Tsang, and thus the four sub-sects took shape: Kama Kagyupa, Tsalpa Kagyupa, Babrum Kagyupa and Pagdu Kagyupa. The Pagdu Kagyupa sub-sect was further divided into eight minor sub-sects, and so the whole of the Kagyupa Sect is generally known as the "four major and eight minor sub-sects."

The Kadampa Sect, or the Commandments, was the earliest sect of Tibet to take form. "Kadam" means "Buddha's commandments," and the sect teaches the Buddhist doctrine through Buddha's own words. Its founder was Domtonpa Gyalwa Jungne who in 1045 invited the eminent Buddhist priest Atisa from Ngari and took him as his Master. After Atisa's demise, Domtonpa founded the Rating Monastery in 1056, and using this monastery as a base, the Kadampa sect was gradually formed. The characteristic of this sect is its stress on discipline; monastic discipline, set steps through meditation, and the regulation of the relationship between tantricism and philosophy. Its principal canon is Atisa's own work "Bodhipathapradipa" (The Lamp That Shows the Path to Enlightenment). In the fifteenth century when Tsongkapa founded the Gelugpa Sect on the basis of the Kadampa doctrine, this sect was gradually merged into the Gelugpa Sect.

Tsongkapa's Religious Reform and the Emergence of the Gelugpa Sect as a Political Power

Tibet's decentralisation had contributed to the establishment of the different Buddhist sects, and it was the revival of religion rather than the emergence of a new royal line that sought to bring unity to the Tibetan plateau. In the thirteenth century, this state of decentralisation came to an end when Pagpa, the abbot of Sakya, unified the whole of Tibet with the support of the Yuan Dynasty.

In the fourthteenth century, as the strength of the Sakyapa Sect gradually diminished, an armed struggle for political and economic paramountcy one again emerged among the different cliques, with the Pagdu Kagyupa Sect at the head. Pagdu Changchub Gyaltsan with an army from Lhoka annexed the Tsalpa and Drikung myriarchies in U and at the same time, taking advantage of internal troubles among the Khon clan of the Sakyapa Sect, attacked the Sakya Monastery and seized control of most of the region of Tsang. Subsequently Pagdu's regional administration was set up and received recognition from the Yuan Dynasty, the Yuan Emperor Shun Di conferring the title of *Da Situ* ˙ on Changchub Gyaltsan.

It was at this time that Tsongkapa came to Tibet in quest of Buddhist studies so as to keep the Wheel of the Law ever turning. Tibet by now was in a state where different religious sects were attaching them-

---

˙ an ancient title equivalent to Chief Minister of the Interior.

selves to different regional feudal powers and making mutual use of one another. Under the mantle of religion some rulers seized both political and religious power. Politically arrogant and domineering, they brooked no opposition and plundered and seized great amounts of wealth. Their lives were given over to ease and comfort, while the people met only with suffering and misery. Production too suffered loss and damage, and peace and security were urgently needed. Moreover, while the Sakyapa and then the Kagyupa sects held sway, there was relaxation of religious discipline which opened the way to all kinds of abuses. Monks and lamas in power together with their many followers neither recited prayers no observed monastic rules, but gave themselves over to drinking, gambling robbery, and licentiousness, committing all kinds of outrages. The prestige of Buddhism fell considerably, and had things continued in this way Buddhism would indeed have suffered a crisis of faith.

It was under such circumstances that Tsongkapa launched his religious reforms. Originally from Amdo (Qinghai), Tsongkapa at the age of sixteen travelled around various regions of Tibet, paying homage to the Sakyapa, Kagyupa and Kadampa sects and acknowledging their high lamas as his own masters. With the energetic support of Pagdu's administration, he founded a new sect, the Gelugpa, which was based on discipline and laid equal stress on philosophy and tantric mysticism. The direct successor to the Kadampa sect, it took all the strong points of the other sects and welded them into one.

Tsongkapa's religious reform can be summarised in the following three points:

I. Monks were to observe strict discipline, behave

differently from secular people, and combat the quest for benefit and power and the unrestrained way of life practised by the Sakyapa and Kagyupa followers. Monks were strictly forbidden to marry or engage in production or to interfere in worldly affairs. Monks were encouraged "to be content with a little and to lead a peaceful and quiet life."

II. The parochial way of the religious sects maintaining contacts only with local communities was to be abandoned. A broader range of "priest and patron" relationships among various regional powers were to be established. Expenses needed for establishing monasteries and providing food and shelter for the monastic communities were to be provided by these "patrons" from different regions.

III. Strict regulations were to be applied to the study of the sacred texts. Special attention was to be paid to the steps of meditation, and stress was laid upon proceeding step by step in an orderly way. Clear divisions were to be made in the management of monasteries. More than two monks were to be chosen to take charge of each monastery and decisions or resolutions were to be reached through joint discussions. No individual was allowed to act arbitrarily in monastery administration.

This all-out movement of religious reform was launched by Tsongkapa in the latter part of the fourteenth century and continued up until the beginning of the fifteenth century. As well as producing a number of books to explain his own religious beliefs, Tsongkapa also continued teaching the dharma wherever he went, laying stress on monastic discipline, explaining the relationship between philosophy and tantric mysticism, formulating orderly procedures for going into retreat, laying down the order of scriptural study, and setting rules for the monks' daily routine, etc. As Tsongkapa's religious ideas were backed by the then rulers of Tibet, the Pagdu Dynasty, his prestige rose higher than ever. In 1409 Tsongkapa instituted the "Great Prayer Festival" (mom lam) in the Jokhang Temple in Lhasa, gathering thousands of monks, distributing alms or donations and spreading Buddhist teachings far and wide. In the same year, under the patronage of the Lord of Nedong, Tsongkapa founded the earliest monastery of the Gelugpa Sect the Ganden Monastery. Soon after, his fourth disciple Jamyang Dhoje Tashi Paldan, under the patronage of the Lord of Newu, founded the Drepung Monastery in 1416 at the foot of Mt. Ganpoi Uze, and in 1419 the fifth disciple, Jamchen Choje Shakya Yeshe, founded the Sera Monastery at the foot of a mountain located just north or Lhasa. These formed the Three Great Monasteries of Lhasa the backbone and basis of the Gelugpa Sect and from then on the Gelugpa Sect become more and more powerful with each passing day. The disciples of the Gelugpa Sect established monasteries and preached Buddhism eve-rywhere, and as a result monasteries sprang up in great numbers in various regions while monks and lamas increased in multitudes, and very soon the Gelugpa Sect became the greatest Tibetan Buddhist sect.

The Gelugpa Sect founded by Tsongkapa, with its strict discipline and high prestige, became the supreme spiritual image of the ruling class of Tibet at that time, and further penetrated into the regions of Kham, Qinghai and Mongolia. In 1643 the fifth Dalai Lama, Ngawong Gyatso, with the support of the Mongolian Goshri Khan, established the administrative centre of the Gelugpa Sect for the first time at the Ganden Podrang (the Prosperous Palace) of the Drepung Monastery.

Tsongkapa reformed Buddhism and gathered many disciples, but his influence was at first limited to the religious sphere. Succession was guaranteed in Gelugpa monasteries through the theory of reincarnation, and head of the sect later became known as the Dalai Lama. However, up until the period of the fifth Dalai Lama, the head of Gelugpa did not come to the fore in political power. Prior to this, the Dalai Lamas resided in the Drepung Monastery and their power could only be used to effect in religious circles. Goshri Khan then handed the state power of Tibet over to the fifth Dalai Lama, who received his title of authority from the Emperor of the Qing Dynasty; and from then on the Dalai Lama became not only the spiritual leader of the Tibetan people but also took over absolute control of Tibetan local administration. A theocracy was now formally established in Tibet. Ngawong Gyatso moved his residence from the Drepung Monastery to the Potala Palace, and all the land and serfs of Tibet were divided into three categories distributed amongst the monasteries (owned thirty-nine percent), serfowners and the local government - the Kashak (Cabinet). It was at this period that the Three Ranks of Nobility came to the fore. The Tibetan theocracy determined that monasteries could own slaves and serfs, know as "monastery retainers." Tsongkapa's revitalisation of Buddhism and the fifth Dalai Lama's strengthening of the unification of state and church had gradually transformed Tibet into a world of Buddhism. From morn till night prayers to Buddha rose from young and old alike, and faith in Buddhism gradually climbed to its zenith.

From the foundation of the Gelugpa Sect, the Three Ranks of Nobility enthusiastically supported Buddhism and encouraged it to rise more swiftly than ever before in Tibet. In Lhasa for example, at the time the monks numbered 16,000 to 17,000. The number of Gelugpa Sect permanent monks to be housed in the Three Great Monasteries was fixed as follows: Ganden, 3,300 monks, Sera, 5,500 monks, and Drepung, 7,700 monks, which gives an idea of the tremendous power of the monasteries. Tashilhunpo Monastery alone was permitted to take in 3,800 monks, and there were over 3,000 monasteries of a fairly large size in the U, Tsang, Ngari, Kham and Amdo regions, harbouring an incredible number of monks and nuns.

The Impact of Buddhism on Tibetan Culture

Though imported from outside, Buddhism was effective in accelerating the development of Tibet's culture. Songtsan Gampo is credited with the invention of the Tibetan script with the aim of spreading Buddhism and translating Buddhist sutras, and in the course of this the Tibetan script itself was improved. Because there are many concepts not of the material world in the sutras, such as "the boundless universe," "the four great world," "the six cycles of beings" and "heaven and hell," new vocabulary had to be created in order to translate such terms and concepts, and so the Tibetan language became enriched in the gradual course of time.

With the development of a script, Tibet's national culture developed in leaps and bounds. Moving on from translation, the compiling and writing of books in Tibet-an became the order of the day. The Kagyur (the translated scriptures) and Ten-gyur (the translated elucidating treatises) are of course well-known both in China and abroad, but other works such as biographies, dramas, poems, astrological, medical and technical treatises are all treasures of Tibetan culture which also appeared as required.

As Buddhism penetrated Tibet, monasteries were established, figures of the Buddha were painted and carvings created to pay homage to the Buddha. Thus, the popularity of Buddhism in Tibet accelerated the development of the architecture, painting and carving, displayed in the magnificent monasteries and temples built amidst tranquil mountain wildernesses in the Land of Snows. Tibetan murals and carvings are no less famous, and originated from paintings of Sakyamuni and Avalokitesvara. With their animated, realistic figures in various postures and brilliant execution, frescoes and sculptures adorn monasteries and temples everywhere. In secular buildings, there are works which show a departure from the bounds of Buddhist doctrine. These artistic works owe their origins to Buddhist doctrine, and were created using the skills gained through painting and carving images of the Buddha. Moreover, there have been men of wisdom like the renowned Yuthok Yuntan Gonpo, who extracted scientific knowledge from Buddhism and formulated a Tibetan body of medical knowledge and the Tibetan calendar.

3

LHOKA CRADLE OF THE TIBETAN PEOPLE

The Sacred Mount Gongpuri

The Five-Headed Dragon and
the Tradrug Temple

The Yumbulagang and the Advent
of Buddhism

Pagdu Re-establishes Lhoka as
the Centre of Tibet

Princess Jincheng

The Tumuli of the Ancient
Tibetan Kings

The First Monastery

Since ancient times Lhoka, "Tibet's granary," has been a centre of importance, a land of enchantment both to the native inhabitants who have lived in the Land of Snows for generations and to tourists and traders from elsewhere. The land here is fertile, rich in resources, and scenic to behold. Many historical ruins still exist in Lhoka and a number of touching legendary tales have been passed down to the present. Lhoka is universally acknowledged as the cradle of the Tibetans.

Between Lhasa and Tsetang lie the mighty Gangdise Range and the torrential Tsangpo River. It was only after the construction of the Chushu Bridge, which spans the Tsangpo River like a rainbow, that the cradle of the Tibetans became linked to the thousand-year-old ancient city.

Sacred Mount Gongpori

On arrival at Tsetang, the first thing you will hear is the legendary tale of how the Tibetans are descended from monkeys. Elders will even point out in all seriousness the caves where their ancestors dwelt in ancient times. People here all believe themselves without the slightest doubt to be the descendants of the monkey and the ogress.

The story centres round Mt. Gongpori, which stands as a backdrop to Tsetang. Mt. Gongpori is a sacred mountain. It is said that anyone who has sincere faith in the Buddha may be lucky enough when he reaches the summit to see the abode of the gods, and in this vision the fortunes and misfortunes of his next life will be revealed. Mt. Gongpori is regarded as sacred because this mountain is said to be suspended in the air by four deities, the Horse to the east, the Elephant to the west, the Peacock to the north, and the Tortoise to the south, separated from both heaven and earth. Because the four deities hold the mountain in mid-air, the abode of the gods and the mortal world can be seen at the same time and the future can be revealed. But a legend always remains a legend, and a myth a myth. No matter how you strain your eyes looking left and right, you cannot see any difference between this mountain and the others. In face of any disbelief, the local elders would vividly describe the sight, pointing out the Elephant, the Tortoise and so on, until one become so dazed with confusion that he begins to imaging Mt. Gongpori is really floating in the air!

Mt. Gongpori has three peaks: Yangkar Uze, Zangmo Uze, and Drupkhang Tse which is the highest of the trio. Each peak contains a cave, all three of which are connected. It is said the monkey lived on Zangmo Uze, the ogress on Yangkar Uze, while Drupkhang Tse contains the cave where Avalokitesvara meditated. When the ogress and the monkey were joined in marriage, Avalokitesvara who lived in the Drupkhang Tse cave acted as the go-between. The plain lying in front of Mt. Gongpori was where the offspring of the monkey and the ogress played, and so it is known as "Tsetang," meaning "playground." Later, these three caves were held to be sacred, and it is said that if incense is burnt in the Zangmo Uze cave, the smoke will issue out of the Drupkhang Tse cave. If you don't believe it, you may climb the mountain and have a try, but be warned, it takes at least half a day to crawl from one cave to the other.

The Five Headed Dragon and the Tradrug Temple

Another story of the region tells of how the famous Tradrug Temple was built. According to the tale, while Songtsan Gampo was proceeding with the construction of the Jokhang Temple, Princess Wencheng, studying the astrological aspects of the Five Elements, calculated that one of the arms of a she-demon was lying to the southwest of Mt. Gongpori. This location was a huge lake then disturbed by a five-headed dragon. In order to subdue the dragon, Songtsan Gampo went up to Drupkhang Tse to meditate. When he achieved liberation, he transformed himself into a hawk and flew to another mountain called Mt. Depori (Mt. Cock), not far from Gongpori. The hawk landed on the summit of this mountain, and at a glance saw the trouble caused in the lake by the dragon. Eyes closely fixed upon the dragon, the hawk swooped and pecked off one of the dragon's heads as it appeared at the surface of the lake. Tired, the hawk then returned to Mt. Depori for a rest. In five such attacks, the hawk pecked off all five of the dragon's heads, and the dragon finally expired. To ensure that the dragon never rose again, Songtsan Gampo filled the lake and built a temple on it which he named the Tradrug Temple. "Tradrug" means "the hawk which roars like a dragon." so chosen because when Songtsan Gampo changed himself into a hawk and fought fiercely against the dragon, he let out great roars which shook both heaven and earth. The Tradrug was the earliest temple to be built in Tibet. It is said that when Songtsan Gampo and Princess Wencheng paid visits to their old home of Lhoka, they spent their time there.

Initially the Tradrug Temple was tiny, not even forty square metres in totality, and scarcely 3 1/2 metres high and 7 metres across. Inside, the walls were decorated with ancient murals, simply drawn. There were six pillars and three windows, none of them particularly large. And a rough floor of stone slabs and earth. Sanskrit inscriptions appeared on the capitals of the pillars as decorations. The main hall of the Tradrug Temple was situated in the centre, and it was here that the "speaking" Tara was enshrined. This image of Tara was said to have been brought here by Songtsan Gampo from Khotan and Mt. Chakri Mukpo, a region of flourishing Buddhism lying to the north of Tibet.

Later, the Tradrug Temple was expanded by adding six more shrines. To the north were built the Shrine of the Lord of Medicine, the Shrine of Lord Amitabha (the Lord of Infinite Light) and the Shrine of the Guardian Deities, and to the south, the Shrine of Lord Avalokitesvara, the Shrine of the Lord Amitayus and the Shrine of the Seven Successions of Buddha, which gave the temple a more imposing appearance. From then on the Tradrug Temple became a holy place, where Buddhist followers came on pilgrimage, and gradually hermitages for meditation also appeared in its vicinity. Not far from the Tradrug is the Sherdrag, the cave where Padmasambhava went into meditation. In the past, Buddhists were expected to make a pilgrim-age to the Sherdrag, and even now it is still visited by pilgrims or by those wishing to meditate. At Mt. Keme, no great distance from the Sherdrag, remains of ruined temples can still be found, and it is said that Milarepa, the famous Tibetan yogi, dwelt in this area. With such a wealth of Buddhist sacred spots in the Tradrug Temple area alone, it is hardly surprising that Tibet is known as the "Second Paradise" of Buddhists.

The Yumbulagang and the Advent of Buddhism

Yumbulagang, Tibet's first palace, is situated about five kilometres south of the Tradrug. It is the royal palace of Nyatri Tsanpo, the first Tsanpo of the Yarlung Valley, and stands looking like a tent pitched on the summit of a hill, narrow at the top and broad at the bottom. The walls are still standing, the windows still in evidence, and only the roof had long since collapsed.*

One day in the distant past when the Bon herdsmen were out grazing their livestock on a mountain called Tsantang Goshi, they came across a young man. The herdsmen carried the youth on their shoulders down to the tribal settlement, where he was deified as the Heavenly Son and unanimously made the chieftain of the tribe. Because he was brought down to the tribe seated on the shoulders of the herdsmen, the name Nyatri Tsanpo or "the Chieftain Seated on the Throne Neck" was given to him and a palace was also built for him. Thus Tibet gained its first Tsanpo and a palace specially built for royal usage.

During the time of Lhato Thori Nyantsan, the twenty-eighth Tsanpo, Buddhism first appeared in the Yarlung Valley. It is said that one day a collection of scriptures, a golden stupa, and a ritual object descended from Heaven all of a sudden. Due to the lack of a script then, the contents of the scriptures remained a

---

* The palace has now undergone extensive restoration.

mystery, but Lhato Thori Nyantsan enshrined the "Hidden Greatness," as the scriptures descended from Heaven were called, in his palace for worship. With the sacred relics from Heaven, there also came a prophecy: "The contents of these scriptures shall be revealed after five generations." Lhato Thori Nyantsan became devout, and although the Tsanpo was already sixty years old, due to the power of the scriptures, his youth once again returned and he lived to the age of 120. This marked the entry of Buddhism into Tibet. The "Hidden Greatness" had descended onto the roof of the Yumbulagang, and so this palace is recognised as a sacred place and is revered by Buddhists.

Pagdu Re-establishes Lhoka

Taking departure from Tsetang and looking across the torrential Tsangpo River, one can see an array of ruined temples to the east of Won District in Nedong Dzong, on the opposite bank. Among these ruins is Pagdu's hermitage, the Dansa Thil, which attracts crowds of Buddhists on pilgrimage and for meditation.

Pagdu's personal name was Dorje Gyalpo. Born in 1110 AD, he was the disciple of Dhagpo Lhaje, a famous Buddhist scholar of Tibet in the Song Dynasty period. Dhagpo Lhaje together with Milarepa had been Marpa's favourite disciples, and on completion of his studies, Dhagpo Lhaje erected monasteries in Dhagpo. It was at this point that three young men came from Kham to pay homage to Dhagpo Lhaje as their Master, and the nineteen-year-old Pagdu was among them.

Pagdu learned the essence of the dharma from Dhagpo Lhaje, and on completion of his studies, he followed his Master's instructions and went wandering in search of a hermitage for meditation. One day, he came to Lugone Ferry not far from Tsetang. Crossing the river he saw a wide plain lying to the east, the mountains and geographical features of which accorded with the instructions given by his Master. He thought of founding a monastery there and went to see the headman to beg for patronage. Pagdu found the headman making merry and drinking wine with a company of friends. Kneeling before him, Pagdu made his request, time and time again, but the headman showed no interest. Finally Pagdu was forced to raise his voice and entreat him loudly when the headman, said impatiently, "If you must built monasteries, then go right ahead! You can erect one hundred to the east and eighty to the west for all I care!" Pagdu was overjoyed on hearing these words and thought his was a good omen for monasteries to be built in great numbers in the future. Expressing his gratitude to the headman, he hastened off in search of sites.

Just as Pagdu was deep in thought over the siting of his monastery, five chirping thrushes flew over his head, guiding his way. When he reached a hillside, the five thrushes suddenly flew into a cave and disappeared. Pagdu believed this was a sign from the Buddha, and went into retreat in this cave, receiving many disciples. The Master and disciples working in unison started building a monastery on this very site. As the numbers of this disciples increased daily and because of his knowledge of medicine, Pagdu's fame grew greater and greater. It was at this time a princess of the emperor of China fell seriously ill. All the famous doctors that lived under the sun were sought and consulted but in vain. The Emperor heard that Pagdu of Tibet had superb skill in medical treatment, and invited him to administer to the princess. Sure enough, much to the emperor's delight, Pagdu cured the princess, and he was showered with gifts of gold, silver and other valuables.

Pagdu went back to his former hermitage on his return from inland China and started construction of the Dansa Thil Monastery which became the largest monastery in Lhoka. Soon death claimed Pagdu, but his work was continued by his successor who also took control over local affairs and became one of the myriarchy chiefs subject to the Sakya Dynasty. In 1349, Pagdu's descendant Changchub Gyaltsan took an army and attacked the regional power of Drigung and Tsalpa, annexed most of the regions in Tibet and tottered the Sakya Dynasty. In 1354, Changchub Gyaltsan overthrew the rule of the Sakya Dynasty and sent envoys to Peking to ask the Yuan Dynasty for recognition. The Yuan Emperor Shundi conferred upon Changchub Gyaltsan the title of "Da Situ"* and ordered him to take over the local administration of Tibet. He reorganised the thirteen myriarchies of the Sakya Dynasty by redividing them into "dzongs" (counties) and sent his men to these "dzongs" to take charge of local administration. This marked the establishment of the Pagdu Dynasty.

The Pagdu Dynasty had resulted from Tibet's separation into different principalities but its emergence during the infighting and eventual decline of Sakya's Khon clan and Pagdu's acquisition of the title from the Yuan and Ming emperors meant that the Yarlung Valley, which had remained a desolate place ever since the collapse of the Tubos, regained its flourishing fame of the past.

---

* An ancient title equivalent to Chief Minister of the Interior.

The ruling clique of the Pagdu Dynasty represented the power of the Kagyupa Sect and for the second time Tibet came under the unified rule of state and church. The manorial system of the feudal serf-owners was continued, the dzong was made the basic unit of administration and thirteen dzongs were set up with Nedong at the centre. Governors of these dzongs were appointed, and subjects who had provided outstanding services were rewarded with hereditary estates. These ennobled families each controlled a monastic community, thus keeping the fate of the monasteries subject to the rise and fall of the feudal serf-owner families.

In 1357, the Pagdu myriarchy was acknowledged as the Pagdu Dynasty by the central government of the Ming Dynasty, and from then on it became the acknowl-edged ruler of the whole of Tibet. This dynasty, with Nedong at the centre, reigned over Tibet for two hundred years or so, but subsequently was defeated by the armed force of Rimpung-pa. The Pagdu Dynasty's slow political decline was also followed by the decline of the Kagyupa Sect. At the beginning of the fifteenth century Tsongkapa started his religious reform, founding the three great monasteries in Lhasa, and Tibet's political centre gradually moved from Tsetang to Lhasa for the second time.

Princess Jincheng

Five kilometres south from the Yumbulagang is the Podrang District of Nedong Dzong. Some aged people in their seventies living in the neighbourhood of the district are eager to tell the visitors the origin and development of the name of their native land.

The story starts at the time of the thirty-seventh

Tubo Tsanpo, Tride Tsugtan. This Tsanpo was the first to erect a palace here and named it Deng-ga Podrang. Later, Jangmo Tritsun, Tride Tsugtan's queen, gave birth to a beautiful son with a broad forehead and a high nose. The ministers believed he was a son of heaven, and hence named him "Jangtsa Lhawon" "The Heavenly Son born to Jangmo Tritsun." When the prince grew to maturity, the royal court thought of getting a good bride for him, but the ministers did not consider the native girls well-bred enough. The boy's ancestor Songtsan Gampo had married the beautiful Princess Wencheng of the Tang Dynasty, and as a consequence the Tubos had become more powerful than ever. The Tang culture was advanced at that time, and there were also a lot of intelligent and versatile Tang princesses. If the Tubos were to ask for the hand of one of the princesses in marriage she would not only be an appropriate match for the great Prince Jangtsa Lhawon but would make a good queen for him in the future. So, the Tsanpo sent his minister Nie Trisang Yangton as an envoy to the Tang court to ask for a princess's hand in marriage. The Tang Emperor agreed with pleasure and soon Princess Jincheng was on her way to Tibet. While the princess was still on her journey, Jangtsa Lhawon unfortunately fell from his horse and was killed. When Princess Jincheng heard the disappointing news of his sudden demise on her arrival in Tibet, she fell to the ground in a swoon. The ministers tried to persuade her to marry the old Tsanpo, but at first she refused because he looked so ugly with his great bushy beard. But with every voice united in persuasion, Princess Jincheng had no alternative but to give way to the old Tsanpo and become his bride. Tride Tsugtan was overjoyed and wrote a letter to the

Tang Emperor Zhongzong saying that as nephew and maternal uncle, they were old relatives. His marriage with Princess Jincheng had now brought him into the Tang family, and he would treat the princess with every care.

Tride Tsugtan built a palace called Pangtan for the princess near his Deng-ga Podrang, and it has been known as the "Podrang" (palace) in memory of her ever since. This place name, together with the famous name of Princess Jincheng, has been passed down to the present.

There is another story about Princess Jincheng which says that she gave birth to a son two years after her arrival in Tibet. The son was Trisung Detsan,[*] a famous Tsanpo in Tibetan history. Nanang, Tride Tsugtan's senior queen, was already past her child-bearing years by then, and she became anxious that Princess Jincheng would rise to power in the future. When Princess Jincheng produced a son, Nanang seized her opportunity, abducted the infant and spread a rumour that the infant had been born to herself. Princess Jincheng, shedding tears with anger and worry, showed her dripping nipples as witness that the infant was her own, but applying a concoction she had already prepared, Nanang also made her nipples drip with milk, and so no one could tell which was the true mother and which the false. Finally one of the ministers thought of an idea: the infant was to be left at one end of an open meadow, Princess Jincheng and Nanang were to run a race, and whichever reached the baby first was to have it. Princess Jincheng, being the

---

[*] Different views are held among Tibetologists on the true identity of the mother of Trisung Detsan. The story here is an excerpt from Ba-she written by Bal Salnang (the manuscript is now kept in the library of the Cultural Palace of the Nationalities in Beijing).

younger and longing to hug own baby to her breast, ran with all her might and main and lifted the infant carefully to her breast and covered its sweet little face with kisses. But though her limbs lacked ability Nanang was very strong and she wrested the infant from Princess Jincheng's breast. The princess dearly loved the child of her own first and blood, and fearing he might be injured, she slackened her hold and let Nanang snatch him away.

The ministers knew very well that the child had been born to Jincheng, but because Nanang was of noble birth and extremely powerful, none dared to speak the truth in fear of stirring up trouble.

Tride Tsugtan, too, was quite clear as to who the child's real mother was. When the child reached one year of age, the Tsanpo gave a feast and invited members of the Tang family and Nanang's family to partake of some wine. At the banquet Tride Tsugtan was seated in the centre with his two queens on either side. The members of the Tang family and Nanang's family were also seated on both sides of the hall, the ministers below the platform.

After three toasts, the Tsanpo, holding a small golden cup filled to the brim with wine, handed it to the little prince and said, "You have two mothers and two families of maternal uncles, but you only have one real mother. This happy day is your birthday. Take this cup and offer it to your real maternal uncles to drink." The members of Nanang's family, brought out pretty clothes and toys and tried to coax the little prince, saying, "Here you are, my darling, these are all yours to keep. Now quickly bring the wine over here for your uncles." But the little prince without even a glance at them, exclaimed, "My real mother is from the family of the Great Tang. Fine wine should be offered to my real uncles." And so saying he took the cup straight over to where the Tangs were seated.

This interesting tale is replete with affectionate memories of Princess Jincheng. Nor is this all; the elders were proud of the present Podrang District because the house in which Princess Jincheng was supposed to have resided was in this locality. Here, everything of historic interest and scenic beauty is connected in some way with Princess Jincheng. Because of Princess Jincheng, even the colour of the grass growing on the mountain slope at the back of the village is said to be of an unusually glossy green. The elders would say, "When Princess Jincheng sank into grief and despair at losing her child, she shed tears for days and nights, neglecting to comb her hair or wash her face. What's more, Nanang made sure that Princess Jincheng was given no water to wash. But the day came when the child reached one year of age, and both queens were sent for by the Tsanpo to the reception hall to entertain guests. She thought it would be a disgrace to the Great Tang if she continued to neglect her hair and face, but since she had no water she used oil to wash her hair. When she finished, the dirty oil was thrown out onto the mountain slope, and that is why the grass is so grassy there."

The Tumuli of the Ancient Tibetan Kings

Following the Shangpo River upstream twenty kilometres from the Podrang District, leads to Chong-gye, once the capital of the Tubo Dynasty.

From Pode Gong-gyal, the nineth Tsanpo, to Esh-oleg, the fifteenth Tsanpo, the ancient Tubos successively built six palaces here: Taktse, Gutse, Yangtse, Tritse, Tsemo Chung-gye and Tritse Pangdo, which are known collectively as "the Six Palaces of Chingwar Taktse." They make up the second biggest fortress built by the ancient Tubos and are the ruins one most wishes to see on arrival at Chong-gye.

Chong-gye Town is excellently situated with the turbulent Yarlung River passing before it and a chain of mountains to the rear. Looking out over the mountain from the town, the ruins of the Chingwar Taktse Fortress could be seen distinctly midway up the mountain, the six palaces linked by a snaking of solid construction. These Tubo chieftains who lived 1,300 years before had really been smart in siting their fortress in a pass where it was sheltered from the wind and protected from attack. During this period the ancient civilisation of the Yarlung Valley made great progress. Not only did division of labour already exist in agriculture and animal husbandry, but metallurgy and handicraft production were introduced. The Yarlung tribe also intermarried and had contacts with other surrounding tribes.

Going uphill, one finds himself in front of the Rio Dechen Temple. To the east of the temple, a stone wall was built along the mountain ridge. About ten feet high, and still sturdy, this is a fortification of the Tubo period, and although a trifle compared to the Great Wall of China, it shows the Tubos were aware of the need to defend themselves and keep the enemy out by erecting a protective wall, and this in itself was a huge stride forward in civilization.

One end of the wall finishes at a towering rocky peak where an ancient fortress stands. Above and below the fortress are two blockhouses, probably for defence. The other buildings had long since disappeared. The fortresses, walls and houses were all built of stone slabs found on these mountains, and it was solely due to these solid stones of the Gangdise Range that the buildings had managed to stand up to the wind and rain for over 1,500 years without being ravaged by nature. Wind, frost, rain, and snow had done nothing but make these stones a little smoother by weathering.

People living here often say that if one leaves Chong-gye, having visited the Six Palaces of Chingwar Taktse but not having a look at the tumuli of the Tibetan kings, he will not be able to verify the actual heroic deeds of the Tubos in the creation of their history.

As early as prior to 1,300 years ago, when the tribes of the Yarlung Valley were rising to prosperity, the ancestors of Songtsan Gampo lived in the Six Palaces of Chingwar Taktse situated near Lhamo Hill, from where they ruled over thousands and thousands of tribal people and opened up the mild and fertile Yarlung Valley. There, Tubo tribes waxed and multiplied, swallowing up the nearby peoples. Then, Namri Songtsan crossed the northern mountain range and defeated the Sumba people who lived in the river valleys of the Kyichu (Lhasa River) and Nyangchu. Spreading his power over the whole of Tibet, he established the Tubo kingdom. Namri Songtsan's son, Songtsan Gampo, moved his capital from the Yarlung Valley to Lhasa, the then political, economic, military and cultural centre, but Chong-gye and its environs still remained the home of the royal line. Even the later Tsanpos who lived in Lhasa dared not forget that their ancestors had originated from the Yarlung Valley, and they frequently came back to reside so as never to forget their ancestors' heroic deeds and meritorious services. The Princesses Wencheng and Jincheng of the Tang court also often spent time there after their marriage with the Tubo Tsanpos. In memory of their origins, the Tubo Tsanpos were all buried at Chong-gye, which explains why so many tumuli are gathered there.

According to historical records there should be of altogether thirteen tumuli of Tibetan kings, but only nine can still be discerned. It is clear that over the passage of time some tumuli must have sunk and disappeared. The nine tumuli which still remain have been reliably identified as belonging to the following: Songtsan Gampo, Gungri Gungtsan (son of Songt-san Gampo), Dusong Mangtsan (grandson of Songt-san Gampo), Tridu Songtsan (son of Mangsong Mangt-san), Tride Tsugtan (son of Tridu Songtsan), Trisung Detsan (son of Tride Tsugtan), Tride Songtsan (youn-ger brother of Trisung Detsan), Muni Tsanpo (son of Trisung Detsan), and lastly Princess Jincheng (wife of Tride Tsugtan).

On the summit of Songtsan Gampo's tumulus there used to be an ancient temple called Tongtsan Luakhang (Songtsan's Temple), which was where the Guardian of the Tombs resided. Within the temple, images of Songtsan Gampo, Princess Wencheng, Prin-cess Bhrikuti Devi, and the Ministers Gar Tongtsan and Thonmi Sambhota were enshrined. Only the ruins now remain.*

Beneath the ancient temple was Songtsan Gam-po's vault. It lay at the mouth of the Chongpo Stream about one and half kilometres from Piro Hill, in a group of tumuli located to the west of the present Chong-gye

---

* This temple has now been restored.

Dzong. Massive in size, the subterranean mausoleum was composed of five chambers, and in all was the length of an arrow-shot and the breadth of a call.* Statues of Songtsan Gampo, Sakyamuni and Avalokitesvara were placed inside the mausoleum along with great quantities of gold, silver, pearls, and agates as funerary objects, and so it was named "the Mausoleum with Inner Decorations." The front gate of Songtsan Gampo's mausoleum faced the southwest, looking towards the birthplace of Sakyamuni. On the left of the tomb itself was buried a suit of golden armour worn by Songtsan Gampo on expeditions; at the foot of the tomb was a cache of pearls, weighing two and half "kals,"** wrapped in satin, which was Songtsan Gampo's share of wealth, and at the head of the tomb was buried a coral statue of Lord Loyak Gyalmo, eight "forearms" (a unit of length from elbow to fingertip) in height, which was supposed to give light to the dead king. Knights and battle-horses made of pure gold were laid out on the right, as the retinue of Songtsan Gampo after his death.

Judging from accounts, the grand burial given to Songtsan Gampo by the Tubo Dynasty slave society, befitted his unparalled achievements and prestige. However, mausoleum containing only funerary objects and without a single sacrificial human victim does not quite conform with the general custom of Tibet at that time, and this probably shows the influence of the Tang Dynasty which then was at its height. Generally speak-

---

* "The distance of an arrow-shot" and "the distance of a call" are ancient Tibetan units of length. Both approximately equal to one hundred kilometres.
** "kal" is a Tibetan unit of weight approximately equal to 14 kilogrammes.

ing, in feudal society human sacrifice was not practised in royal burials, but Songtsan Gampo reigned during the latter part of a slave society which must have been well advanced judging from the fact that no slaves were reportedly sacrificed as funerary objects. As yet the tomb has not been excavated, and the details given here come solely from records or oral traditions. This ancient tomb, undisturbed for over a millenium, still holds its secret for future discovery.

The tumulus of Princess Jincheng's husband, Tride Tsugtan is another huge one, which is a six-metre high mound. Forty metres away a stone tablet erected more than a thousand years ago stands in a deep shaft covered by a small shelter. At that time the Tubo Dynasty was still in its golden age. When the Tsanpo died, a stone tablet was enacted to his memory, as was done to his maternal uncles (the Tang Emperors), which shows the influence of Princess Jincheng.

The ten-metre high stone tablet had withstood the ravages of wind and rain for over a thousand years, and the ancient Tibetan writings on the front of the tablet, recording Tride Tsugtan's achievements, are still decipherable. The top of the tablet is carved with vivid decorative patterns, and on one side of the tablet an upright flood dragon is still clearly discernible. The other side, however, had been already weathered completely smooth. Why only one such tablet stands amongst the tumuli of the Tibetan kings remains a mystery.

The tomb of Gungri Gungtsan, Songtsan Gampo's son, was built while his father was on the throne. It is the biggest in size and best in location. The site chosen for Songtsan Gampo's own tumulus was not as good as his son's.

On the Molari Hill, there are two tumuli joined together, which at first appeared to be one single tumulus. About 40 metres high and 170 metres across, the burial mounds look like a pair of square hills. Two successive generations were buried here: Mangsong Mangtsan (Gungri Gungtsan's son) and Dusong Mangtsan, his son. These two tumuli are notable because a pair of carved marble lions stood guard before them about two hundred metres apart. The one on the left lacked only a leg, but otherwise was quite complete and still maintained its air of grandeur, while the right-hand lion was still sitting firmly at the front of the tumulus, loyal to its post although its head was missing. The two lions were seated facing the tumuli, tails curled to the left, and were carved out of solid stone in clear, un-trammelled lines. Unmarked by the passage of time, their carved designs were still distinct.

At present apart from these tumuli no other cemeteries and burial places have been found in Tibet. Owing to the widespread practice of celestial and water burial, the existence of these tumuli seems very strange. One possible explanation is that during the Tubo epoch, interment was considered the noblest form of funeral, and the idea of "sacrificing one's body" was not yet upmost in the minds of the Tubo people.

The First Monastery

According to the Tibetan tradition a complete monastery should have three precious things: the Buddha, the dharma, and sangha (monks). With no monks in permanent residence, monasteries can only be considered as temples. Therefore the Samye Monastery in Lhoka can be regarded as the forerunner of the Tibetan monasteries for it harboured the first community of monks who renounced their homes and took to monastic life.

In fact, the Samye Monastery is made up of a cluster of buildings. Around the Assembly Hall were a number of temples of all sizes. It is said that aside from the monks' living quarters, temples alone number 108 all told, some of which have already collapsed into ruins although their foundations can still be seen. It is quite a surprise to come across such a large monastery complex in such a sparsely populated area at the foot of Mt. Hapuri.

Long before the founder of Samye, Trisung Detsan, ascended to the Tsanpo's throne, his father Tride Tsugtan was already a follower of Buddhism. During his reign, Tride Tsugtan spread Buddhism claiming that he had his ancestor's testament and prophecy: "Five generations after Songtsan Gampo, when a Tsanpo with the syllable 'de' in his name comes to the throne, Buddhism will rise and flourish." The king dispatched Sangshi, one of Princess Jincheng's attendants, to Mt. Wutaishan in inland China to study the dharma. After undergoing innumerable hardships, Sangshi obtained the knowledge of the dharma. But before he returned to Tibet, Tride Tsugtan died, and so the duty of spreading the dharma fell onto the eight-year old Trisung Detsan's shoulders. Although in name he was the Tsanpo, the real power was in the hands of a group of treacherous ministers who were opposed to Buddhism. They placed all the blame for the former king Tride Tsugtan's violent death on his faith in Buddhism, but before they managed to wipe out Buddhism, one by one they all died of natural causes. Subsequently, Trisung Detsan accepted the advice of his minister Ba Salnang to place his faith in Buddhism, and then sent him to Nepal to pay homage to the eminent monk Shantarakshita and seek to become his disciple. When Ba Salnang arrived in Nepal on his mission, Shantarakshita gave him the religious name of Yeshe Wangpo.

After becoming well-versed in Buddhism, Yeshe Wangpo invited his Master to return with him to Tibet to preach Buddhism and raise its prestige. Shantarakshita replied, "We shall go to Tibet and act in accordance with its climate and topographical advantages." The Master thought that for Buddhism to make a swift recovery in the land of Tubos, it would be necessary to build a monastery at the foot of Mt. Hapuri near the Tsangpo River as a base for preaching Buddhism.

Thereupon Yeshe Wangpo and Shantarakshita returned together to Tibet and busied themselves in the Samye region building a monastery. However for some inexplicable reason the construction never met with success. It might have been due to an insufficient knowledge of the geological structure or some fault in the method of construction, but no sooner was anything built than it collapsed. At that time it was automatically assumed that the destruction was caused by evil spirits. Shantarakshita proposed that he should leave for the Pure Land to invite Padmasambhava, who was an expert exorcizer of evil spirits, to Tibet. Padmasambhava probably knew something about architecture, and after his arrival the construction of the monastery was amazingly completed. Modelled on India's Odantapura Monastery, Samye combined the craftsmanship of central China, Tibet, and India. The Tubos were now in possession of their first monastery, and Padmasambhava, Shantarakshita and Trisung Detsan who had made such a great contribution to the spreading of Buddhism became honoured as the "Trio of the Abbot, the Master, and the King."

The main building, Tsuglhakhang, stands conspicuously towering above others resembling a stupa with its broad base and pointed top, and glistening golden roofs. Originally three-storeyed, the third storey was removed in the last decade because it had been on the verge of collapse. Fortunately in one of the shrines on the second floor, there is a panoramic picture of Samye as it had been which showed the size and position of the original monastery. It is said that the first floor was built by Tibetan craftsmen according to Tibet's own national pattern of architecture and the second floor was designed by monks of the Han nationality in the style of monasteries in central China. On the door lintel of the second floor hung a dark green panel with carved characters painted in gold which read: "Brightness to the Boundless Universe." With its bold strokes and skillful style, this looked rather like calligraphy of the Ming period. The third floor had been built under the supervision of Indian monks, and hence it had borne the features of an Indian monastery. To the north of the main building three temples were located on the slopes of a hill called the Uze Risum (Three Peaks). Surrounding the main building were eight huge temples with an outer ring of four stupas; while outside the monastery there were three palaces called Jomo Lingsum, built by Tisung Detsan as residences for his queens when they came on pilgrimage. In addition there were monks' living quarters, storehouses, side halls, and the like which made this place worthy of its name "forest of monasteries."

Southwest of the main building is a square where

the translation of the sacred texts took place. Many lotsavas (translators of sacred texts) from the whole of Tibet, from the Han regions and from other lands were gathered here in those times to translate the Buddhist scriptures into Tibetan and so promoted the spread of the Buddhist doctrine throughout Tibet. To begin with, Trisung Detsan sent seven men Ba Salnang, Verotsana, Khon Luyi-Wangpo, Ma Rinchen Chog, Tsang Legdrup, Gyawa Chog-yang, and Chim Shakya Tawa to study Buddhism as a trial to see whether the Tubos really could stand up to renouncing the world and observing monastic discipline as did eminent monks of the Pure Land. These seven scholars proved to be obedient, diligent and well-versed in Buddhist sutras. Thereupon Trisung Detsan once again invited more eminent monks and lotsavas from the Pure Land and the Han regions to supervise the Tibetan monks in their translation of the Buddhist sutras. From that time on, Buddhism spread throughout the length and breadth of the land of the Tubos.

A number of attractive murals still graced the translation courtyard. In these paintings, scholars from different countries site in the lotus position in groups of three, one reciting loudly, another carefully taking notes, and the third seated in an elevated position engaged in proofreading. It is said that the proofreaders were the wisest of the panditas (pundits), and the name of each pandita was recorded below his picture. These paintings reproduced the working style of translation at that time, and they are of great reference value to later researchers of the history of religion and translation in Tibet. This translation courtyard was established by Trisung Detsan, and was the training ground for a group of Tibetan scholars and lotsavas.

One of them was Verotsana, who was regarded as one of the three greatest lotsavas in Tibetan history.

Like other monasteries, Samye possesses a lot of priceless relics, "Tangkas," and images. The monastery's most valued possession was a huge bronze bell cast in the Tang period, inscribed with the contribution made by Trisung Detsan in spreading Buddhism.

Tibetan Buddhism and Tibetan culture go hand in hand. The development of Buddhism brought with it rapid progress in Tibet's architecture, carving, painting, script, translation, and the like, and with the founding of monasteries and wide-scale translation of sutras during Trisung Detsan's time, Tibetan culture took great steps forward.

Lamas gathering for a sermon

Long prostration, a common scene

A dance to communicate with the Buddha

A religious procession

Unfolding the thangka

Hanging of the giant thangka at the Shoton Festival

Lamas at the Great Prayer Festival

The 26-meter high Maitreya Buddha at
Tashilhunpo Monastery

The Statue of Buddha at Jokhang Monastery

A lama music band

Unique Tibetan rock art

Carving the Buddhist scripture

One of numerous devout Buddhist believers in the crowd

Enjoying the Picnic Festival

An ego-slaying practice
(Tibetan: chö)

4

LHASA "ABODE OF THE GOD"

Songtsan Gampo Shifts His Capital to Lhasa

Filling in the Wotso Pool to Build the Jokhang Temple

The Potala Palace Landmark of Tibet

The Norbu Lingka the Jewel Park

The Three Great Monasteries of Lhasa

Memorial Tablets in Lhasa

The Uncle-Nephew Alliance Tablet

Takdra Lukong's Merit Tablet

The Kangxi Tablet and the Qianlong Tablet in the House of the Serpent

Nestled amidst the eight auspicious mountains, Lhasa well deserves the name given it by the Tibetans "Abode of the Gods," and her ancient and dignified appearance has charmed countless visitors and pilgrims alike. The Jokhang in the heart of the city still appears as tranquil as ever it had been in the past, though its surroundings have long since taken on a new look. Along the Bharkor, Lhasa's ring road, shops and markets flourish and a recently constructed tar road paves the way for those on pilgrimage. Mingling with the golden roofs of the Jokhang, the Potala Palace stands majestic to the west of the city, its lofty walls rearing up on the towering sacred hill, the Red Hill, known to Buddhists as "Mt. Potala the Second." Tsongkapa, the founder of the Gelugpa Sect, established the Ganden Monastery amidst a cluster of mountains to the southeast of the city, while his two senior disciples successively founded the Drepung and Sera monasteries north of the city, and these further provide the city with a number of stories of Buddhist miracles and age-old historical tales.

Songtsan Gampo Shifts His Capital to Lhasa

Whenever scholars of Tibetan history speak of Lhasa's origin, they recall the forerunner of the Potala, the "Chogyal Drupug" (Cave of the Religious-king). Sources say that this cave was the first major construction Songtsan Gampo undertook when he moved to Lhasa at the beginning of the seventh century. In actual fact it is scarcely thirty square metres in area. It is said that this cave later became an ideal hermitage for meditation and mental cultivation for Buddhist disciples. Today the statues of Songtsan Gampo, Princess Wencheng, Princess Bhrikuti Devi and the ministers of the Tubo Dynasty, Gar Tongtsan and Thonmi Sambho-ta, still stand well preserved in the cave. This spot is one of the few remaining treasures of ancient Tibet. But it is to the smoky Jokhang Temple that one must turn if one really wants to delve into the history of Lhasa.

The Jokhang was first built in the mid-seventh century and was constructed solely of timber and mud. The main section of the temple is three storeys high, topped with golden roofs found nowhere else except in Tibet, which glint in the sun creating a splendid scene of grandeur. The image of Sakyamuni brought by Princess Wencheng is enshrined in the central section of the main building, and the temple also contains all sorts of murals, sculptures and architectural features of a singular style, with gorgeously carved and painted beams and pillars. For more than a thousand years incense has filled the Jokhang, to be supplemented in more recent years by a continuous stream of tourists.

It seems incredible that this magnificent ancient temple which pious Buddhists liken to the "Kaaba of Mecca" was originally built over a pool called the Wotso. Tibetan historical records show that 1,350 years ago the site of the Jokhang was a marshland with a pool in the centre known as the Kyishod Wotso. At that time, the Kyishod Wotso was a desolate place inhabited solely by wild goats. At the time when Tibet was still divided into separate fiefdoms, Tubo might had not yet penetrated to the Kyishod Wotso which then formed part of the territory of the powerful Sumba people. However, this broad and splendid plain had escaped the notice of the Sumba chieftains, who had centred their administration in Yuna, many kilometres away from Lhasa, southeast of today's Panpo Farm.

At the beginning of the seventh century, the Tubo people living in isolation in a corner of Lhoka abruptly rose to power. They undertook a number of projects, popular at the time, in agriculture, connecting lakes, digging canals and channelling water to cultivated fields. By the time of the thirty-first Tubo Tsanpo, Takri Nyansik (grandfather of Songtsan Gampo), the great cause of the unification of Tibet had commenced and was carried on by the Tsanpo's son, Namri Songtsan, when he succeeded to the throne.

Born at a time when the Tubos' nascent power was starting to make itself felt, Songtsan Gampo was the only son of Namri Songtsan. He was regarded as a great gift from heaven, and considered the most fortunate of men among the Tubos, who believed he would bring glory and victory to the tribe. But when Songtsan Gampo reached the age of thirteen, disaster struck. Dissent grew among the Tubo ministers and they hatched a plot; Songtsan Gampo's father was poisoned by evil-intentioned nobles, and tribes formerly subject to the Tubos broke away one by one. And so this enigmatic prince assumed the throne at a troubled period. Taking up the challenge of the former nobles, he very soon put an end to internal strife and fulfilled the great cause of unification by extending his power along the length and breadth of the land.

On one auspicious day at the height of summer, the ambitious prince happened to be bathing in the limpid waters of the Kyichu River. As he raised his head and looked into the distance, his attention was aroused by the abundance of water and grass and the beauty of the valley in the centre of which rose the prominent features of the Red Hill and Chagpori Hill. Geographically, the place was of great strategic importance. Moreover, the spot was traditionally held to be a holy place as Songtsan Gampo's ancestor Lhato Thori Nyantsan, who was an incarnation of a heavenly god, had gone into meditation in seclusion on the high and solitary Red Hill as an example to later generations. Songtsan Gampo resolved forthwith to shift the capital from Gyama Migyurling to the Kyishod Wotso, ostensibly because of the legend of his ancestor, although in actual fact the young Tsanpo had his political aims in mind.

The Yarlung Valley, where the former capital of the Tubos had been sited, was now in the hands of rebellious former nobles of the Tubo Dynasty. Resentful at the crushing move made by the Songtsan clan, they hatched a sinister plot against the Tsanpo. The Tuguhan people in the north and the Shangshung people in the west were also eyeing Tubo territory covetously. This external trouble obliged Songtsan Gampo to abandon his out-of-the-way southern stronghold to accomplish his determined aim of occupying that strategic spot the Kyishod Wotso.

Filling in the Wotso Pool to Build the Jokhang Temple

After moving his capital to the Kyishod Wotso and unifying the whole of Tibet, Songtsan Gampo took further steps to realise his general plan. First he dealt with internal trouble, consolidated his royal power, reorganised the troops, developed the economy and improved agricultural techniques, and then sent Thonmi Sambhota abroad to study and create a script for

Tibetan, and enriched the national culture. From then on, the might of the Tubo kingdom increased day by day. Under such circumstances, Songtsan Gampo sent an envoy to the Tang court in 634 AD to ask for the hand in marriage of an imperial princess. After a number of delays and setbacks, Princess Wencheng of the Tang court eventually made her journey to Tibet in 641 AD as the bride of the twenty-five year old Songtsan Gampo. The arrival of the noble Princess Wencheng in Tibet marked the speedy development of the Kyishod Wotso and its transformation from a deserted swamp into a prosperous, thriving city.

Before his marriage to Princess Wencheng, Songtsan Gampo had already taken Princess Bhrikuti Devi of neighbouring Nepal as his queen. Princess Bhrikuti Devi had moved into the cave dwelling on the Red Hill, so when Princess Wencheng arrived she had to take up residence on the sandy soil near the Wotso Pool, east of the Potala, where the image of Sakyamuni she had brought with her had to be left amidst a dense grove of willows. A traditional tale says that Princess Wencheng observed the aspects of the heavens and the earth of the place, and concluded that the sandy land where she was living was situated over the mouth of a dragon, and hence a temple should be constructed there. The Tsanpo wholeheartedly agreed with her suggestion to build a temple to house the image of Sakyamuni.

No sooner had this news reached Princess Bhrikuti Devi than she too conceived the idea of building a temple for the worship of Buddha. The Nepali princess chose the southeast part of the sandy area for the site of her temple, but no matter how closely she supervised the construction during the daytime, the whole thing collapsed as soon as night fell. She had no alternative but to beg Princess Wencheng's assistance. Princess Wencheng generously agreed to help, and calculated through divination and astrology the right site for the temple.

Skilled in Tang astrology and well-versed in the theory of the Five Elements, Princess Wencheng examined astronomical phenomena by night and topographical aspects by day, and found that the land of the Tubos appeared like an ogress lying flat on her back, which was highly unfavourable for the establishment of the kingdom. In order to prevent any violent changes of ill omen, the princess deemed it necessary to build temples to pin down the four limbs of the ogress. Princess Wencheng next examined the Wotso Pool and found it was the heart of the ogress, and the water in the pool the blood. Therefore it was necessary to fill in the pool to block the circulation of the blood, and build a temple over it to suppress it. Examining the harmonious or contradictory nature of the Five Elements, Princess Wencheng then advised Songtsan Gampo to use white goats to carry earth when filling in the pool. Finally, the enormous construction project got under way. The flocks of goats loaded with earth swarming round the Wotso Pool gave the spot its new name. As the word "goat" is "ra" and "earth" is "sa" in Tibetan, the temple got the name of "Rasa" (goat-earth). Subsequently, this unprecedented majestic feat of construction became the prominent symbol of the capital and the town itself took the name "Rasa."

A number of fascinating tales still exist about the construction of the Jokhang. Tradition has it that Songtsan Gampo regarded Princess Wencheng as the incarnation of the goddess Tara. While the Jokhang was being built , Songtsan Gampo himself took his axe and climbed up to work on the building, which so alarmed the gods of the Heaven that they came down one after another to offer assistance. On one occasion a maidservant happened to take some food to the construction site, but when she arrived all the men working above and below looked identical to Songtsan Gampo, and she had no way of distinguishing the real one from the false. Turning pale with apprehension, she ran back to inform Princess Bhrikuti Devi, who, half-believing and half-doubting, went in person to take the food. When she discovered it was exactly as the maidservant had described, she let out a word of exclamation, "Strange!" At this, all the Songtsan Gampos seated on the beams looked down, and carelessly dropped their axes which, as they fell, struck off the noses of the sphinxes they were making. Today, visitors to the Jokhang will notice that everyone of the one hundred and eight sphinxes has a flat nose.

Many of the murals of the Jokhang are clearly in the Han style. In figure and attire, the warriors in the murals in the shrines of the Four Guardian Kings and the God of Serpents look very much akin to warriors of the Tang period, while the flag of the "Rising Lion" and the image of Sakyamuni to the west of the God of the Serpents Shrine are also painted in the Han style.

When the Jokhang was completed, Songtsan Gampo further asked Princess Wencheng to survey the astronomical phenomena and geographical aspects of Lhasa. After observing the aspects, Princess Wencheng said, "The sky is like the Eight Wheels of the Law, a sign of good omen; the earth is like the Eight-Petalled Lotus, a sign of fortune; the mountains are like the Eight Auspicious Emblems, a sign of prosperity." So saying, Princess Wencheng pointed out the Eight

Auspicious Emblems of the mountains surrounding Lhasa: the Lotus, the Parasol, the Conch Shell with a Rightward Spiral, the Wheel of the Law, the Knot That Has No End, the Vase of Great Treasure, the Pair of Goldfish, and the Banner of Supreme Excellence. Princess Wencheng then described the features of the four directions as seen from Lhasa in a poetic verse:

The eastern mountain peaks rise in waves,
Like angry tigers about to leap;
The two mountains to the west press
into the gorge,
Like the outstretched wings of an eagle;
In the south the Kyichu River winds by,
Like a wriggling turquoise dragon;
The northern peaks rise in gentle folds,
Like a tortoise crawling on all fours.

Princess Wencheng also named the four great mountains situated in the four directions. The southeast mountains she named Mindrug Zari, those to the northeast Jomo Sishi, the northwestern mountains she called Ganpoi Uze, and the southwestern ones Jomo Ulha. Today, over 1,300 years later, these names are still used.

In 648 AD the majestic Jokhang was finally completed. Together, Princess Wencheng and Songtsan Gampo planted a willow tree at the front gate of the Jokhang, which became known as the famous Jowo U-tra (The Buddha's Hair). The images of Sakyamuni brought by the two princesses were separately enshrined in the temples each had built, and ever since devout Buddhists from every region have flocked there on pilgrimage. At the end of the seventh century, over a dozen inns had appeared around the temple to cater for pilgrims. Gradually more residential houses were built, and so the Bharkor with the Jokhang at the the centre began to take shape, and the ancient city of the plateau started its rise to fame.

Under the influence of Princess Wencheng, herself a devout Buddhist, Songtsan Gampo too adhered more and more closely to Buddhism. Monasteries started to appear throughout Tibet's various regions and monks came forward to take Buddhist vows. Monks from the Tang Empire and the Pure Land too streamed into Lhasa. The rise of Buddhism coloured many Tibetan place-names. The prosaically named "Rasa" (goat-earth) had been transformed into a sacred place, and its name changed to "Lhasa," "Abode of the Gods."

Political struggles play an indispensable role in the rise and fall of a political and economic centre. The breakup of the Tubo royal family which started in the mid-ninth century led to the beginning of disregard for royal authority, and eventually Songtsan Gampo's two-century old slave system totally collapsed. In the latter half of the ninth century, Tubo society was confronted with an enormous uprising of common slaves which accelerated the decline of the Tubo slave system. Tibet then fell into separatist rule which lasted for four hundred years and was eventually succeeded by the dynasties of Sakya and Pagdu both of which set their capitals not at Lhasa but in Sakya and Nedong respectively. In the religious sphere, with the assumption of Lang Darma to the throne the persecution of Buddhism commenced: monks were massacred, monasteries were destroyed, and sutras were burnt. In keeping with the division of political power among separate states,

Buddhism broke up into different sects such as the Kadampa, Kagyupa, Nyingmapa, Sakyapa and so forth. During these four hundred years, Lhasa the once-flourishing capital became a dreary desolate place. Even famous buildings like the Potala were destroyed by natural and man-made calamities.

Notwithstanding, the royal capital Lhasa, "Abode of the Gods," had not been completely forgotten by the people. Even though incense burning at the Jokhang had been reduced to the minimum during those dark centuries, the trickle of pious Buddhist followers could not be entirely stemmed. In 1409, the eminent monk Tsongkapa from Qinghai organised the Great Prayer Festival ("mon lam") of the Gelugpa Sect in Lhasa for the first time, and the Jokhang regained its former opulence and prestige. Later, Tsongkapa and his disciples successively founded the monasteries of Ganden, Drepung and Sera, and Lhasa once again became the centre of religious activities. Later, the Fifth Dalai Lama rebuilt the Potala, while the Seventh Dalai Lama built the Norbu Lingka, and thus Lhasa entered another epoch of prosperity. With the establishment and development of the system of unification of state and church, Lhasa gradually became the centre of Tibet's politics, economy, culture and religion. For four hundred years after the fifteenth century, monasteries and monks became more and more numerous in Lhasa, which gradually gained fame far and wide as the "Second Paradise." Buddhists from Sichuan, Yunnan, Qinghai, Gansu and neighbouring countries came flocking to Lhasa, especially at the exceptionally grand occasions which were held every year during the Great Prayer Festival and Illumination Day, when the lines of pilgrims stretched for miles, Lhasa became enveloped in clouds of incense smoke, tents were pitched everywhere at the outskirts of the city, and monks in deep red robes with law-keeping staves in their hands swaggered along the streets and alleyways. At times like these, the ancient city of the plateau was indeed a sight to behold with its lofty buildings, crowds of merchants, swarming visitors, horsecarts manoeuvring everywhere and a hubbub of voices.

In 1637, Tibet came under the rule of Goshri Khan, a Mongol prince, also a follower of the Gelugpa Sect. He suppressed religious rivals, gave his support to the Fifth Dalai Lama to unify the whole of Tibet, and gradually strengthened the unification of state and church. In 1645, the Fifth Dalai Lama put the Desi (Regent) in charge of rebuilding the Potala, which took eight years to complete. Today, the Potala Palace stands prominently to the west of the city centre. Thirteen storeys high, it measures 117.19 metres in height, covers 130,000 square metres, and contains 999 halls and rooms, a masterpiece of architectural genius in Lhasa. After the rebuilding, the Fifth Dalai Lama moved his residence from the Drepung to the Potala, and it was at this time that the Serpent-God Temple situated north of the Red Hill also took shape, which added to the splendour of Lhasa's architecture.

From the time of the Fifth Dalai Lama, the Jokhang underwent numerous large-scale repairs and extensions, reaching its present size in the seventeenth century. By this period residences in Lhasa had also increased greatly, and as the Jokhang occupied a central position, numerous private mansions of monk and lay officials appeared in its surroundings. The urban district of Lhasa now extended as far as the Yuthuk Bridge (Glazed-Tile Bridge) in the west, the Moslem

mosque in the east, southwards to the July First Agriculture Machinery Plant, and northwards to the Muru
Monastery. Offices of the Town Magistrate had also
appeared.

In the 1750s, the Seventh Dalai Lama initiated the
construction of the Norbu Lingka on a marshy area
where thorny shrubs and willows grew, about two
kilometres west of the Potala. During the time of the
Eighth Dalai Lama, the Norbu Lingka was further
extended to the south, so that it covered a total area
of 350,000 square metres with 374 rooms. Within the
park, shady trees, fragrant flowers, sweet-voiced birds,
terraces and pavilions are to be found everywhere. The
Dalai Lamas used this park as their summer palace.

At the time of the Third Dalai Lama, the system
of reincarnation of the Dalai Lama was established.
The Fifth Dalai Lama subsequently strengthened the
system of the unification of the state and church and
established the Gandan Podrang's administration, and
thereafter during each interval between reincarnation
of the Dalai Lama, hereditary regents ruled the country. The emergence of the system of regents paved the
way for further establishment of monasteries. For
example, monasteries such as the Tan-gye-ling, Shide,
Tsemeling, Kundeling and Meru which owned vast
tracts of land and harboured hundreds of monks all
belonged to the regents. From the emergence of these
monasteries we can deduce that the urban district of
Lhasa was growing while religion was developing and
flourishing.

Starting from the Fifth Dalai Lama, family members and relatives of the Dalai Lamas all moved to
Lhasa from their native places and became members of
the nobility, and in consequence many spacious man-

sions appeared one after another. At the turn of the century, senior noble families not only built mansions within Lhasa but also constructed villas in lovely natural parks along the banks of the Kyichu (Lhasa) River and in the outskirts of the city. Along the northern bank of the Kyichu River alone there were a dozen of these villas. In this way the urban district of Lhasa continued to grow.

From the seventeenth century, Lhasa began to arouse the attention not only of the Hans and Moslems and other nationalities of inland China, but also of the merchants of neighbouring countries such as Bhutan, Sikkim, Nepal and India. Many of these merchants made the long journey to Lhasa in order to trade, and Lhasa evolved into a small-scale international market. Many of these Han, Moslem and foreign traders gradually settled in Lhasa and played a definite role in the expansion of the city.

However, for 1,300 years or so in pre-liberation days, Lhasa's construction was in fact restricted to monasteries, government headquarters and mansions for the nobility, with no concept of city planning or provision for public buildings. Since liberation, the construction area has risen fifteen-fold over that of the previous 1,300 years.

The Potala Palace Landmark of Tibet

Standing loftily above the Lhasa basin, the Potala Palace is not the symbol of Lhasa alone but of all Tibet. No journey to the "Roof of the World" is complete without a visit to the world-famous Potala.

The thirteen-storeyed ancient building built only of mortar, timber and stone dates back 1,300 years. As well as being of great historical value, the architecture itself of the Potala, and in addition its murals, stupas, carvings, sculptures and the like are witness of its being a treasury of art. The palace contains such invaluable treasures as pearls, cultural relics, "tangkas," scrolled texts and ancient chinaware, making the Potala a repository of inestimable worth, and it is a mecca to which the visitor can return again and again, each time experiencing fresh understandings and gains.

Toiling up the stairs leading to the Potala, step by weary step, you indeed feel yourself a small and insignificant creature in the face of this gigantic palace. Arriving at the huge front entrance, the Puntsok Donam Gate, you may marvel at the great bar across the gate which is made out of an entire tree trunk. As you pass through the gate you enter a narrow passage, and then a high-walled tunnel-like corridor which allows a rare glimpse of the massive palace walls, built solely of stone and mortar and several metres thick, which date back over a thousand years.

The passage gives out onto a huge courtyard, sixty to seventy metres above ground level, which was specially built for ritual dance performances. The even, 1,600 square metre floor is paved with "arka," a special type of Tibetan flooring like concrete. Low yellow-walled galleries line the northern and southern sides of the courtyard, while directly opposite, a short but steep triple flight of steps leads up to the antechamber in the western front of the Deyangshar Mansion. The flight of steps in the centre was reserved for the Dalai Lama's sole use, while those to either side were for ordinary people and officers. This is the only way to the other halls, and it is said "a troop ten thousand strong cannot pass through the entrance though it be guarded by a single man." In the antechamber, the visitor's attention is caught by a pair of hand prints under a glass cover to the left on the southern wall. These prints were left by the Fifth Dalai Lama at the height of the construction of the Potala in the mid-seventeenth century. By then the Fifth Dalai Lama was advanced in age and did not take much interest in political affairs, so all arrangements were put in the hands of Sang-gye Gyatso, (the Desi or the Regent). But the Desi at that time did not have much prestige, and consequently the Fifth Dalai Lama, realising that people were unlikely to recognise the Desi's authority, left the Desi prints of his own hands as a symbol of his authority over monk and lay officials in government affairs. Ever since then, these historic hand prints have been preserved.

Turning to the eastern walls, familiar murals of Songtsan Gampo asking for the hand in marriage of Princess Wencheng and scenes from her journey to Tibet can be seen. After unifying Tibet for the first time and founding the powerful Tubo Dynasty, Songtsan Gampo sent his trusted minister Gar Tongtsan to Chang'an, the capital of the Tang Dynasty, to ask the Tang Emperor Taizong for the hand of the princess in marriage. From these murals we can see a contemporary sketch map of the Tang Dynasty capital Chang'an, and also how Emperor Taizong posed five tricky questions to test the intelligence of the envoys from neighbouring minority nationalities who had all come to the Tang Court to seek the princess in marriage. Gar Tongtsan, the Tubo envoy, being the most intelligent of the lot, succeeded in cracking all five riddles, gained first place and consequently won the hand of Princess Wencheng for the Tubo Tsanpo. Murals depicting this part of history can also be found in many other monasteries and temples.

Leading on next to the murals on the northern wall, we can see a portrayal of Princess Wencheng's journey to Tibet and the scene of great rejoicing on her arrival in Lhasa. In 710 AD, following in the footsteps of her royal sister of a previous age, another Tang princess, Princess Jincheng, made her journey to Tibet. Princess Jincheng's deeds too are portrayed in the murals of the Potala, and a painting of Princess Jincheng's journey to Tibet appears on the east wall of the Tsomchen Shar (the East Audience Hall).

The Tsomchen Shar is the largest hall in the White Palace section of the Potala. Major political and religious events such as ordinations and coronations of the Dalai Lamas were held in this audience hall. Here are preserved the gold slab and gold seal inscribed with the title offered to the Fifth Dalai Lama by Emperor Shunzhi of the Qing Dynasty. The inscription reads: "Preceptor of Lord Buddha's Doctrine, Keeper of Peace in the West, Uniter of the Buddhist Faith Beneath the Sky, Superior of the Ocean, Holder of the Thunderbolt."

From Tsomchen Shar if you climb up to the topmost part of the White Palace section, you will find yourself in another world. Full-length glass windows face south so that the rooms are bathed in brilliant sunshine from morning till evening. Respectively named East Sunny Room and West Sunny Room, these were the Dalai Lama's living quarters and are crammed with precious jewels, luxurious furnishings, gold basins, jade bowls, brocades and satins. Stepping out onto the balcony, Lhasa seems to be just beneath one's nose; fold upon fold, mountain ranges rear up, the Kyichu River gurgles along below, footpaths crisscross the fields and villages studded with green trees, creating a scene of genuine majesty.

The whole of the Potala is divided into two sections, the White Palace and the central Red Palace. From the very beginning, the two sections of the Potala were strictly distinguished by their different colours, being white-washed and red-washed. The Red Palace mainly consists of funerary stupas of the Dalai Lamas and various shrines and temples. There are altogether eight funerary stupas in the Potala containing the embalmed remains of the Fifth to the Thirteenth Dalai Lamas, excluding the Sixth. The funerary stupas are more or less akin to each other in structure, but they differ greatly in size, and those of the Fifth and Thirteenth Dalai Lamas are the most splendid of the lot. Built in 1690, the funerary stupa of the Fifth Dalai Lama is the largest at 14.85 metres high. It is entirely covered in sheets of gold, and studded with countless pearls, jade and agate. 110,000 ounces of gold were used for this stupa alone, excluding the jewels.

Although the large majority of Tibetans dispose of their dead through celestial and water burials, the bodies of religious leaders who are apt to preach to others about "sacrificing one's body" are preserved for posterity. Whenever the Dalai Lama passed away, the body was smeared with salt to absorb moisture, and then anointed with perfumes. When dessicated, it was placed in a stupa. This is one kind of stupa burial. In Tibet, stupa burials are only given to the Dalai Lamas and "Hutogtu" lamas'. No other monk or lay officials are permitted to be treated in this way after death. In

---

· "Hutogtu" is a Mongolian term meaning "high lama." In Tibet, lamas with the title "Hutogtu" are qualified to act as regent should the Dalai Lama die.

keeping with his rank, a golden stupa is accorded only to the god-king, while others are given silver, brass and clay stupas respectively.

The shrines containing the funerary stupas lead off from the huge central Sishi Puntsok Hall, with a floor space of nearly seven hundred square metres. Displayed here is the panel presented by Qing Emperor Qianlong with its Chinese characters written in gold which read: "Holy Spot of the Emerging Lotus." The murals in this hall mainly include works of the Fifth Dalai Lama during his lifetime and events of his reign, and his famous visit to Beijing and interview with Emperor Shunzhi in the mid-seventeenth century appears conspicuously on one of the walls. The frescoed corridor on the floor above the Sishi Puntsok can be rated as an art gallery. Here, nearly seven hundred murals are displayed covering every aspect of life of the Tibetan people and showing different scenes from the construction of the Potala.

Two storeys up from the Sishi Puntsok Hall is the Chogyal Drupug (the Cave of the Religious-King). This cave-like shrine is said to have been built to commemorate Songtsan Gampo's meditation on the Red Hill in his youth. Constructed in the seventh century, it is the most ancient part of the Potala. According to written records, when it was built 1,300 years ago, the Potala had 999 rooms, with the addition of this cave shrine making the figure up to 1,000. Formerly, the Potala was built on a vast scale, but due to fire damage caused by lightning strikes and sudden attacks, the original construction was almost levelled to the ground leaving only the Chogyal Drupug Cave and the Pagpa Lhakhang Temple. Looking around at the Chogyal Drupug's shiny walls blackened by incense smoke, you can faintly see that all four walls have been dug out to form a cave. Under the gloomy electric light, the lifelike sculptures of Songtsan Gampo, Princess Wencheng, Princess Bhrikuti Devi, and Gar Tongtsan and Thonmi Sambhota could be real! This tiny cave shrine scarcely thirty square metres in area will take you back 1,300 years in history.

The Pagpa Lhakhang, on the next level directly above the Chogyal Drupug, is also one of the earliest parts of the palace. The central image enshrined inside is said to be a manifestation of Songtsan Gampo. A panel with the inscription "Blissful Soil Nourishing Miraculous Fruits' written in Chinese by the Qing Emperor Tongzhi hangs above the entrance to the shrine. From the time of the Fifth Dalai Lama, the Qing Dynasty strengthened its control over Tibet, and the Dalai Lama in return developed his relationship with the central government. Other proofs of this close relationship can be found elsewhere in the Potala, and include a portrait of Emperor Qianlong and an imperial longevity tablet written in four languages Han, Tibetan, Mongolian and Manchurian both of which are kept in the Sasum Namgyal Hall. Later reincarnations of the Dalai Lama paid their respects annually to the portrait and tablet to express courtesy from a minister to a monarch.

It would be impossible to mention one by one all the jewels and antiques that are preserved in the Potala, but one item that deserves to be remarked on is a pearl mandala composed of 200,000 pearls. It is not only priceless but a precious work of art.

When visit to the Potala Palace is over, one might be pondering this question: from its murals, sculptures, "tangkas" and gifts, the Potala seems no different from other monasteries in Tibet, so why is it that the others are called "monasteries" while the Potala alone is called a "palace?" The reason is because that the Potala was originally built in the Tubo era when Buddhism had not yet attained its dominant position in Tibet. Moreover, the unification of the state and church had not yet been effected. The imposing buildings of the Potala were erected merely as a palace for the kings, built against a hilly backdrop so as to give a majestic impression of standing aloft. In those days there were not as many images and stupas as there are today, and so there was no reason for people to come and worship and burn incense. After the Fifth Dalai Lama received his appointment from the Qing Emperor and rose to the leadership of both state and church, the residential palace for the Dalai Lama was moved from the Drepung Monastery to the Potala Palace. As a consequence, the identity of the Potala underwent a change: it became the seat of not only local government but also the greatest Buddhist lama of Tibet. The Potala therefore obviously took on a deeper religious colouring, and as it was the seat of the Dalai Lama, the incarnation of a god, the Potala also became a sacred place for people to prostrate themselves in reverence.

With the strengthening of the unification of state and church, the Potala not only took on the functions of seat of government, ministries and monastery, but also became the leading military headquarters for the pre-liberation local army. A prison was built under the Potala, adding to its complex nature.

The Norbu Lingka The Jewel Park

On the banks of the Kyichu River, two kilometres west of the Jokhang Temple, there is a tree and flower filled park known as the Norbu Lingka or the Jewel Park. Covering a total area of 360,000 square metres, the park was originally laid out in the 1750s during the time of the Seventh Dalai Lama Kalsang Gyatso. Before then, the Norbu Lingka was just a stretch of wasteland containing a spring in which Kalsang Gyatso took treatment baths for his frequent bouts of illness. At this time, the Amban bestowed favour by building a rest pavilion for Kalsang Gyatso, named the Uyap Podrang. In 1751, the Seventh Dalai Lama built the first palace close to the Uyap Podrang and named it the Kalsang Podrang, after himself. It was the forerunner of the Norbu Lingka. The Kalsang Podrang is three storeys high and built of block stones. Within the palace, there are shrines, a chamber, a reading room, a shrine for the Guardian Deities, and an audience hall. Murals adorn the shrine of the Guardian Deities, and depict the three greatest Tsanpos of the Tubo Dynasty Songtsan Gampo, Trisung Detsan and Tritsug Detsan (Ralpachen) painted together with various guardian deities, as well as commemorative portraits of representative personages of major religious schools of Tibetan Buddhism.

Following the construction of the Kalsang Podrang, successive Dalai Lamas, before reaching their maturity (before the age of eighteen), were tutored in elementary Tibetan and religious knowledge, and gave audiences and blessings in this palace. When the Dalai Lama took power, the Norbu Lingka was used as the summer palace and the Potala as the winter palace. Every year from the middle of the third month to the beginning of the tenth month, the Dalai Lama took up residence in the Kalsang Podrang where he recited religious texts, learned history, went over documents, appointed officials, and held discussions on state affairs. His leisure time was spent in amusements a-round the park.

The Norbu Lingka was extended with almost every new succession of the Dalai Lama. During the time of the Eighth Dalai Lama, considerable additions were made to the park in the form of a courtyard for sermons, the House of the Serpent, a reading room, and the Chamber of Surveying Over the Three Realms. When the Thirteenth Dalai Lama took power, the Norbu Lingka was further extended by establishing the Chansal Park and the Chansal Podrang. The Norbu Lingka lies to the east and the Chansal Park to the west, with a number of buildings, terraces, pavilions and verandas in between.

The three-storeyed Chansal Podrang contains shrines, chambers, storerooms, a courtyard for sermons, audience hall, the office of the lord Chamberlain, and the like. Like the Kalsang Podrang, the palace is filled with murals depicting Mt. Wutaishan and Mt. Longevity, and also showing symbols of happiness, wealth, longevity and fortune painted in the Han style. The style of the art is a mixture of Han and Tibetan. The Chansal Podrang further possesses a number of carvings, while glazed tiles, the Medogongka's folk art form, are used for roofing.

In 1954, the Norbu Lingka was once again extended with the building of the Dalai Lama's new palace, the Taktan Migyur Podrang (popularly known as the New Palace). The New Palace is a magnificent work of art; on the rooftop the Wheel of the Sacred Law and Banners-of-Victory glint golden in the sun, writhing dragons and flying phoenixes are poised over arched windows, and the topmost edge of the outer wall is bordered with a frieze several feet wide and made from stained tamarisk wood. To find a frieze in a Tibetan monastery or palace is very unusual as they are only permitted in monasteries in possession of the three precious jewels, the Buddha, the Dharma, the Sangha, and the palaces or residences of the Dalai Lama, the Regent and high lamas of the "Hutogtu" rank. In order to add solemnity and majesty to the friezes, they are ornamented with the Eight Auspicious Emblems and the Seven Royal Insignia in brass and gilding.

Stepping onto the porch of the New Palace, the visitor will notice a pair of long cylindrical tigerskin lashes hanging prominently on either side of the door. The symbol of power, they serve to prohibit entry without permission. These one-metre-long tigerskin lashes were formerly carried by the palace guards to clear the way for the Tsanpo during the reign of Trisung Detsan. Later, officials were specially assigned to carry these lashes at the head of the Dalai Lama's procession to drive people out of the way. Opening the stout red wooden door and stepping onto the deep red carpet, the visitor will notice two huge paintings of a lion and a tiger which indicate that this is the residence of the head of state and church in Tibet.

The murals of the Norbu Lingka's New Palace are painted in a composite style of various monasteries and temples. The richness of artistry is evident in the superb collection of beautiful sacred murals, images, "tangkas," stupas and butter lamps. On the southern wall of the corridor there are some intriguing "crossword poems," arranged in both squares and rounds, which appear as verses read either horizontally or vertically. Among the attractive murals, there is a scene of Songtsan Gampo sending Gar Tongtsan to the

Tang Court with an offer of marriage. One group of murals vividly depicts Trisung Detsan at the age of one picking out his real mother by recognising his maternal uncles at a grand banquet. The paintings capture the happy and surprised expression of Trisung Detsan's natural mother, Princess Jincheng, when the infant king confidently approaches the envoys sent by the Tang court. Among the murals of the New Palace there is also a scene of the Fifth Dalai Lama's visit to Beijing in 1652, where he is in audience with Emperor Shunzhi, receiving the title of Dalai Lama and accepting the gold diploma and the gold seal. This event is of great significance to the Gelugpa Sect as it was from this time that it gained ground in dominating the whole of Tibet. The newest murals in the palace describe the historical events of the Fourteenth Dalai Lama's visit to Beijing along the newly-opened Kham-Tibet Highway to attend the National People's Congress of China, and his visits to other places in China. Also depicted are the gifts presented by the Central People's Government.

The collected architecture, murals and decorations of the Norbu Lingka's New Palace represent the cream of Tibet's monasteries, temples and palaces. A visit to the New Palace is like a visit to every architectural sight in Tibet. In style, the New Palace has a strong air of a monastery or temple with the set-up of a palace or mansion. In all aspects it outshines both the Kalsang Podrang and the Chansal Podrang.

The parkland surroundings of the New Palace form a colourful scene of rockeries and fountains. Deep green pines and cypresses and numerous different kinds of fresh flowers in various colours set each other off against a carpet of meadows, while all around there are fountains, pavilions, terraces and stone tables and stools where visitors may rest amidst the flowers, and gaze at the snow-clad mountains rearing up in the distance.

The Three Great Monasteries of Lhasa

In the northern, eastern and western suburbs of Lhasa, "Abode of God," are the three great world-famous monasteries of Ganden, Drepung and Sera. These three monasteries, known collectively as the "Dansa Sum" (Three Great Seats of Monks), were founded by Tsongkapa, the founder of the Gelugpa Sect, and his disciples. According to the traditional rule, the "Dansa Sum" were to harbour monks as follows: Ganden, 3,300 monks; Sera, 5,500 monks; and Drepung, 7,700 monks. In fact, the monks housed in these monasteries greatly exceeded these quotas. Judging from such a great multitude of monks, one can well imagine just how vast these monasteries were. The Ganden Monastery was totally razed to the ground during the "cultural revolution," but Drepung and Sera are still preserved in their former state, and their buildings can be seen clustered against the mountains from a distance of five kilometres.

Ganden was founded in 1409 by Tsongkapa Lobsang Dragpa, who was born in Tsongka, near Xining in Qinghai. Tsongkapa means "a native of Tsongka" and Lobsang Dragpa was his personal name. He became a monk at the age of eight, and at sixteen he came to Tibet to study Buddhism. Tsongkapa arrived just at the time when Tibet was facing rivalry among the different schools of religion, the Nyingmapa, Kadampa, Kagyupa, Sakyapa and Bon, each with its own subsects. During his twenty years in Tibet, Tsongkapa paid homage to eminent lamas of different schools, studied the strong points of these schools, and finally achieved profound attainment in doctrine. In his view, many monks of these different schools did not observe discipline, lived dissipated lives, sought benefits and wealth, committed all kinds of outrages, and thus had already lost sight of the aim of religion. If this were to continue, the people would lose faith in Buddhism and it would plunge into an unfathomable chasm. Thereupon Tsongkapa made up his mind to reform Buddhism, found a new school and widely spread Buddhist doctrine.

At the age of thirty-six, Tsongkapa began his wanderings from place to place, delivering sermons and accepting disciples. In 1409, under the patronage of Drongchen Rinchen Pal, the Internal Minister of the Nedong Principate, Tsongkapa founded the first monastery of the the Gelugpa Sect, the Ganden Monastery, as a place for his followers to settle down and concentrate on their studies of the scriptures.

After the establishment of Ganden as his base, Tsongkapa's activities became considerably strengthened. The year 1409 also saw the institution of the Great Prayer Festival in Lhasa on a massive scale. The Gelugpa Sect was gaining strength daily, and in 1416 Jamyang Choje, Tsongkapa's fourth disciple, under the patronage of Rinchen Sangpo, the Lord of Newu, founded the Drepung Monastery at the foot of Mt. Ganpoi Uze in the western suburbs of Lhasa, and he himself became the first abbot of the monastery.

"The Yellow Glazed Tiles," an historical religious text, records that when construction of the Drepung Monastery began, Tsongkapa dug out a conch shell from the "buried treasure of Gopo Hill" and gave it to

Jamyang Choje with the prophecy that the building of the monastery would meet with success, and with this monastery as the base, Buddhism would spread and monasteries and religion would flourish. Jamyang Choje regarded the conch as a gift from the enlightened Bodhisattvas and kept it in the monastery. This pure white conch shell is preserved in Drepung to this day.

After its completion, the Drepung Monastery soon became the most powerful monastery of the Gelugpa Sect. Right from the beginning, besides the Assembly Hall it had seven colleges: the Gomang, Losaling, Tosamling (also Jepa), Shargo, Dowa, Deyang and Ngagpa with altogether 7,700 monks.

Drepung was also the seat of the foremost Dalai Lamas. The Fifth Dalai Lama resided here before he received his appointment from the Qing emperor, and only after the expansion of the Potala Palace did he move to Lhasa. The Third Dalai Lama, Sonam Gyatso, started off as merely the Abbot of Drepung, but later he accepted the Mongolian Altan Khan's invitation and set out for Qinghai where he delivered sermons, spread Buddhism and achieved outstanding successes. In 1558, Altan Khan conferred on Sonam Gyatso the title "Dalai Lama, the All-Knowing" which has been retained ever since. After receiving this title, Sonam Gyatso further requested that the title be extended to his two predecessors. The First to the Fifth Dalai Lamas all successively held the position of Abbot of Drepung.

The Sera Monastery was founded in 1419 by Jamchen Choje, another disciple of Tsongkapa, but before its completion, Tsongkapa passed into nirvana. Jamchen Choje, then the head lama of Sera, had twice travelled to inland China. His first visit took place in 1409 when the Ming court sent a four-man party as imperial commissioners to Tibet to invite Tsongkapa, the Great Master, to Beijing to preach Buddhism. But Tsongkapa was unable to accept the invitation owing to his advanced age, and sent his disciple Jamchen Choje in his stead. Jamchen Choje was given the title of "Great Religious-King" during this visit. After the completion of the Sera Monastery, Jamchen Choje paid a second visit to Beijing, and then went on to Mongolia where he delivered sermons on Buddhism. The Ming Emperor Xuanzong offered him the additional title of "Imperial Preceptor." Jamchen Choje brought back numerous imperial gifts including a set of scriptures on Buddhist philosophy written in gold, the great canons written in cinnabar in the Han and Tibetan languages, images of sixteen arhats carved on white sandalwood, and a scrolled painting of Sakyamuni's Wheel of the Law painted in gold. These treasures are safely preserved in Sera to this day as important relics of the monastery.

Sera had a proud history of its own during the Ming Dynasty, while in more recent times it was also involved in the out-of-the-ordinary "Rating Incident" which caused something of a sensation during April and May of 1947. Rating Lama became the Regent at the death of the Thirteenth Dalai Lama. During the few years of his reign he had taken some measures to strike at the separatists, which resulted in the discontent among some of the political figures. While he was living in seclusion in the Rating Monastery having retired from political life, those people in power in the Kasha (the Cabinet), accused him of intentionally scheming to assassinate the acting Regent, the Takdrak Lama, and dispatched troops to arrest him. On hearing the news, the monks of Sera feared that misfortune might befall the Rating Lama, and they organised an armed force of monks and made preparations to ambush the escorting troops and rescue him. But the monks took the wrong route while in the meantime the Rating Lama had already reached Lhasa as a captive of the local troops. Consequently, the monks of Sera organised a larger armed force and made a charge on Lhasa intending to rescue him by armed force. On the way the monks were stopped by local troops and a battle resulted in the northern suburbs of Lhasa which lasted for seven or eight days. When their ammunition finally ran out, the monks were defeated and driven back to their monastery. This clash between Sera and the Kasha is one of the major incidents in contemporary Tibetan history.

Memorial Tablets in Lhasa

As an ancient city with a history of over 1,300 years, and many time the capital of the whole of Tibet, Lhasa has experienced a host of political events, a number of them worthy of record. Rulers of the past always like to erect tablets to themselves, which, as historical documents and everlasting memorials, are of great value. Lhasa has quite a number of these tablets, and at the front entrance of the Jokhang alone we can find two of them. Representing the past is the Uncle-Nephew Alliance Tablet erected by the Tsanpo in the Tubo period, while more recent history is preserved on the Monument to Prevent Pestilence and Protect Infants erected by the Amban of the Qing government. Apart from these, there is the Doring Chi-ma Tablet in front of the Potala on which the merits of Tagdra

Lukong are recorded, the blank tablet at the foot of the Potala, and the Doring Nangma Tablet, the Kangxi Tablet and the Qianlong Tablet inside the House of the Serpent in the Norbu Lingka. Just outside Lhasa there is the Shal Lhakhang Tablet to the northeast of Medro Gongkar, near the Kyichu River, and the tablet in the Karkyung Temple on the southern bank of the Kyichu River. These tablets are valuable documents for the study of Tibetan history and the relationship between the Tibetan and Han nationalities. The below are brief introductions to the most important tablets; the Uncle-Nephew Alliance Tablet, the Tablet of Doring Chi-ma, the Kangxi Tablet and the Qianlong Tablet.

The Uncle-Nephew Alliance Tablet

This domed tablet stands in front of the Jokhang, enclosed by a stone wall. All four faces of the tablet are covered with inscriptions. The front and both sides are inscribed in Han and Tibetan while the rear face contains the oath of alliance inscribed in Tibetan. It is generally known as the Changqing Tablet or the Uncle-Nephew Alliance Tablet.

The tablet records the marriage of Princess Wen-cheng and Princess Jincheng to the Tubo Tsanpos and the establishment of the uncle-nephew alliance between the Tangs and the Tubos. It was erected in the Third Changqing Year of the Tang Dynasty which corresponds to the Ninth Kyitak Year of the Tubo Dynasty, or 14 February 823 AD. The alliance was established between the Tang Emperor Muzong and the Tubo Tsanpo Tritsug Detsan in 821 AD.

After Songtsan Gampo's marriage to Princess Wencheng, later Tsanpos acknowledged themselves as nephews of the Tang emperors as a mark of respect from the bridegroom's side. Hence the relationship between Emperor Muzong and Tritsug Detsan became that of uncle and nephew, and on behalf of the "good relationship between uncle and nephew" Tritsug Detsan and the Tangs erected this tablet of uncle-nephew alliance.

Between the seventh and ninth centuries, the Tang Dynasty was at its zenith, and Chinese feudal society had entered into a period of prosperity. China's economy and culture at the time ranked among the most advanced in the world. The Tang Empire was bordered by several dependent nations, among which the Tubos were the most powerful, their power extending to the Pure Land (India) in the south, Nancho (Yunnan) to the east, Taksig (Persia) to the west, and the Huihe (Ouigours) to the north. Like the other dependent nations, the Tubos allied themselves with the Tang Dynasty through marriage, but though they set up friendly relations, border disputes and friction nonetheless cropped up now and then. With the aim of creating an everlasting friendship, the Tang rulers and the Tubos concluded a formal alliance. In 821 when Emperor Muzong was enthroned, the Tubo Tsanpo Trisung Detsan twice sent envoys with greetings for the Tang Emperor. Later he again dispatched envoys to Chang'an to ask for an alliance, to which the emperor expressed agreement. In the ninth month of the same year, a team composed of seventeen ministers headed by the Prime Minister was appointed to meet with the Tubo envoys in the western suburbs of Chang'an. The Chang'an negotiations met with success, and subsequently envoys accompanied the Tubo party on their return, finally reaching Lhasa in the fourth month of the following year (823). In the fifth month a plinth for the tablet was set up while final agreement was reached. The next year the tablet was formally erected as an everlasting commemoration.

The erection of the tablet was completed in 823. The Tang court, being much interested in the occasion, sent an envoy name Duzai with an entourage to take part in the grand ceremony. Thus, on the fourteenth day of the second month, the whole of Lhasa was decorated with butter lamps and banners, and citizens ecclesiastical and secular alike celebrated the erection of the tablet with singing and dancing. Approximately 3.5 metres high, 1 metre wide and 35 cm thick, the tablet stands erect in front of the Jokhang to this day.

The inscription on the Uncle-Nephew Alliance Tablet is still clear despite 1,100 years of weathering. The full text appears in the Appendix 1. The tablet gives ironclad evidence of the thousand-year-old relationship between the Hans and Tibetans, and clearly shows that from ancient times Tibetans took a keen interest in Princesses Wencheng and Jincheng's remarkable contributions. After the establishment of this alliance between the Tangs and the Tubos, friendly visits and economic and cultural contacts became more and more frequent, forming a basis for Tibet's formal entry into the motherland's territory in the thirteenth century.

Takdra Lukong's Merit Tablet

This tablet was erected during Trisung Detsan's reign, some time between 763 and 775 AD and stands just south of the Potala, opposite the Tibet Exhibition Hall. The tablet is in the form of a square pillar and stands upright above others. Despite the ravages of the weather over 1,200 years, the principal inscriptions on the tablet can still be seen distinctly (inscriptions cover three sides of the tablet facing north, south and east).

The inscriptions on the south face eulogize the merits of a certain Takdra Lukong, praising his "loyalty" to the Tsanpo, his "outstanding achievements" in his expeditions both within Tibet and elsewhere, and his deeds of valour in battle performed so that "the Kingdom of the Tubos might last forever." The tablet was therefore erected as "an everlasting memorial" of his merits. The inscription on the north side consists of a citation written by Trisung Detsan in praise of the contributions of Takra Lukong, and forgiving him and his descendants for any past or future misdeeds save that of disloyalty to the Tsanpo. Even in the latter case, the offender was "not to be sentenced to death." The inscription is continued on the east side of the tablet and records the special privileges granted to Takdra Lukong and his descendants by Trisung Detsan. All this shows the Tsanpo's generosity towards Takdra Lukong and his future descendants, to be ever remembered so they would continue to put forth efforts for the Tubo Kingdom.

The tablet is of very great value for modern scholars conducting research into the political situation of the Tubo slave society, for checking historical texts, and for studying the development of the Tibetan language.

The Kangxi Tablet and the Qianlong Tablet in the House of the Serpent

Flanking the main entrance of the House of the Serpent stand twin tablets, over three metres high and preserved in two small rooms built of stone. These were erected by the Kangxi and Qianlong emperors during their reigns, and hence are known as the Kangxi Tablet and Qianlong Tablet respectively. Inscriptions on these two tablets are complete and orderly. They originally stood on either side of the front entrance at the foot of the Potala, but following the pacification of the 1959 rebellion in Tibet, Lhasa has been undergoing large-scale urban reconstruction, and so the tablets were moved to the House of the Serpent at the beginning of the 1960s for safekeeping, and are still there on display for visitors.

To the right of the front gate of the House of the Serpent is the huge stippled stone Kangxi Tablet set up to commemorate the pacification of Tibet. The inscription is an edict of Emperor Kangxi written in 1721. The tablet was erected in front of the Potala by a team of seventeen men headed by E-ji, a cabinet member and a scholar, after the Qing government had sent troops to Tibet to suppress the invasion and harassment by the Dzungars of Mongolia.

The Dzungars, a Buddhist Mongol tribe, originally one of the four major tribes of the Oirat Mongols living in the northern part of China, wandering about the Ili region of Xinjiang in quest of pastures. Beginning from the time of the Fifth Dalai Lama, the Regent Desi Sanggye Gyatso, in order to extend the range of his power, secretly contacted the chieftain of the Dzungars and urged him to sent troops into Qinghai and Tibet so as to drive out his formidable adversary Lhasang Khan, the grandson of Goshri Khan, who then held the ruling position in Tibet. However, before the scheme could be carried out it was uncovered by Lhasang Khan who had Sanggye Gyatso put to death. Undeterred, Sanggye Gyatso's subordinates continued to collaborate with the Dzungars who launched an expedition to Tibet and killed Lhasang Khan. Tibet once again fell into disorder with various groups fighting one another. To pacify Tibet, the Qing government dispatched troop in 1717 and again in 1720 and drove out the Dzungars, restored the social order of Tibet, consolidated the southwestern border, and defended the unity of the country. After the pacification of Tibet, some Dzungar tribal chieftains who lived in Qinghai and had taken part in the pacification of Tibet demanded that Emperor Kangxi set up a monument in commemoration of the victory. The emperor signed his own name on this tablet, "erecting this monument to last forever." In it he recorded Tibetan history of the past eighty years from the reigning period of Emperor Shunzhi to his own, elucidated the close relationship between the local power of Tibet and the central government, and explained how the Dzungar invasion and harassment of Tibet had been put down.

At the left of the front entrance to the House of the Serpent stands the other tablet, the Qianlong Tablet. In 1791, Tibet's southern neighbours the Gurkhas launched a large-scale invasion of Tibet. Making intrusions into Tibetan territory and occupying the regions of Kyirong, Dingri and Shigatse, the Gurkhas looted the Tashilhunpo and other regions of Tsang, and forced the Seventh Panchen Lama to withdraw from Lhasa. In consequence the Tibetans suffered a severe national disaster, and the Dalai Lama and Panchen Lama sent an urgent request for help to the central government. Emperor Qianlong then dispatched simultaneously Fu'an Wang with massive forces to Tibet via two routes, Qinghai and Sichuan. This campaign against invasion had the support of the Tibetan people and won speedy success. Finally, the Gurkha forces were completely routed. In 1783, Fu'an accepted the surrender of the Gurkhas, and at the same time met with local Tibetans and with them jointly reached an agreement as to the rules of rectification of the administration of Tibet, the twenty-nine point "Regulations Dealing with Problems Arising From the Invasion of Tibet." Henceforth, the Qing government strengthened its hold over Tibet by setting up a lottery system using a golden urn to select the reincarnations of the Dalai Lama and Panchen Lama, as well as instituting a system of training Tibetan troops, and a system of reforms in finance and trade.

The Qianlong Tablet records not only the events of the Qing government sending its troops into Tibet, driving out foreign invaders and consolidating the southwest border of the country, but also the substantial content and significance of the series of reforms concerning the running of Tibet. It is a monument tablet of great historical value.

5

THE FAMOUS SCENIC SPOTS OF TSANG

The Yamdok Yumtso the Sacred Lake

The Ancient Town of Gyantse and Its Chorten of Hundred-Thousand Buddhas

Dzong Hill British Battle Site

Shigatse, Capital of Tsang

The Magnificent Monastery of Tashilhunpo

The Assembly Hall Which Took Twelve Years to Complete

The Gyanag Lhakhang, Shrine of the Hans

The 26-Metre High Bronze Statue of Maitreya Buddha

Golden Roofs and Funerary Stupas

Shalu Monastery, Han Sytle Eaved Roof

Nartang the Library of Tibet

The Sakya Monastery a Treasury of Art

The Origins of the Khon Family Sakya and the Sakyapa Sect

The Five Forefathers of Sakya and the Striped Sect

The Sakya South Monastery and the Sakya Dynasty

Tsang derives its name from the Tsangpo River which has its source in this region. Nowadays the region covers an area of 300,000 sq. kilometres mostly lying at the foot of the Himalayas and around the upper part of the Tsangpo River.

Tsang contains several world-renowned peaks and rivers. Mt. Jomo Langma (Mt. Everest), known as the earth's "third pole" lies on the border of Tsang and Nepal, while the Tsangpo River, the highest river in the world, also rises in this area. A good number of Buddhist monasteries well-known throughout the ages lie within Tsang. In short, with its numerous famous historic sites and vast size, Tsang can only be described as magnificent.

Yamdok Yumtso, The Sacred Lake

Driving west from Lhasa, crossing the huge Chushur Bridge over the Tsangpo River, one will travel south along the Lhasa-Yatung Highway for 170 kilometres until he come to Yamdok Yumtso, one of the three largest sacred lakes of Tibet.

The Chushur Bridge not only joins Lhasa and Lhoka but the regions of U and Tsang as well. Chushur lies 3,700 metres above sea level, and forms the juncture of the Himalaya and Gangdise Ranges. But the real road into Tsang only begins after Chushur and one has to climb up to the Kampala Pass, which is 5,000 metres above sea level. From the bottom of the gorge the way winds up the mountain to the top which is at 1,700 metres height.

Once across the ridge, the magnificent Yamdok Yumtso appears before eyes. In winter time Yamdok Yumtso is enveloped in ice. Folk tales describe Yamdok Yumtso as a transformation of a goddess. In summer the lake takes on another appearance, blue water, rich pastures and abundant sources of fish and animals in water and on shores and island. In the distance, backdrop of towering peaks clad in silvery armour. The lake and the mountains, each reflecting the other's radiance and beauty, present a scene of incomparable charm. The local inhabitants praise the lake in their folk songs in these terms: "Paradise in heaven and Yamdok Yumtso on earth."

Like a fan, Yamdok Yumtso spreads out to the south, narrowing to the north. The lake edge is crenellated by many tiny inlets penetrating into every nook and cranny of the mountainous shore like the legs a spider. West and north of the lake there are two mountain ranges covered all year round with snow. These two snow-clad ranges are permanently shrouded in mist, and only on a clear morning at sunrise can one catch a fleeting glimpse of the pace of the snows as the clouds part. The lake contains a dozen or so hilly islands, rearing there heads above the surface of the water, which range in area from 3,000 square metres to eight square kilometres. Densely covered with juniper shrubs on which wild pigeons gather in flocks, the islands form natural grazing lands with rich pastures. At the start of summer, local herdsmen take their livestock to the islands in hide boats and fetch them back only when winter approaches. Yamdok Yumtso is also a natural fish pond. There you can find shoals of fish with delicate skins and tender flesh, delicious in flavour and not too large. Every year from April till October the fish from this lake are transported to Lhasa markets in great quantities.

Unfathomable in depth, and 621 sq. kilometres in area, Yamdok Yumtso forms a huge reservoir.

The Ancient Town of Gyantse and Its Chorten of Hundred-Thousand Buddhas

The ancient town of Gyantse lies about ninety kilometres or so to the west of the shores of Yamdok Yumtso. The Nyangchu River rolls swiftly through Gyantse Plain at one side of which the famous ancient monastery, the Palchor with its Chorten of Hundred Thousand Buddhas, stands. Traditionally the Chorten is also known as the "Bakhor Chorten," or the Chorten formed by the whirlpool of the river. The "Bakhor Chorten" over the years of its construction and expansion has collected 10,000 images of Buddha in the form of clay sculptures or paintings. An octagonal structure, the Chorten is also known as the "Eight-Cornered Chorten." This magnificent structure is the king of Tibet's chortens and has been the emblem of Gyantse since earliest times.

The foundation of the ancient town of Gyantse dates back six or seven hundred years. In ancient times Gyantse was a quiet and fertile valley, its inhabitants engaged in stock raising and agriculture. It is said that when Princess Wencheng came to Tibet, the two giant men named Lhaga and Luga who pulled the cart carrying the image of Sakyamuni, settled in Gyantse.

Following the decline of the Tubo Dynasty, Tibet fell into a period of decentralization for four hundred years during which regional chieftains set up independent principalities. It is recorded in the "Nyang Chu Jung" (Penetration of Buddhism Into the Nyangchu Valley) that the earliest religious-king of the principality, Palchor Tsanpo, erected a fortress on Dzong Hill and took up residence there. At the time this religious-king thought Dzong Hill and the geographical features of Gyantse appeared unusual and considered this to be a good omen. In the east it resembled a delicate drooping bough of a fruittree, to the south there was a lion about to leap in the air, in the west floated a white silk scarf (this referred to the Nyangchu River rolling westwards), and to the north the land took the shape of herdsmen presenting livestock products. From a distance, the waves of golden wheat fields gave the valley the appearance of an oblong-shaped golden depression, considered a sign of a land of fortune. Gyantse at the time therefore was known as "Nyangtoi Sershong Ringmo" (Nyangtoi meaning "the upper part of the Nyangchu," indicating where the town is situated; Sershong meaning "the golden basin;" Ringmo meaning "long."). There, Palchor Tsanpo laid the foundations of his palace.

North of the Nyangchu lies a strange mountain as clear as rock crystal known as Dzong Hill. Here, "Nangchen'" Pagpa-pal at the age of forty-eight, in the Wood Serpent Year, built a fortress. On the completion of the fortress, Bhoton Choglas Namgyal (a famous lama of Tibet and the founder of the Bhoton Sect), praised this magnificent fortress, as the "bright pearl" of the mortal world which could be compared with the "immeasurable palace" of the immortal world, and hence the fortress was fit to be named the "Gyalkhartse" ("Gyal" king; "Khar" fortress; "Tse" peak). "Gyalkhartse" therefore means "the peak of the king's fortress," better known by its short form "Gyaltse," written as "Gyantse" in accordance with its pronunciation. Thus, the place-name "Gyantse" originated from the name of the fortress, at times also known as the "Shelkar Gyantse" (crystal Gyantse), because of the

---

· Title of the Minister of Internal Affairs during the Sakya Dynasty.

crystal rock of Dzong Hill.

In the Iron Horse Year, Kunka-pal, the thirty-four-year-old son of Pagpa-pal, established Changra Castle as a memorial to his ancestors. Later, Raptan Kunsang, the son of Kunka-pal, at the age of twenty-six built a bridge with six arches across the Nyangchu in front of the fortress of Gyalkhartse. Thus we can judge the Nyangchu at that time ran just beside the foot of Dzong Hill. Raptan Kunsang also built a magnificent chorten with 100,000 images, the present Palchor Chorten.

Not long after, Raptan Kunsang further expanded the Palchor Monastery, and ever since pilgrims have flocked there in crowds. Moreover, as Gyantse is situated to the east of Sakya and Shigatse, and to the north of Yatung, it was on the only route to Lhasa from these three regions, and hence, it became a focal spot for pilgrims, merchants and tourists. Gyantse quickly grew to its present size and became a renowned city of Tibet. The Palchor Monastery was founded at a time when the various rival religious schools matched each other in strength. The monastery therefore has the unique characteristic of different sects coexisting peacefully in one community, each sect having five to six colleges. Construction of the monastery took ten years. Inside the three-storeyed central Assembly Hall, amidst numerous hanging "tangkas" stands a bronze image of Buddha, eight metres in height. According to historical records, 14,000 kilograms of brass were used in the casting of this image. The eastern and western side halls on the second floor of the central hall contain clay arhats, famous throughout Tibet. The lifelike sculptures are modelled in various postures, and are precious artefacts of the Ming period. The bronze image of the Buddha and the shrines of arhats are dimly lit by glimmering butter lamps while wisps of incense smoke rise to the ceiling and swirl back again, creating an atmosphere of mystery and awe in the Assembly Hall and giving strong impression of the celestial realm.

Next to the Assembly Hall stands the Chorten of Hundred Thousand Buddhas, well-known both in China and abroad. Nine storeys and thirty-two metres in height, the Chorten has a total number of 108 niches and contains an enormous number of images in the form of statues or paintings. It is traditionally said that altogether 100,000 images are enshrined, which explains the origin of the name of the Chorten: "Kumbum," or the 100,000-image Chorten. The Chorten can be considered a magnificent museum of images. Besides the numerous figures in paintings, thousands of clay, bronze and gilded sculptures are also on display. The images include the Buddha, Bodhisattvas, Vajrapani, Tara, the Lord of Death, etc., and also Songtsan Gampo, Tri Ralpachen and the founders of the different religious schools. Each of these images is distinct, with its own characteristics. The architecture of the Chorten is unique in style: up to the fifth floor the building is octagonal, while from the sixth floor it becomes round. The pagoda's many niches are decorated with carvings of flying dragons, leaping lions, and lumbering elephants, all exhibiting highly lifelike modelling and carving. The architecture and the style of sculpture and painting are unique to Gyantse, and quite different from those found in Lhasa, Lhdka, and elsewhere. At present, restoration work is underway in the monastery.

Dzong Hill The Site of the Battle Against the British

At the summit of the hill in front of the Palchor Monastery stands the ancient fortress of Gyantse Dzong. Here, in 1904, the people of Gyantse put up a resistance against foreign aggression. The battery used in the resistance against the British is still preserved to the present. In the mid-nineteenth century British imperialists invaded China along the southeastern coastline, while at the same time also making a vain attempt to open China's southwestern gate by invading Tibet. In 1903, the British dispatched a force of six hundred men to seize Gampa Dzong. Taking advantage of the Tibetans being off guard, a 1,400-strong force from Yatung simultaneously broke through the boundary of Gyantse Dzong to the north. As the invaders made a deep push into the interior, the people of Gyantse resisted gallantly. When Gyantse was occupied by the British troops, the people of Gyantse in cooperation with the local troops constructed a battery and fortifications on Dzong Hill, armed themselves with muzzleloaders, swords, spears, bows and arrows, and held out for several months. Then one night at the beginning of May, 1904, over a thousand soldiers and civilians took advantage of the enemy's unpreparedness and made a sudden attack on the British garrison stationed in Gyantse under the command of Younghusband. In June, the British dispatched reinforcements from Yatung and besieged Dzong Hill with an enormous number of troops. The soldiers and civilians of Gyantse armed with inferior muzzleloaders and swords and stones did not concede an inch to the enemy even when the fortress was shelled by huge cannon. Cut off from their supplies of ammunition, food and drinking water, the defending forces nevertheless refused to relinquish their arms or take one step in retreat. To solve the problem of water they slid down ropes at the dead of the night to fetch water from a filthy pool at the foot of the hill. Even under such hardships the military units and civilians of Gyantse repulsed several enemy assaults. Unfortunately the powder magazine on the fortress was hit by a shell and exploded, but even so the military defenders and the people of Gyantse, using stones as weapons and occupying a commanding position, kept up their resistance regardless of the danger to their own lives. The battle continued for three days and nights and caused the enemy to suffer heavy casualties. In the end owing to the disparity in strength, Dzong Hill was captured by the enemy. Rather than be taken prisoners, the defenders jumped from the cliff gallantly. The remains of the battery can still be seen on Dzong Hill as a reminder of the Tibetan people's heroic defence of Gyantse.

Shigatse The Capital Town of Tsang

Driving westwards alongside Tsangpo River one can reach the point where its tributary the Nyangchu joins the main flow. It is here that Shigatse, the central town of Tsang, is located.

The history of Shigatse stretches back five hundred years. Apart from its geographical situation and economic and political factors, there is another reason why Shigatse should have become the heart of Tsang. It is said that in the eighth century when the Tibetan king Trisung Detsan invited the eminent monk Padmasambhava of India to come to Tibet to supervise the founding of the Samye Monastery, the great sage travelled via Shigatse where he practised and preached Buddhism and spread the Buddhist doctrine. During the course of his journey into Tibet from the Pure Land (India), Padmasambhava prophesied that Lhasa would become the heart of the Land of Snows, with Lower Nyang (Shigatse) in second place. He observed that Nyima Rio Hill of Lower Nyang was in the shape of a male lion springing fiercely into the sky, and said that if a palace could be erected on this spot and Buddhist doctrine spread from it, it would be highly beneficial to the people of the Land of Snows. Devout Buddhists subsequently established a fortress on this hill, which later developed into the capital town of Tsang. If you were to take a stroll along the old section of the town, you would notice the remains of a lofty fortress perched high upon the hill which used to be the administrative office of the Dzong (county). Before its destruction, this fortress, like the Potala, was built against a hilly backdrop, to give it the appearance of standing majestically aloft above everything else.

Shigatse did not rise to fame until after Gyantse. Prior to six or seven hundred years ago, although the region was inhabited, it was still a remote wilderness. Known to begin with as Lower Nyang (the lower part of the Nyangchu River), It is recorded in the historical book *Nyang Chu Jung* (The penetration of Buddhism into the Nyangchu Valley) that the geographical features of Lower Nyang resemble the Eight-Petalled Lotus; to the east its sweet dew (the Nyangchu River) the gift of the Buddha, ripples along gently like a silken sash; to the south flowers and plants flourish like the garden of paradise; to the west the mountains, baring their teeth as if in defence of the gods of the celestial realm, face the valley as if paying their sincere respects to this holy land; and to the north the Tsangpo River wriggles like a black snake and roars endlessly; such is the magnificence of the region's geography, making it a worthy site for the future.

In the fourteenth century, Changchub Gyaltsan, the "Da Situ," triumphed over the Sakya Dynasty and established the Pagdu Dynasty. Gaining support from the Yuan and Ming dynasties, Changchub Gyaltsan divided Tibet into thirteen "dzongs" (counties), the last of which was named Shiga-samdup-tse (the estate that fulfills one's wishes). The name expressed Changchub Gyaltsan's hope that his ambition of ruling over the whole of Tibet had been fulfilled. And this is how Shigatse got its name of Shiga-samdup-tse, later abbreviated to Shigatse.

But Shigatse did not actually begin to flourish until Karmapa's reign over Tibet which lasted for twenty four years. During this period, the Karmapa Dynasty established its capital in Shigatse, and as a result Shigatse became the centre of Tibet's politics, economy and culture for a time, with a constant flow of visitors and uninterrupted growth. According to accounts in the *Nyang Chu Jung* at that time four parks were created around the town of Shigatse; the Tashi Kyitsal to the south, the Rigyatso to the east, the Ri Gawatse to the north and the Ludingtse to the west. At Kapgye to the rear of the Shigatse fortress there is a secluded grotto where it is traditionally said that Padmasambhava took refuge from life's turmoil and went into meditation, preached the dharma and chanted incantations. Later, Tsogyal, one of his disciples, achieved enlightenment here which inspired the Serpent God to create a spring not far from the cave. Ever since then, the cave has been regarded as a sacred place. Every year in summer the men of Shigatse, mounted on donkeys, go on pilgrimage to the holy place of Kapgye. The wives and children await the return of their menfolk at the outskirts of the town, and the pilgrims race their donkeys to meet them. Over the years the spot has changed into a race track for shooting and racing events held at the outskirts of the town. This tradition has lasted up to the present.

The Magnificent Monastery of Tashilhunpo

A visit to the Tashilhunpo is a must for every visitor to Shigatse. This city-like monastery is the seat of the Panchen Lama, and may be compared with the Dalai Lama's Potala Palace. It houses more than five hundred and seventy monks even to this day.

Located in the western suburbs, the Tashilhunpo backs onto Nyimari Hill, in the shape of a galloping elephant, which acts as a protective screen for the town. The monastery buildings mount the hillside one above the other, some adjoining and others scattered separately, creating a magnificent scene of grandeur when viewed from a distance. The Tashilhunpo certainly deserves its name as the greatest monastery of the Yellow Sect in the Tsang region. The monastery buildings cover an area of 300,000 sq. metres, while the perimeter wall, which connects with the hill at the back of the monastery, has a length of more than 1,500 metres. It takes several days to look round the monastery in any detail.

The Tashilhunpo was founded in 1447 by Gedun Drupa, Tsongkapa's disciple, with the financial backing of two nobles of the Tsang region, Chushong Nangpa

Sonam Palsang and Chungye-pa Sonam Paljor. Originally the monastery was named "Gangchen Chopel" (may Buddhism flourish in the Land of Snows), but after its completion, Gedun Drupa renamed it "Tashilhunpo" (the auspicious Sumeru mountain).

The Assembly Hall Which Took Twelve Years to Complete

The Assembly Hall is the earliest building of the Tashilhunpo which took twelve years to build.

Stepping through the entrance, one will find himself in an extensive courtyard covering an area of five hundred square metres, paved with slabs of stone from the Himalayan foothills.

The courtyard was used by the Panchen Lama to deliver sermons to the monastic community, and as a debating ground for points of Buddhist philosophy. All four walls were covered with thousand stone Buddha reliefs. The images differed from one another in detail but they were all more or less the same size and depicted Buddhas in meditation in Grottoes. The atmosphere was deeply imbued with a sense of the practice of the Law of Buddhism.

At the top of the tone steps stood Assembly Hall. This forty-eight pillared hall could hold more than two thousand monks during prayer time, or over half of the monastery's prescribed number of monks. The Panchen Lama's magnificent golden throne stood in the Assembly Hall. Lifting the satin cover, the exquisite carvings of the seat, back screen and armrests were revealed. Inside the Assembly Hall there were shrines of Sakyamuni, Maitreya Buddha, and Tara. The Sakyamuni image was erected by Gedun Drupa, the founder of the monastery, in memory of his tutor, Sherab

Seng-ge. On either side of the Sakyamuni image were the figures of the Eight Spiritual Sons of Buddha.

To the left was the shrine of Maitreya Buddha built in 1461 under the patronage of Jodrag Bumde, the Guge King of Ngari. An eleven-metre statue of Maitreya Buddha stood in the centre which was modelled by Tibetan and Nepalese craftsmen working together in cooperation. The statue stands as an historical witness to Sino-Nepalese friendly cooperation. On either side of Maitreya Buddha were the images of Shariputra and Maudgalyana, the oldest sculptures in the monastery. sculpted by the first Dalai Lama, Gedun Drupa himself.

On the right was the shrine of the Tara. Within this shrine a two-metre bronze image of the White Tara stood in the centre with a pair of clay sculptures of the Green Tara to either side; behind these images were murals of the Tara.

Besides these, there were a good number of ancient frescoes inside the Assembly Hall, including the well-known paintings of Tsongkapa and his two spiritual sons, the eighty great disciples of the Buddha, dakinis floating in the air in different poses and other Bodhisattvas. These paintings of various figures were beautifully posed, meticulous in execution, bright and lustrous in colour, and unique in style; many were the works of famous painters of the time.

The Gyanag Lhakhang, The Shrine of the Hans

Not far from the Assembly Hall is the Gyanag Lhakhang, the shrine of the Hans, a structure found in no other monastery. It was specially established to show the relationship between the Panchen Lamas and the Qing emperors. A number of gifts presented to the

Panchen Lamas by the Qing emperors are on display within the shrine.

On the second floor of the Gyanag Lhakhang there is a huge portrait of Emperor Qianlong, an original painting in the Forbidden City in Beijing. In front of the portrait was a panel on which was written in Chinese characters: "Long life, long long life to the Gracious Emperor." The shrine was established during the time of the seventh Panchen Lama and the enshrinement of this panel indicated that the Tsang region was subject to the Qing Dynasty.

The side-hall next to this shrine served as a parlour where the Qing Dynasty's Amban was received by the Panchen Lama. The parlour was decorated in the style of the past. Whenever the emperor passed down imperial edicts, the Amban brought them into the shrine where the Panchen Lama received them. After hearing the imperial edict, the Panchen Lama would kowtow and express gratitude in front of the emperor's portrait and the panel, and then retire into the parlour and chat with the Amban over tea.

Passing through a small door from the parlour, we entered an exhibition hall, one of the major parts of the Gyanag Lhakhang. In the hall were displayed gifts from the emperors presented to successive Panchen Lamas on their visits to inland China to pay their respects to the emperors. The gifts arranged in glass-fronted cabinets included ancient China of the Ming Dynasty's Yongle period (1403-1424), fabrics of the Yuan and Ming Dynasties, jade objects, gold and silver wine cups, teacups and saucers, images of Buddha and prayer beads,etc. Among them there was a string of prayer beads inlaid with jewels presented to the seventh Panchen Lama by the Qing emperor which is well preserved to the present.

Apart from these treasures, the Gyanag Lhakhang also contained many cultural relics of rarity, most from the Sui and Tang periods. One such item was a specially made glass box, well-sealed with lock upon lock and preserved with care, which contained many tiny figurines. Within it there are only ten bronze figurines. The latest one dated from the Yuan Dynasty and depicted a naked Tara seated on a wild boar, while all the others were works of the Tang period. The bronze figurines, ranging in size from ten to twenty centimeters, were all precious relics of the monastery.

In the past the Tashilhunpo was extremely rich in precious relics, but the monastery was plundered a number of times, and only a part of its treasures remains today. The most tragic plunder took place in the eighteenth century when the Gurkhas invaded Tibet and made off with loot including the jade diploma and jade seal presented to the sixth Panchen Lama by Emperor Qianlong, a Buddha of Infinite Light inlaid with pearls, ritual objects, sacred texts and the like. Later, the Qing government dispatched troops led by Fu Kang'an to Tibet who drove out the invaders and demanded that the relics be returned. Nevertheless, the Gurkhas only handed back the golden diploma and golden seal and the jade diploma and jade seal, whereas the rest were either lost or destroyed. Thus, the Tashilhunpo suffered an irreparable loss.

The 26-Metre High Bronze Statue of Maitreya Buddha

At the western extreme of the Tashilhunpo there is a lofty temple, the Jamkhang or Temple of Maitreya Buddha, which towers seven storeys high, attaining a height of thirty metres, and covering more than 860 sq. metres. The Jamkhang was built in 1914 by the nineth Panchen Lama, Chokyi Nyima, who took charge of the construction in person.

The giant Maitreya Buddha inside the Jamkhang was the most spectacular statue of the Tashilhunpo. The bronze statue towers 26.5 metres high, with the pedestal alone standing 3.8 metres in height, the middle finger 1.2 metres in length, and the shoulders 11.5 metres across. The sacred white hair between the eyebrows of the Maitreya is made of thirty-one precious stones of various sizes and one thousand four hundred pearls, pieces of amber and turquoise, an amazing quantity indeed. One hundred and ten craftsmen laboured for four years to complete the statue, using 6,700 ounces of gold and 115,875 kilograms of brass. The amount of other ornaments is incalculable.

The statue of Maitreya is majestic and lifelike, and technically superbly structured, reflecting the Tibetan people's marvellous inventive talent and the high technical standards of the time.

Golden Roofs and Funerary Stupas

Almost every major monastery of the Gelugpa Sect has glistening golden roofs and sumptuous stupas.

As we climbed to the topmost part of the Assembly Hall of Tashilhunpo golden roofs shone in the sun, while the carved beams and painted pillars below were in no way inferior to those of the Potala in structure. Northwest of the golden roofs was a towering "wall" standing nearly a hundred metres high and built in 1468 solely of stone blocks for the display of the great appliqued tangka. Every year the great appliqued Tangka is put on display on this giant "wall" so as to let the faithful see it exposed in the open air.

There were also funerary stupas in the Tashilhunpo, in which the bones of the First Dalai Lama, Gedun Drupa, and the complete bodies of successive Panchen Lamas were preserved. The most sumptuous tomb was that of the fourth Panchen Lama, Chokyi Gyaltsan (1567-1662), who made a great contribution to the Tashilhunpo. When the Tashilhunpo was first founded by the First Dalai Lama, only the ground floor of the Assembly Hall was in existence. Small in size, it could hold a mere hundred or so monks. During the fourth Panchen Lama's time, the Assembly Hall was extended to the third storey and the other shrines were built. This was the biggest extension of the Tashilhunpo. Later extensions added by successive Panchen Lamas built the Tashilhunpo up to its present size. With its fifty-six shrines, two hundred and thirty-six rooms and halls, and the tombs of the fourth to the ninth Panchen Lama, the whole place has become a monastic city, a cluster of buildings peeping one over the other when seen from a distance.

Lobsang Chokyi Gyaltsan, the fourth Panchen Lama, lived to the age of ninety-four. In gratitude for his enormous extension of the monastery, his disciples erected a beautiful funerary stupa in his honour. The tomb was completed in 1666 after four and a half years. The stupa is eleven metres in height, and materials used in its construction include 2,700 ounces of gold, 33,000 ounces of silver, 39,000 kilograms of copper, and 9,000 ft. of satin as well as about 7,000 precious stones such as coral, pearls, agates and turquoises. Nevertheless, the stupas preserve important historical evidence and art treasure of the time.

The Shalu Monastery
with its Eaved Roof
in the Han Style

Turning southwards twenty kilometres east of Shigatse, we came to the famous monastery of Shalu.

As we entered a narrow valley, the Shalu Monastery could be seen in the distance, its green tiled roofing glistening under the radiant sun. The monastery looked quite different from Tibet's other monasteries as it had the same style of slanting ridged roofs with guttering at the eaves as the monasteries of inland China. At close quarters, we saw the construction differed from the Han style, and was built in the Tibetan style after all out of irregular stone slab. Judging from its exterior appearance, Shalu was a singular mixture of the Han and Tibetan style.

When the door of the central hall opens, one can notice the interior is well preserved, the statues intact, and the full complement of bronze and clay images, tangkas and stupas are present, while incense is kept burning before the altars.

Though small in size, the monastery has a long history. In the Song Dynasty (998 AD), Tibet entered into the era of the Latter Prosperous Period of Buddhism. It is said that ten Buddhist followers headed by Lumi from Tibet fled a thousand miles to Heyuan, in Qinghai Province, to pay homage to Lachen Gongpa Rabsal after Lang Darma's persecution of Buddhism. One of the ten named Dorje Wangchuk subsequently returned to Tibet having achieved distinction in his studies and founded a tiny monastery called the Gyalgong in present-day Gyatso district, Shigatse. Although small, the monastery preached the dharma and took in disciples. Among the followers there was a certain Jetsun Sherab Jungnas who, following his master's example, also intended to found a monastery and preach Bud-dhism. One day when he asked where he should site his monastery his Master replied: "I shall use my walking stick as an arrow and shoot it into the air. Wherever it lands shall be the site for your monastery." The Master's "arrow" landed on a newly-sprouted sapling not far from the Gyalgong Monastery, and in accordance with his Master's instructions Jetsun Sherab Jungnas built his monastery on that very spot. This was in 1087 AD. The new monastery was named Shalu, meaning "sprout."

It is traditionally said that the Bengali sage Atisa took up residence in Shalu and delivered sermons there on his way to Tibet. Thus the prestige of the monastery grew with each passing day. By the Yuan period, Jetsun Sherab Jungnas, descendant Jigtsal became the myriarch of the Shalu area, one of the thirteen myriarchies of the Sakya Dynasty. As Jetsun Sherab Jungnas was of the royal lineage of the Tubo Tsanpos, Pagpa's younger brother, Drogon Chagnang, therefore lavished much attention on Jigtsal and introduced him to the Yuan emperor. In 1329 the Shalu Monastery was almost washed away by an exceptionally big flood, but the Yuan emperor gave Jigtsal a large sum of money and ordered him to undertake repairs. In 1333, Jigtsal asked for a number of Han craftsmen to be sent from inland China, and they in cooperation with the local craftsmen rebuilt the monastery which has lasted to the present day. It is said that in the same year some of the glazed tiles, porcelain, and fired bricks were brought from inland China, while the glazed tiles used on the roofs of the central hall and other side-halls were made in Tibet under the supervision of the Han craftsmen.

Climbing upstairs and making a careful examination of the architectural detail, we could see from the curved roof beams, the overhanging guttered eaves, and the roof ridge porcelain sculptures and mouldings, that everything looked exactly the same as in the monasteries of inland China. Such is the proof that Shalu was a product of the Yuan period.

Inside the central hall and the side-halls there were some beautiful ancient murals depicting lively scenes, vibrant with colour, which were still in an excellent state of preservation. The style of painting was similar to that of Song and Yuan murals. The figures in the frescoes, their attire, implements and furniture, also resembled those of inland China. The results of cultural exchanges between the Tibetan and Han nationalities were thus revealed in the architecture and painting of Shalu.

There are four treasures in the monastery. One of them is a printing board. This two foot square wooden board is composed of one hundred and eight small wooden blocks stuck together, each one carved with a word. The history of the wooden board dated back seven hundred years or so. A warning had been passed down by word of mouth for generations that the board should not be broken up into pieces or else no one would be able to put it together again, and as a result the board had been preserved for posterity. Pilgrims to Shalu believe themselves most fortunate if they can obtain a print from this board. The second treasure is a copper jug sealed with a red cloth affixed with two seals. The water in the jar is changed only once in a dozen years and changing water is the only time it is permitted for the jug to be opened. After the jar is opened, the water inside is considered "holy water," and curiously enough not a drop of it evaporates. Pilgrims who are lucky enough to be present at the opening ceremony and receive a cup of this "holy water" can "wash off" one hundred and eight different kinds of impurities. At the entrance of the central hall there is the next treasure, a huge stone basin supposed to have been used by Jetsun Sherab Jungnas, the founder of the monastery, for washing his face. It is said on rainy days when the stone basin fills to the brim with rain water, it is impossible to empty it as the water will not flow out. The last treasure is a stone slab in front of the central hall inscribed with the six syllable prayer "om mani padme hum" in the centre and with four small stupas engraved at the margin. It is said that the stone slab was unearthed while digging the foundations of the monastery. This naturally occurring treasure became the foundation stone of Shalu. The stories behind these four treasures may sound rather fantastic, but their value lies in their long history, as they have been preserved from generation to generation for six or seven hundred years.

Though Shalu seems small compared to the great Yellow Sect monasteries which have been in existence for three to four hundred years, it enjoyed a period of fame and prosperity when Puton Rinchen-drup, one of Tibet's Buddhist scholars, became abbot. The author of the famous book "History of the Puton Sect" and many other explanatory works, he was greatly renowned for his scholarship. During this period, monks from various places came crowding to Shalu out of admiration for the famous master and to listen to his teachings. The number of visitors reached more than three thousand

and eight hundred when Shalu was at its height. Those who had studied Buddhist doctrine and were able to preach Buddhism gradually increased in number until the monastery became the centre of a religious sect called the Shalu or Puton Sect.

Nartang, the Library of Tibet

Twenty kilometres along the highway from Shigatse to Sakya, lies Nartang Monastery, "the Library of Tibet," Though smaller than the Tashilhunpo, its history is longer by about four hundred years.

The history of the founding of the Nartang Monastery is wreathed in tales of fantasy and mystery. It is said that Atisa, the Bengali sage, passed by Nartang on his way to Tibet. He observed that the spot was remarkable as it had been visited by the god of the tenth heaven, making it a place of incomparable auspiciousness indeed where in the future a monastery was bound to be established which would spread Buddhist doctrine. Atisa's wish was passed down to his followers as if it were a command, and his instructions became engraved upon the minds of subsequent generations of his disciples. Eventually in 1033, Tumton Lodrodrag, an eminent monk of the Kadampa sect, founded the Nartang Monastery.

After the completion of the monastery, several renowned monks preached Buddhism at Nartang. For example, Chenmo Namkadrag, Pagpa's tutor, had his residence at Nartang, and Gedun Drupa, the First Dalai Lama, spent seventeen years there fulfilling his religious vows and pursuing his studies in Buddhism. Only after the establishment of the Tashilhunpo did Gedun Drupa move to Shigatse.

The most remarkable contribution of Nartang is its

establishment of a printing house. In 1730, Polanas, a cabinet member of the Tibet local government who was also in charge of the Tsang region, directed the establishment of a printing house at Nartang in order to preserve and expand the ancient books of Tibet. It took more than twenty years to set up this enormous printing house, and in order to complete the massive project, Polanas exacted corvee labour from all over Tibet, brought together calligraphers, engravers, and painters from the whole country, and gathered a group of youngsters to learn the art of wood carving. After a long period of painstaking work, the preparation of the block prints was completed and Buddhist canons were then printed in great numbers. All 108 volumes of the "Kagyur," the Translated Scriptures, and the 215 volumes of the "Tengyur," the Translated Elucidating Treatises, were carefully carved onto wooden blocks, which not only contained print but also coloured woodcuts. In addition many great works such as the "Hundred Deeds of Sakyamuni" were carved and printed in this printing house. The printing blocks of Nartang were so numerous that they formed a huge mound right up to post-liberation times. Compared to the printing houses of Dege and the Potala, Nartang is far superior both in quantity and quality. Over the years the Nartang printing house also trained a large number of carving and printing craftsmen which had an inestimable effect on Tibet's printing techniques and cultural development.

Nartang suffered damage during the "cultural revolution," and moreover the old printing methods have been superseded by modern techniques, but even so, the Nartang printing house, the "Library of Tibet," still remains important from an historical point of view.

The Sakya Monastery Treasury of Art

No visit to Tsang is complete without a trip to the Sakya Monastery. Sakya, once the centre of Tibet's politics, economy, military affairs, culture and religion, has long been an attraction to dedicated researchers of Tibetan history and tourists alike.

Leaving Shigatse, and crossing the Gyatsola Pass, one turns southwest and drives for sixty kilometres until he enters the Sakya region, situated at the mouth of a river valley. The valley lies like a huge curving vase. A wide plain at the mouth of the gorge narrowed as two peaks facing one another closed in and then opened out to another plain, about ten kilometres long, at the end of which two more peaks once again narrowed the valley.

The scene recalled an ancient folk song of Sakya composed by a Sakya man returning home on horseback:

As I look down from the Adruk-la Pass,
I see Sakya as clear as crystal,
The Damo* seated in the crystal vase,
Outshines even a goddess in beauty.

Do not underestimate the value of Sakya,
For she has been blessed by the Buddha,
Though her outer stone walls may collapse,
Her inner sutra walls will never give way.

Prior to the building of motorable roads in recent years, whenever the people of Sakya made a journey,

---

* The wife of the Abbot of Sakya was addressed as "Damo." The hereditary abbots of the Sakya Sect were allowed to take wives.

they had to cross the Adruk-la Pass on horseback so it seemed to them as if they were emerging from "the mouth of a vase." Even those who came from the direction of Shigatse had to first cross the Adruk-la Pass and then "drill through the bottom of the vase" again. On the northern and southern sides of the "vase" there were two monasteries established by the ancestors of the Sakya Dynasty which gave Sakya a unique air of beauty, and numerous scriptures, the pride of the Sakya people, were preserved within their walls.

The Origins of the Khon Family

The Sakya Monastery had been the seat of the Khon Family who ruled the Sakya Dynasty and the Sakya Sect. The most interesting thing about the origins of the Khon family is that the original ancestors were actually enemies.

The founding father of the Khon family came from a huge tribe in Ngari region. The tribe was immensely powerful and the chieftain Yapang-kye, continuing in the footsteps of his forefathers, conquered the east and suppressed the west, took over several tribes, and finally made his conquest of Sakya. The chieftain of Sakya was a man named Kyareng Tragme who had a beautiful wife. Yapang-kye defeated and killed Kyareng Tragme and took his wife by force. The new couple produced a son and named him Khon-par-kye, meaning "born between enemies" who became the ancestor of the Khon family.

More than 1,200 years ago, a later generation of Khon-par-kye's clan produced a man of exceptional wisdom, called Khon Palpoche. At that time, the Tibetan plateau was under the rule of the Tubo Dynasty in the person of one of the most outstanding Tubo Tsan-

Gorshae, a most popular Tibetan folk dance

Drosu Chemar, a cereal container prepared for
the New Year symbolizing the wish for happy life
and good harvest

Butter sculptures at the Greater Prayer Festival

Getting ready for the race

A Lhoba hunter

Yamdok Lumtso, the sacred lake

Yaks, a common means of transportation

The pastoral area of Tibet
Grassland at Nakchu

Right and Middle At the bank of Lhasa River during the Bathing Week

Bottom Scarf-picking at the Horse-racing Festival

Local handicraftsmen at work

Out to a hunting trip

pos, Trisung Detsan. Khon Palpoche gained even more prestige when he served as a minister for the Tubo Dynasty, while one of his sons, Khon Luyi Wangpo, was also one of the first seven monks who were sent to the Samye Monastery. The Khon family therefore held prestigious positions in administrative and religious affairs and their influence spread all over Tibet, the family name being carried down for fifty generations to the present.

Sakya and the Sakyapa Sect

Luyi Wangpo took his monastic vows and applied himself to Buddhist studies, and became the first generation of Tibet's famous Buddhist scholars. The Khon family continued to be zealous in spreading the dharma, particularly the seventh generation descendent Khon Konchog Gyalpo who paid homage to Drogmi Lotsava Sakya Yeshe as his master, painstakingly studied the new tantric mysticism, translated vast amounts of the new doctrine and gradually abandoned the traditional mystic order of the old translations.

In order to properly teach his new doctrine Khon Konchog Gyalpo founded a monastery called Palchen Podrang (situated opposite the North Monastery, the ruins can still be seen today) at Dawolung on the southern bank of the Drongchu River in the Dongto region. One day, as he stepped out of his monastery and raised his head to look into the distance, Konchog Gyalpo noticed that north of the Drongchu River was an unbounded chain of mountain ranges, looking just like a massive elephant lying on the grassland. At what appeared to be the belly of the elephant, in front of a hill of white earth with the Drongchu River flowing tempestuously below, a fertile spot caught his eye.

Konchog Gyalpo believed that if a monastery were to be erected at the belly of the elephant, it would be bound to receive the blessing of the Buddha, the dharma would spread as if it had taken wing and the new doctrine would develop faster than ever.

Konchog Gyalpo therefore crossed the Drongchu and went to see the landlord who owned all the mountains and plains to ask for this portion of the land to build a monastery, persuading the landlord that it would not harm his interests.

The landlord was in favour of Buddhist teachings and generously set aside a vast stretch of land for Konchog Gyalpo saying: "Since you think this bit of land resembles a supine elephant, I'll make you a gift of all the land from the Baldrog region at the head of the elephant to the Mondrog region at the tail of the elephant site of your monastery."

Khon Konchog Gyalpo was overjoyed at hearing this, and in his fortieth year (1073 AD) set about large-scale construction on the hill situated on the north bank of the Drongchu and built the White Palace, known as the Gurong Monastery to later generations. People also called the monastery Sakya, or White Earth, because it was built on a white hill. It is the Sakya North Monastery known today which was successively extended by later generations of the Khon family and grew into the present cluster of buildings. By the time of Khon Kunka Nyingpo, the son of Konchog Gyalpo, the new doctrine of the Sakya Monastery had become widespread and as it developed its own system, it became known as the Sakyapa Sect.

A child of extraordinary talent, Kunka Nyingpo showed an amazing aptitude for learning from an early age. In his childhood he visited many places with his father in quest of Buddhist studies. He was widely respected as a famous master, devoted himself to the study of the sacred texts, and extended the Sakya North Monastery, gathering followers from all around. He continued the systematization and perfection of the Sakyapa Sect doctrine initiated by his father.

The Five Forefathers of Sakya and the Striped Sect

Owing to Kunka Nyingpo's outstanding contribution to the formation of the Sakyapa Sect, people completely forgot his father Konchog Gyalpo and respected the son as the first of Five Forefathers of Sakya. In the mid-twelveth century Khon Sonam Tsemo, the second son of Kunka Nyingpo, became known as the second of the Five Forefathers of Sakya for fulfilling his father's will and accepting many followers.

The third forefather was not Sonam Tsemo's son but his younger brother Dragpa Gyaltsan. He had a thorough knowledge both of Buddhist philosophy and tantric mysticism, and was strict in religious discipline.

These three are known as the Three White Forefathers because they took wives. Later, Kunka Gyaltsan and Pagpa were added to the trio. They took religious vows and remained celibate and so were known as the Two Red Forefathers. Altogether there are five forefathers who were the men who made the greatest contributions to the Sakyapa Sect.

The Sakyapa Sect also called the Striped Sect. In the Sakya South Monastery, there are three stripes of red, white, and black on the wall which are the symbols of the Sakyapa Sect. Some say the sect is called the Striped Sect because of these three colours are arranged in stripes but as a matter of fact each colour has its own significance.

In Buddhist religious imagery red symbolises Manjusri (the Lord of Wisdom), white symbolises Avalokitesvara, and black Vajrapani. This is the true essence of the Striped Sect to the Buddhist mind. In the latter period of the Sakyapa Sect, monks did not observe monastic rules and gave themselves over to ease and comfort, and so in the eyes of the secular world such monks were considered as "striped" or "fancy." But this is a misrepresentation of the original meaning.

The Sakya South Monastery and the Sakya Dynasty

The establishment of the Sakya South Monastery was the contribution of Pagpa, the last of the Five Forefathers of Sakya.

In the Sakya South Monastery, the Lhakhang Chenmo or the Assembly Hall was an enormous building, 5,500 sq. metres in area and 11.6 metres high, containing forty giant pillars (historical records claim 108 pillars, but in fact there are not as many as that). The largest pillar in the Assembly Hall is so giant that three men were needed to encircle it with arms fully stretched. With a diameter of 1.5 metres, the biggest pillar was called "Gyanag Sechen Kawa" the Kublai Khan Pillar; and there were three other pillars respectively called "the Tiger Pillar," "the Bloody Black Pillar," and "the Wild Yak Pillar." Each pillar ran the whole way from floor to ceiling. These wooden pillars had been transported from the forest regions of Trintang in Tengkye Dzong, one hundred kilometres away. A mural even depicted a record of the monastery's construction. The painting showed the massive scale of the work: with a sea of people engaged in lumbering, transporting earth, quarrying stones and ramming wall foundations. It is said that corvee labour was gathered from all over Tibet for this undertaking.

A statue of the famous Pagpa on the altar indicates that he is the very person to construct the Monastery. In 1264 Kublai Khan established the central power of the Yuan Dynasty in Peking, and appointed Pagpa, who had been at his side for nine years, as "Dishi," or Imperial Preceptor, and assigned him to take over the Buddhist affairs of the whole of China and the administration of the Tibetan-inhabited regions. The next year Pagpa received instructions to return to Tibet. On his arrival in Tibet he extended the Sakya North Monastery, appointed the "Ponchen" (minister) to handle the administration of Tibet, and established the Sakya Dynasty, which became the local government of Tibet subject to the Yuan central government.

Pagap divided Tibet into thirteen myriarchies, took a population census and promulgated laws. In 1288, when Pagpa was about to depart for Peking after fulfilling the task given to him by Kublai Khan, he inspired "Ponchen" Shakya Sangpo to build the Sakya South Monastery. Since at that time the Sakyapa Sect had risen to power in Tibet in both the political and religious spheres, Shakya Sangpo gathered a huge pool of labour and material resources from the thirteen myriarchies of Tibet and built the monastery on a massive scale.

The fortification wall is over ten metres high and 3.5 metres thick. It runs from east to west for about 170 metres, and north to south for about one hundred metres. There are forty forts and four watchtowers along the wall and four gatehouses facing north, south, east and west. Outside the fortification wall there used to be a moat, and its vague outline can still be seen even now.

It is said that many master craftsmen were invited from the Han regions and Mongolia to supervise the construction of the monastery, and the proceedings were recorded on tangkas preserved to the present.

There are many precious goods and treasures preserved in the Monastery. In the rear of the Assembly Hall where light was rather dim there is a great library; on all four sides of this hall were walls of sutras. More than 10,000 sutras, most of which had been copied by professional copyists gathered from the whole of Tibet during Pagpa's rule form a treasury of calligraphic skill in liquid gold and silver, cinnabar and black ink.

To the right side of the sutra walls there is one of the sutras. About one metre square, with projective slats top and bottom, the sutra was written in liquid gold, a rarity in the world. There are tiny bells hung all around the protecting slats, probably serving as alarms in case of theft.

Sakya could be seen as the second Dunhuang with its 40,000 volumes in the entire monastery. There are also some recently discovered sacred texts written on "pattra" leaves kept in store on the upper floor.

The Sakya Monastery was indeed a real treasure-house. In the Assembly Hall one can see ancient chinaware of the Song and Yuan periods including vases, cups, figurines, and the like, which could have formed a museum display in their own right. To the right of the Assembly Hall there was a half-metre tall holy bell which served as a shade for the ever-burning butter lamp in front of the altar. There was also a rectangular jade slab on which was inscribed a poetic verse written in the Han language with the writer's name Xing Shi carved on it. Both of these were invaluable treasures. In addition there was armour and ancient ritual objects dating from the Yuan Dynasty; religious vestments and Mongolian long boots presented by the Yuan emperors, brocades of the Yuan and Ming period, so on and so forth, too numerous to mention.

Murals too made up some of art treasures of Sakya. Upstairs, a good number of enormous murals including huge portraits of the Five Forefathers of Sakya, several paintings of religious subjects, and other designs are well preserved. The unique mandalas especially draw visitors interest. There are altogether 139 mandalas upstairs, all works of the Yuan period.

Some twenty or thirty tangkas are well kept in a box, which were drawn more than six hundred years ago. Each tangka is densely dotted with animated figures of men three or four centimetres in size, or mountains, rivers, forests, and roads all in clearly defined colours with brief descriptions noted in Tibetan under each scene. It is obvious that the tangkas were painted as a narrative, and the stories depicted included Pagpa's audiences with the Emperor, the building of the Sakya Monastery after his return from Peking, his travels to different places to deliver sermons; and lastly, his second visit to Peking to receive the title of the "Dishi" or Imperial Preceptor. Each tangka narrated one story in pictures.

There is one of the Pagtang* ("tangkas" about Pagpa) which are the records of the deeds of Kunka Gyaltsan, the fourth of the Five Forefathers of Sakya.

---

* In these tangkas biographies of the Five Forefathers of Sakya are recorded in picture-form in scrolled paintings. There are forty-nine tangkas in all. Among them the biography of Pagpa is painted in especial detail.

Kunka Gyaltsan was the first person to visit Koko-nor (Wuwei region of present Gansu) in 1246, where he gained recognition and support from Godan, the son of Genghis Khan. From that time on the Sakyapa Sect held a dominant position both in religious and political affairs in Tibet. Kunka Gyaltsan therefore was the cornerstone of the Sakya Dynasty.

Another tangka recorded Kunka Gyaltsan's outstanding achievements in his studies of Buddhism. As his fame rose in Tibet, an Indian Buddhist scholar named Drodon Gawa and some other scholars, quite sceptical that there could be such a wise man in such a wilderness as the Land of Snows, came to Kunka Gyaltsan's very door to engage in debate with him for thirteen days. The Indians lost the debate, and Drodon Gawa had no alternative but to pay homage to Kunka Gyaltsan as his Master. From then on Kunka Gyaltsan became more celebrated than ever and he became known as "Sakya Pandita" (the pundit of Sakya).

This "pandita" (pundit) was a gifted erudite and wrote many books such as "The Mottoes of Sakya" written in the style of folk songs containing mainly feudal ethics and reflecting a bourgeois philosophy of life, which has been reprinted contless times. Kunka Gyaltsan's Buddhist works such as "Detailed Interpretations of the Three Religious Voes" and "Interpretations of Lord Buddha's Teachings" became compulsory scriptures for the Sakyapa Sect. Kunka Gyaltsan genuinely proved himself an excellent scholar, and importance has been attached to his great achievements in his studies both at home and abroad. As well as being invited to inland China to preach Buddhism, he also created a script of more than forty letters for the Mongolians and thus laid the foundation for Pagpa to popularize the same script.

Everything about the Sakya Monastery from the buildings themselves exquisite murals, precious religious vestments, armour and ancient chinaware to its ancient sutras, scrolled texts, and tangkas, is imbued with artistic value. Sakya truly is a great treasury. Almost every single item within it shows the Tibetans close relationship with the Hans, Mongolians, and Manchus during the Yuan Dynasty or during the Ming and Qing dynasties and a good number of its art treasures are the fruit of the cooperation of various nationalities.

6

NGARI THE ROOF OF THE WORLD ENVELOPED IN MYTH

Gang Rinpoche the Monarch of the Sacred Mountains

The "Sacred Mountain"

Where the "Sacred Lake" Joins the "the Sacred Mountain"

The Ancient Kingdom of Guge

People say the Tibetan plateau is "the Roof of the World." In that case, Ngari, the western part of the plateau where mountain ranges rise one upon another, and rivers tumble down for thousands of miles, indeed deserves the name of "the Roof of the Roof of the World."

Thinly populated, Ngari's remoteness adds a touch of adventure to a visit there, while tales of its "sacred mountains," "sacred rivers," and "sacred lakes" give Ngari even more of an air of mystery. Amidst the sea of ice and snow of the Himalaya Range lying to the south, stand five great peaks which have given rise to oft-told tales of "goddesses descending to earth." Folks say Mt. Jomo Langma (Mt. Everest) and the four other peaks are five heavenly dakinis. Mt. Jomo Langma itself is the Tingki Shalsangma (Blue Joyful Goddess), while the others are Tashi Tseringma (Auspicious Longevity Goddess), the Goddess of Health and Prosperity; Miyo Losangma (Constant Benevolent Goddess), the Goddess of Croplands; Chopan Dinsangma (Harmonious-Voiced Goddess), the Goddess of Wealth; and lastly, Tadkar Dosangma (Reliable Passionate Goddess), the Goddess of Animal Husbandry.

However, the legendary tales of the Himalaya Range are not as mystical and fantastic as those of the Gangdise Range.

The Gang Rimpoche* The Monarch of the Sacred Mountains

The towering range of Gangdise runs between the Kunlun and Himalayas. With its countless precipices and crisscrossing glaciers it looks nothing but majestic.

---

* Mt. Dise is known as the Gang Rimpoche in Tibetan language.

The name of the range has its origin in two separate languages. "Gang" is a Tibetan word meaning "snow" while the word "dise" comes from the Sanskrit for the same. The Gangdise Range is indeed an icy forest of snow peaks. Caves with sparkling icicles, crystal palaces, and ice mushrooms are common sights deep within the mountain range, while "ice suspension bridges" spanning two peaks are often seen, too. With the exception of its massive crags and huge, piled up boulders, the Gangdise Range is a world of ice and snow.

The main peak of the Gangdise Range is called the Gang Rimpoche (Mt. Dise). At a height of 6,714 metres above sea level, it is situated within Porang Dzong and its summit remains covered with snow the whole year round. "Gang Rimpoche" in Tibetan means "Precious Mountain of the Heaven," while its Sanskrit meaning is "the Heaven of Siva" or the "Heaven of Gods." In his book *An Account of the Mountains and Waters of Gangdise*, the famous lama Jetsun Taktse-wa describes Mt. Dise and the four rivers originating from this range in this way; "in appearance, the Gang Rimpoche resembles an olivetree. Its summit, sharp as a splinter, penetrates right through the clouds or even the blue skies. White clouds roll along to the south as if bowing low in worship to the peak. The peak is surrounded by a rainbow halo, while its flanks are crystal, transparent and sparkling. Struck by the rays of the sun, it gives off a fantastic radiance, while from its heights tinkling crystal spring-waters splash down the cracks creating melodious rhythms as delightful as music of the celestial realm. At sunset, as the rays of the sun strike the lofty peak from the western horizon, reflections through the clouds blend to form rings of light which

147

make the peak seem as if it is enveloped in a strip of coloured silk. By this time the mountain is girt with rainbows forming a belt of many colours. At high noon when the sun's rays fall perpendicularly from overhead, the Gang Rimpoche seems to be clad from top to toe in a robe of colours. At the foot of the mountain, the robe's hem is bordered with green grass and colourful flowers, creating a beautiful velvet embroidery."

The eminent monk continues, "the Gang Rimpoche stands majestically in the centre surrounded by mountain peaks like the Eight-Petalled Lotus. The back of the mountain, known as the Scented Mountain, is rife with medicinal herbs, while in front lies the crystal 'sacred lake,' the Tso Mapham, whose limpid azure surface resembles a giant mirror in which the image of the Gang Rimpoche is reflected. Toward evening, the condensation creates a filmy mist which sways to and fro in the gentle breeze over the surface of the lake like a sheet of pure white silk. At this time the radiance of the peak and the colour of the water appear more ethereally beautiful than ever. All around the lofty Gang Rimpoche stand snow-clad companion peaks of various sizes."

Continuing his description Jetsun Taktse-wa writes, "The Palace of the Immeasurable Heaven lies at the summit of the Gang Rimpoche where, for the sake of mankind, the 'yidams' of tantric mysticism gave birth to the four rivers: the Tachog Khabab (out of the horse's mouth), the Sengge Khabab (out of the lion's mouth), the Langchen Khabab (out of the elephant's mouth) and the Macha Khabab (out of the peacock's mouth). These four rivers of the Ngari region flow out north, south, east and west from the Gang Rimpoche. The sources of these rivers bear resemblance to the four animals, the horse, the lion, the elephant, and the peacock, from which the names of the rivers are derived."

Jetsun Taktse-wa's description of the Gang Rimpoche soars in hyperbole, but as a whole, because of its main peak, the Gang Rimpoche, the Gangdise Range really does appear mystical and fantastic. The four rivers originating in Mt. Dise are named after the four animals which are said to be incarnations of heavenly deities. Since everything is described in terms of Buddhist worship, Buddhists everywhere believe Mt. Dise to be a "sacred mountain," the Tso Mapham a "sacred Lake," and the four rivers "sacred rivers." The whole region therefore has become one of the famous sacred places of Buddhism, every year attracting hundreds and thousands of pilgrims from China and abroad. Just as Moslems save up for years to go on pilgrimage to Mecca, so many Buddhists hope that they will be able to visit Mt. Dise on pilgrimage once in their lifetime. A person is considered most fortunate if he dies in the course of his pilgrimage, as he is believed to achieve enlightenment from the sacred place. If he returns home he is received with great respect and is considered a man of merit and virtue for having set foot in a "sacred place," having tasted "sacred water," and having touched "sacred soil." A couple of years ago, one high official of neighbouring country even made a special pilgrimage on muleback to the Gangdise region.

The "Sacred Mountain"

Mt. Dise has been deeply coloured with mysticism due to the mediation, teachings, accumulation of merit and doctrinal debates of numerous famous Buddhist priests from China and abroad in this region in the past.

According to *An Account of the Mountains and Waters of Gangdise*: "Atop the sharp peak of the Gang Rimpoche, the paramount peak of the whole range, stands the Palace of the Immeasurable Heaven below which, midway up the mountain, five hundred yogins are in retreat in caves. Below this are countless dakinis in attendance on the enlightened ones and taking care of the palace." Hundreds of years ago when Atisa, the Bengali sage, came to Tibet to preach Buddhism, he travelled through this region. Arriving at the foot of the mountain, he hesitated, realising he did not know the hour of the day. Just then, he thought he heard the sound of bells and drums from the mountain above, and so he judged the hour must be the recreation and meal time for the five hundred yogins who dwelled on the mountain and thought he too should stop and take some sustenance. Ever since then, those among the Mt. Dise pilgrims who are favoured by fortune will hear the sound of sandalwood clappers while those who are not so favoured will fail to catch the sound. Obviously, no one is likely to admit to not hearing the sound of the sandalwood clappers for he or she will then be considered unlucky. The following story about Milarepa adds further splendour to the sacred mountain.

Milarepa was born into a poor family of Lhatod in the Tsang region. When he heard people say that in Lhodrag, Lhopa, there lived a great Master named Marpa who had accumulated great merit and virtue, he underwent untold hardships and made a special trip to Lhodrag in order to pay homage to Marpa as his Master. There, he endured bitter sufferings for six years and eight months till his body had wasted away to bone and sinew, and his mind had become fully cultivated and filled with understanding. Only then did Marpa place his confidence in him and teach him the dharma. After receiving the dharma, Micarepa left for Ngari where he dwelt in a secluded cave on Mt. Dise and concentrated on meditation by living on nettles as his daily fare. It was at this very place that he relayed his doctrine to his disciples Rechungpa and others in the form of lyric poems. Collected and recorded by Rechungpa, they became known as "Milarepa's Lyric Poems."

One day, a young Bon adherent named Naro Bonchung came to see him. As he possessed super-natural powers of transformation, Naro Bonchung thought himself superior in religious consciousness, and challenged Milarepa to a doctrinal debate. He thought in this way he could win control of the region and become the Master of Mt. Dise, the sacred mountain. But Naro Bonchung met his match in Milarepa, so next he challenged him to a mountain-climbing contest on the auspicious fifteenth day of the lunar month. Whoever was to reach the summit first, was to become the Master of the sacred mountain. Milarepa accepted the challenge with calmness. And so, early in the morning of the fifteenth day, Naro Bonchung, mounted a drum, and using the drum stick as a whip, galloped towards the peak. Meanwhile Milarepa, as calm as ever, remained seated firmly in his cell and went on with his teaching. Seeing this, his disciples were driven wild with anxiety, and urged Milarepa to take his leave forthwith, but to no avail. Not until it was already broad daylight, did Milarepa step out of his cell and look into the distance. Far away he saw Naro Bonchung toiling up the path to the summit as if his life depended on it. Then Milarepa returned to his cell and said to his disciples, "What a fool!" A moment later Milarepa flapped his shawl and made his ascent of the summit, where he found himself in a wonderland. Chanting prayers, he went into meditation at the entrance to the summit. A long time afterwards, Naro Bonchung approached the summit, in a state of absolute exhaustion. When he discovered Milarepa had been there in meditation long beforehand, he felt highly embarrassed, his legs gave way and he sank to the ground, thinking to rest for a while. Unfortunately, at the very moment of respite, he tumbled downhill drum and all, leaving on the Gang Rimpoche a deep gash still visible to this day, which is never covered with snow even after heavy snowfall. At the foot of the Gang Rimpoche the hollow formed where Naro Bonchung and his drum landed can still be seen on a huge rock.

After his fall from the summit, Naro Bonchung admitted defeat and acknowledged Milarepa as his Master. He asked to be given a place where he could go into meditation and so Milarepa gave Naro Bonchung a grotto near his own landing spot. Today, a cell still exists near the huge rock where Naro Bonchung paid his respects to the Master and did his meditation.

Stories and legends about the religious antagonism between Milarepa and Naro Bonchung may have been fabricated and exaggerated by Buddhists, but the characters actually existed. The story shows the beginning of the "Persecution of Buddhism Period" in Tibet after the decline of the Tubo Dynasty. The struggle between Milarepa of the Kagyupa Sect and Naro Bonchung of the Bon religion took place right at the time of Tibet's breakup into separate states when each sect was engaged in a life-and-death struggle.

Milarepa's religious victory further increased the

might of the Buddha on Mt. Dise, and pilgrims flocked there in growing crowds. In particular the huge rock lying at the foot of the mountain became a spot on which every pilgrim had to set foot. Over the ages, the imprint of so many feet left their mark on the huge rock, leading later generations to believe that these footprints were left by gods and dakinis to guide their the way. It was said: "One circumambulation of the rock can wash off the sins committed in this life; ten circumambulations can wipe out the sufferings of hell for five hundred lives; while one hundred circumambulations can turn one into a bodhisattva and allow one to achieve enlightenment."

The interesting tales of Buddhist sages such as Atisa and Milarepa, have heightened Buddhist faith in the holiness of Mt. Dise and as a result, it has become one of the sacred places of Buddhism. Every year thousands of pious Buddhists from all over the world visit the place on pilgrimage. The Horse Year of the Tibetan calendar is the luckiest year to go on pilgrimage because it is the memorable year of Milarepa's triumph over a non-Buddhist. In such a year, Mt. Dise is packed with pilgrims and is the scene of great excitement.

Where the "Sacred Lake" Joins the "Sacred Mountain"

Like a pair of giant dragons, the Himalayas and the Gangdise Range wriggle across the Ngari plateau, while crushed between these two towering snow-clad ranges, the River Tachok Khabab (out of the horse's mouth) roars eastwards. Like the other three rivers, the Sengge Khabab (out of the lion's mouth), the Langchen

Khabab (out of the elephant's mouth), and the Macha Khabab (out of the peacock's mouth), from its source curving like the head of a horse, spring water oozing from the mouth, the Tachok Khabab passes through wide grain fields and uninterrupted snowy mountain ranges, flows through Drongpa Dzong of Shigatse Prefecture, and eventually becomes the upper part of "the Heavenly River," the Tsangpo. The other three rivers pass through Kashmir, India, and Bengal respectively before emptying into the Indian Ocean.

The full name of the Tsangpo is the Yarlung Tsangpo River, meaning "The River of the Highlands." It is also known as the "Heavenly River" because the upper part of the river, the Tachok Khabab, flows at an average altitude of 5,200 metres above sea level. The Tsangpo, which has the total length of 2,057 kilometres, is therefore the highest great river in the world. Glaciers collected from the Gangdise and Himalayan ranges form a huge reservoir of solid ice, which, as it melts and becomes a river, connects the numerous lakes formed by ice and boulders and becomes the Tachok Khabab, the head waters of the Tsangpo. In this region, a cluster of snowy peaks, the crystal glaciers and queer-shaped icebergs, all make the river and lakes of this scantily populated area even more fascinating.

Northwest of the Tachok Khabab and southeast of Mt. Dise lies a "sacred lake" named Tso Mapham (Manasarowar). One of the highest fresh water lakes in the world, it has an area of more than four hundred square kilometres, and forms a huge natural reservoir.

According to historical and Buddhist accounts, Tso Mapham is the king of the world's "sacred lakes." Fed by the ice and snowmelt from Mt. Dise, the lake appears especially blue and limpid, so that fish can be seen to a depth of fifteen metres or more. Hence, the water of the lake is known to Buddhists as the "Sweet Dew," the gift of the Buddha. This "sacred water" can wash off the "five vices" (avarice, anger, idiocy, sloth and envy) as well as the filth of the body. Anyone who bathes in the lake gains baptism for the soul, purity and longevity for the body. Every year from summer to autumn numbers of pious pilgrims, young and old, visit the "sacred lake" to bathe. After bathing, they take home treasured gifts of clear lake water for their friends and relations.

An Account of the Mountains and Waters of Gangdise has this to say about the lake: The Dragon Palace of the wealthy Dragon King lies beneath the lake, where vase treasures of the world are gathered. People who come on pilgrimage to this place will receive from the wealthy Dragon King the gift of everlasting wealth for the rest of their lives if they only make one single circumambulation of the lake, or capture one single fish, or pick up one single pebble, or even pick up one single feather from a bird living on the lake. Thus, nine hundred years ago, this lake was known as the Matutso which referred to the name of the wealthy Dragon King. In the eleventh century, when the Kagyupa Sect, the representative of Buddhism at that time, triumphed in its fierce fight against Black Bonism, Buddhists marked the religious victory of Buddhism by changing the name of the lake to Tso Mapham, the ever-victorious lake.

In fact, it was Tso Mapham's wonderful scenery of the snows and the lake which probably exerted fascination over people. As long ago as before the advent of Buddhism into Tibet, Xuanzhuang, the eminent

Tang monk, in his book *Journey to the West of the Great Tang* described Tso Mapham as the "wonderous lake of the Western Paradise." Thus, it is clear that the region had long been admired for its beautiful scenery of mountains, rivers and the lake as well as the richness of its produce. Later, as time went by and the Buddhist faith deepened, the lake became more and more "heavenly" and "sacred" in people's minds.

The Ancient Kingdom of Guge

On the northwestern slopes of Mt. Dise, the main peak of the Gangdise Range, there is a spring resembling an elephant drawing up water through its trunk. Natives call the stream which flows from this spring the River Langchen Khabab (out of the elephant's mouth). The Langchen Khabab rushes towards the northwest between the Himalayas and the Gangdise Range, and after passing through Tsanda Dzong of Ngari Prefecture, enters Indian territory and finally empties itself into the Indian Ocean.

Within the territory of Tsanda Dzong, Ngari Prefecture, at Yiprang on the southern bank of the Langchen Khabab, there lies a mound of yellow earth about three hundred metres in height. On this hill lie the ruins of a wall and a castle, the most important remains of the ancient Guge Kingdom. Built against the hillside, the castle penetrates the skyline at its highest point, while on the northeastern side of the hill there are seven earthen forts and three temples each about ten metres high. The hillside is honeycombed with more than three hundred caves, while at the centre stand a number of red and white striped walls. Taken together, these make a magnificent cluster of temple buildings, preserved intact. Inside, tunnels run in all directions and the entire complex is surrounded by a fortification wall built of yellow earth on which many carvings of the Buddha can still be discerned. It is not difficult to see that this ancient kingdom was once prosperous and splendid.

Taking a zig-zagging route up the earthen hill, bypassing the broken walls, and looking into the distance from the top of the hill, one can see chains of mountain peaks lying to the south of the castle while a vista of mountain ranges, studded with pagoda-like rocky peaks, unfolded to the north of the glistening Langchen Khabab.

Looking up and down the castle's overhanging fortification wall, we noticed heaps of pebbles gathered both on top of and at the foot of the wall. These were said to have been used as weapons at the time. Tradition has it that at the beginning of the seventeenth century the Guge Kingdom was attacked by some outside force. Taking advantage of his favourable position, the King of Guge held out in the subsequent siege, while the attackers, too, fortified themselves by building high walls in order to make a breakthrough over the fortification wall and moat. As both sides remained at an impasse, facing one another, sabres and spears, bows and arrows ran short and eventually both sides turned to the stones that covered the whole mountain wilderness as effective weapons.

To the south of the castle are the remains of a building. The roof had long since collapsed, and it now lay open to the sky. The walls were blackened by smoke and fire, but the vestiges can still be seen distinctly. Behind one wall there is a room stacked full of firewood and sheep droppings. This probably serves as the king's kitchen and the cook's living quarters.

Northwards from the kitchen is a courtyard covering four or five thousand square metres. This courtyard, like the Deyangshar courtyard of the Potala, is used for song and dance performances and other entertainments. North of the courtyard is a large hall whose roof had long since caved in leaving only the walls still standing. Their smooth and shiny mortar surface is in perfect condition, and the odd trace of paintings of the period can still be seen. The floor is covered with a thick layer of leaves. Apparently it is in this hall that the king and his ministers held their official discussions.

Outside the castle, there are three temples; the Red Temple, the White Temple, and the Samsara Temple, situated midway up the hillside. The upturned eaves of the temples are decorated with carvings of animals such as the lion, elephant, horse, dragon, and peacock. These carvings are directly linked with the legends of the four "sacred rivers" which rise in Mt. Dise. The walls and upper part of the scripture hall are covered with frescoes depicting Buddhist anecdotes, naked figures, flowers, grass and trees, animals such as lions, elephants, horses, dragons, peacocks, and so on. The figures and animals are realistically painted, and bear distinct expressions of pleasure, wrath, sorrow, or fear. Depicted in standing, sitting or fighting postures, the figures are painted in harmonious shades of red, blue, indigo, and white, all natural pigments extracted from indigenous minerals and plants. There is no doubt that the Guge Kingdom, too, is a Buddhist state, and that its people worshipped animals such as the lion, elephant, horse, and peacock, which even to this day are still objects of veneration in Ngari.

Near the castle and temples are more than ten

caves in which are stored extremely valuable historical relics such as various ancient weapons, gunpowder, agricultural tools, cooking utensils, and scriptures written in Tibetan. It is quite certain that these caves were used as storehouses during the time of the Guge Kingdom. Some items kept in these storehouses are porcelain bowls, copper alms bowls, wooden basins, wooden ploughs and wooden hoes, as well as saddles, armour, helmets, arrows, firearms, swords, spears, rattan shields, and the like. The arid climate and the rarefied atmosphere of the Tibetan plateau have helped preserve these relics in excellent condition, undamaged for centuries.

According to Tibetan historical records, Lang Darma, the last Tsanpo of the Tubo Dynasty, persecuted Buddhism but was unable to wipe it out completely, and instead lost his own life at the hands of Lhalung Paldor, a Buddhist monk. Lang Darma left behind a queen and a concubine. The queen was childless while the concubine had a son, and so as a consequence a struggle for the inheritance of the throne developed. The queen became envious of the concubine for having a child, and the concubine, fearing that her precious son might be murdered, kept the palace lighted day and night in order to protect him against any evildoer. She named her son "O-sung," meaning "protected by the light." The queen realised that it was impossible to murder the child, and so she hatched a scheme whereby she claimed an infant of common blood as her own, spreading the news that the child was a posthumous child of Lang Darma among the diehards at court. With the intention that this child should inherit the throne, the queen named him "Yumtan," meaning "relying on the mother." Yumtan schemed and plotted to the fullest and succeeded in making O-sung the target of public criticism. The straightforward and honest O-sung realised on reflection that his father's persecution of Buddhism had lost the hearts of the people, and so he intentionally restored certain Buddhist religious activities. Yumtan, on the other hand, obstinately carried on Lang Darma's policy of persecution. In the end the two brothers had no option but to scramble for the two regions of "Dburu" and "Gyoru." In the meantime other regions of Tibet such as Kham and Yarlung rebelled one after another, and as a result the whole of Tibet was thrown into disunity with the rise of separatist states.

The fighting between the two brothers was continued by their sons, and in the end O-sung's son Palkhortsan was killed by Yumtan's lackeys. Palkhor-tsan's two sons, Jide Nyimagon and Tashi Tsepal, both fled from Lhasa to the western regions of Tibet during the persecution of religious ministers. The religious ministers exhorted them to flee as far away as possible for the sake of continuing the family line, and further advised them that only by fleeing to Ngari region could they gain a firm foothold. Following this advice, Jide Nyima-gon fled to Mang-yul, a region near Tso Mapham, and joined forces with a tribal chief called Tashi-Tsan, whose daughter he took to wife. She later bore three sons, Palde-gon, Tashi-gon, and Detsug-gon. When the three sons grew to maturity Jide Nyima-gon divided his land among the trio. Palde-gon was to take over the region around the lake in Mang-yul, near Tso Mapham (nowadays Porang Dzong); Tashi-gon was given the area around Mt. Sangpo, near Mt. Dise; while Detsug-gon received jurisdiction over the rocky region around Guge of Shangshung (the region where the Guge ruins are located in Tsanda Dzong). Later generations called these areas "the three regions of the three Gons." Ngari is divided into three regions even today, although the present divisions are not as same as the ancient ones mentioned in historical records which are the region of water (in Ritu and Gar), the region of mountains (in Tsanda and Porang), and the region of grasslands (in Getsa and Tsoleg).

Thus it is clear that the present remains of the Guge Kingdom are the remains of the kingdom founded in Tsanda Dzong by Detsug-gon, the third son of Jide Nyima-gon. Whether anything is left of the kingdoms established by the other two brothers awaits further investigation. Judging from the Buddhist images and scriptures, and the temples found among the Guge ruins, it is inferred that O-sung's descendants continued to respect his belief that the wholesale destruction of Buddhism was unwise. According to the records given in *A Mirror of the Genealogy of Kings*, the Guge Kingdom lasted for sixteen generations, while the ancient castle we saw in Tsanda Dzong was built and continuously enlarged between the tenth and sixteen centuries. The Guge Kingdom occupies a very important position in Tibetan history as a powerful kingdom during the four hundred years of decentralization in Tibet after the decline of the Tubo Dynasty. While it lasted, the Kingdom of Guge made a great contribution in standing up to foreign invasions, safeguarding the territorial integrity of Tibet, and defending the motherland's southwestern frontier. At one time its power even extended westwards towards the regions around Ladak.

Ngari to this day has remained a region of mystery and exceptional fascination. Valiant mountaineers are obviously proud of setting foot upon "the Roof of the Roof of the World," while natural science and social science researchers are keen to probe this region of profound mystery. As of old, Buddhists, still yearn for the "sacred mountains" and now curious tourists, too, will surely feel the deep fascination that the scenery of Ngari has always exerted on people.

7

CHAMDO A STRATEGICALLY IMPORTANT TOWN IN EASTERN TIBET

The Karo Archaeological Site and the History of Chamdo

The Famous Jampaling Monastery of Chamdo

Chamdo Takes on a New Look

Crisscrossed by high mountain ranges and deep ravines channelled by angry torrents, the Chamdo Prefecture is airily situated on the Kham Plateau of Eastern Tibet at an altitude of between three and four thousand metres above sea level, except for the Puro Region and certain river valleys which are comparatively lower in altitude. Major watercourses include the Yangtze, Zachu (Mekong), Gyamo Ngulchu, Yigong Tsangpo and Powo Tsangpo. Historically, Chamdo was once part of the Tibetan Tubo Dynasty. Later, during the Ming and Qing dynasties, it became known as Kham, and then as Dokham during the time of the former Tibetan Kashak (Cabinet). Today the region forms a prefecture under the administration of the Tibet Autonomous Region. Covering an area of approximately 300,000 square kilometres, Chamdo runs 850 km eastwards until it meets the Gyamo Ngulchu River and the Gangtse Autonomous Prefecture of Tibetan Nationality (Sichuan Province). Northsouth, Chamdo stretches 470 km down to Yunnan, partially bordering on Indian and Burmese territory in the south, while to the north it joins with the Yushu Autonomous Prefecture of Tibetan Nationality in Qinghai Province. To the southwest it meets Kongpo at Serkye-La Pass. At the juncture of mountain ranges deep within the region lies the strategically situated town of Chamdo. It is at the exact of the Sichuan-Tibet Highway, about five days journey from both Lhasa and Chengdu.

Agriculture, animal husbandry and forestry are important resources of Chamdo. The regions of Dray-ag, Lhorong, Sang-ngag Choling and Powo are mainly agricultural areas. Animal husbandry covers the whole prefecture, with Tengchen and Chamdo ranking foremost. Forestry regions are found everywhere throughout Chamdo. Geological surveys have shown that the region is also extremely rich in mineral resources such as gold, silver, copper, iron, tin, lead, coal, petroleum and gypsum.

The Karo Archaeological Site and the History of Chamdo

The history of Chamdo stretches way back in time. Evidence of settlement in neolithic times is still preserved at Karo, situated twelve km. southeast of Chamdo on the northern bank of the Gyamo Ngulchu River. The discovery of Karo, which dates back mare than 4,600 years, was made a few years ago. A rich variety of ancient artefacts were excavated from the 10,000 sq. metre site, including the remains of settlement, stone and bone implements, pottery, and grains. This discovery has proved highly valuable to archeologists, geologists, palaeoanthropologists, zoologists and botanists all over China.

The Karo discovery provides evidence that the primitive aborigines of the Tibetan plateau had close times with the inhabitants of the Yellow River settlements more than four or five thousand years ago, and is also of great importance to research on Tibet's early history and other scientific questions. The discovery also gives us a clue as to the origins and development of this strategically important town of the eastern Tibet.

According to historical accounts Chamdo's history as a town goes back only two hundred years. However, Chamdo shows clear signs of human inhabitation since ancient times. Tools such as stone axes, scrapers and augers, and a large quantity of ashes from millet and other grains excavated from the Karo site prove that people had been living in the area and opening up this rich bit of land several thousand years before. Records from the Zhou Dynasty (eleventh century-221 BC) state that grain had been cultivated from earliest times in central China. Thus it eventually spread to the banks of the Gyamo Ngulchu River where judging from the cultivation of millet it is quite clear there was an early settlement, the precursor to Chamdo. Chinese records show that by the time of the Han (206 B.C-220 AD) and Wei (220-265 AD) dynasties Chamdo had already arisen to fame, known in those days as "Kham." The area it covered was not the same as the later Kham which included the whole territory of the former Shikham Province, and Kham originally probably referred to the area round about the juncture of the two rivers, the Zachu and Angchu, where Chamdo town is now situated. In Tibetan, "Chamdo" means "the lower part of the river," and brief accounts of Chamdo appear in writings of the Han, Jin and Sui dynasties.

At the beginning of the seventh century, the Tubo Dynasty rose abruptly in Tibet, conquering the tribes that lived in the Yarlung valley, taking over the Sumba people who lived in the Nyangchu valley, and reaching as far east as the Kham region. From then on Chamdo became subject to the Tubo Dynasty. Following the decline of the Tubo Dynasty, Tibet underwent a period of decentralization which lasted four hundred years. During this period the Chamdo region was also divided among local headmen. When the Sakya Dynasty became the ruler of Tibet in the thirteenth century, Chamdo came under its domination, and subsequently in the fourteenth century as the Pagdu Dynasty rose to power in the U-Tsang region of Tibet, Chamdo's allegiance was transferred accordingly. Starting from this time, the Ming and Qing dynasties implemented a policy of control through conciliation and restraint. Emperor Shunzhi of the Qing Dynasty conferred upon the great lamas who were in control of both political and religious power the titles: "Great Master of Compassion" and "Hutogtu*." Subsequently these great lamas regularly paid tribute to the imperial court. In 1719, Emperor Kangxi sent a general named Gaerbi with an army to Tibet by two routes from Yunnan and Sichuan to drive out the Dzungar invaders from Mongolia. Gaerbi advanced as far as to Chamdo where he acted as representative of the Qing court and presented diplomas and seals inscribed in Manchurian, Mongolian and Tibetan to Pagpa-lha Hutogtu, the abbot of the Jampaling Monastery, and Shiwa-lha Hutogtu, the abbot of the Pambar Monastery. These gave the two high lamas the authority to exercise religious and political power over the region of Chamdo, centralised in Chamdo town. The Qing court helped the two "Hutogtus" to select military and civil officials to take charge of the granaries, guerrilla forces, garrison forces, and thousand-household administrative units, and stationed several hundred troops from Sichuan and Yunnan in Chamdo to keep control over the neighbouring counties. Over the next two hundred years, Chamdo developed from this basis into an important town amidst mountain ranges.

The Battles for Chamdo

Chamdo occupies a vital strategic position situated as it is between Sichuan and Lhasa, Qinghai and Yun-

---

*"Hutogtu" is a Mongolian title for a high lama.

nan and Burma. The town itself stands against an imposing mountain backdrop with clusters of peaks jutting into the sky, and looks down over a flat winding valley, where the Gyamo Ngulchu and Zachu Rivers worm their way through fold after fold of mountains and valleys. Chamdo's important strategic position in its mountain fastness has meant that it has often been contested by strategists. Leaving aside the remote past, in recent history, when the Qing general Gaerbi set out to suppress a rebellion raised by the people who sided with the Dzungars in 1719, Chamdo was the first place he took along the eastern route. Stationing his troops there he completely destroyed all the monasteries and villages for hundreds of miles around. Later, in the first year of the Qing Emperor Xuantong's reign (1862), when Zhao Erfeng, the Minister of the Sichuan and Yunnan border regions, exercised the policy of abrogating hereditary land ownership and turning the land over to imperial officials appointed to the region, once again Chamdo was the first spot where he stationed his troops, and from where he carried out reactionary massacres which resulted in longstanding antagonism between nationalities. In 1950, to drive out the powers of imperialist aggression and unify the sacred motherland, the People's Liberation Army marched into Tibet. In an attempt to stop the People's Liberation Army's march into Tibet, the former upper strata serf owners of Tibet, backed by the imperialists, put up a desperate resistance at Chamdo. The losing of the battle resulted in their final acceptance and signing of the 17-Point Agreement for the peaceful liberation of Tibet. The battle at Chamdo scored a victory in bringing Tibet into the bosom of the motherland.

The Famous Jampaling Monastery of Chamdo

Looking down from the top of the Tamala Pass, the Chamdo Monastery appears tucked within the crisscrossing mountain ranges on a knoll composed layers of red earth formed by ancient glaciers between the Zachu and Angchu Rivers. This monastery was founded during the Ming period by a disciple of Tsongkapa after Tsongkapa's religious reform in Tibet. According to Gelugpa Sect rules, the Chamdo Monastery should harbour 2,500 monks.

When Tsongkapa made his journey into Tibet via Chamdo in 1373, he predicted that in the future a monastery would be erected and Buddhism would flourish in the area. Later, in 1437, Sherab Sangpo, one of Tsongkapa's disciples, founded the monastery on a rocky hill between the Angchu and Zachu Rivers, and modelled it on a flying eagle about to land. The main relic is the statue of the Jampa (the Future Buddha) from which the name of the monastery, Jampaling is derived. The monastery is the largest of the Gelugpa Sect monasteries in the Chamdo region and is divided into five colleges: the Lingtod, Lingme, Nupling, Kuchuk, and Chagra-khapa. Heads of the monastery have included such great Buddhist lamas as Chowang Dragpa of Shangshung, Namkha-pal of Tsurton, Jedrung Kunka Tashi of Drongtse in Upper Nyang, and the third Dalai Lama Sonam Gyatso. Famous all over Tibet, Jampaling Monastery had thirteen successive abbots, until it was taken over by the reincarnations of Pagpa-la, starting from the Third Pagpa-la, Thongwa Dondan. By this time the monastery had one hundred and thirty subordinate monasteries in the

Kham region, mostly concentrated in Chamdo, Drayak, Pagshod, Shopado, Sang-ngag Choling, and Powo.

Chamdo is the gateway between Sichuan and Tibet, and so is an important trading centre. The monastery, too, engages in trade, and distributes its profits equally among the monks in the form of daily necessities such as butter, "tsampa" (barley flour), brick tea etc.

Chamdo Takes on a New Look

More than thirty years have elapsed since the peaceful liberation of Tibet, a mere twinkling compared to the lengthy process of history. As we climbed midway up the northern slope of the grazing pastures from where we could enjoy a bird's-eye view of this mountain-girt town, age-old Chamdo appeared before our eyes bursting with vitality. The town has indeed taken on a new look. The Sichuan Bridge and Yunnan Bridge, double-curvature arch bridges built in recent years, span the turbulent waves of the Zachu and Angchu Rivers joining the ancient town to the new development zone. In the past, the river banks, strewn with the bodies of the starved, presented a scene of desolation, but today more than twenty small and medium-sized factories and plants providing electric power, cement, farm implements, foodstuffs, printing and tanning processes have sprung up one after another like bamboo shoots after a springshower. These factories and plants produce daily necessities and construction materials from natural resources of the locality. Once piled high with rubbish, the old town now boasts rows of houses built in the local style, and a vehicle repair and spare parts plant as well as a bus station. On the wild and sandy areas erect the prefectural departments, prefectural commissioner's offices, the bank, and the general store. The old and new town are joined by interlacing cement roads. By day, Chamdo bustles with traffic and pedestrians, while in the evening bright lights gleam against the mountains and river, creating a magnificent scene.

To the south of the town, on the eastern side of the Zachu River, a cultural and educational zone has been established on about 140,000 sq. metres of former pastureland. Here, a middle school, a normal school, a school of hygiene, a rediffusion relay station, etc., are energetically engaged in training various types of qualified personnel.

The development area of Chamdo at present, runs from the Yunnan Bridge to the Sichuan Bridge, from the Angchu River to the banks of the Zachu River, and extends to the terraces of the mountain slopes, and further. The new construction area totals more than 500,000 sq. metres, or forty-five times the size of old Chamdo. Apart from dozens of mansions with spacious courtyards belonging to wealthy merchants, feudal nobles and their managers, there were no dwellings in old Chamdo for the one or two thousand labouring people. Occupied with heavy labour or given to wandering the streets by day, when night fell, they curled up within stone stockades or slept in shacks cobbled together out of planks and ragged pieces of felt rug, while some even lived their whole lives in rudimentary caves dug under hillocks.

Chamdo has witnessed great changes in its history; from being a town on the verge of extinction, it has become a burgeoning centre of growth, glowing with vitality.

8

THE NORTHERN GRASSLANDS OF THE CHANGTANG

Lakes Without Number

Hot Springs and Geothermal Regions

A Rich and Beautiful "No-Man's Land"

Tanglba the Legendary Mountain
and Source of China's
Two Longest Rivers

A folksong provides the key to a real understanding of the Northern Grasslands which occupy half the area of Tibet.

> The lonely bleakness may bring sadness
> When the Changtang first you roam,
> But once within her warm embrace
> The grasslands soon become your home.

Excerpt from a folk song of the northern grasslands

The Changtang presents a forbidding appearance (the name "Changtang" means "northern wilderness") and covers an area of 600,000 sq. km. It is the major natural pastureland of Tibet and is home to the famous yaks and wild yaks of the region. To its north lies the boundless Kunlun Range, and to the south snake the Gangdise and Nyanchen Tanglha Ranges. This vast stretch of grassland forms the heart of the Qinghai-Tibet Plateau, and lies at an average altitude of 4,500 metres above sea level, while average temperatures remain at 5 or 6° C below zero and often drop to minus 30 or 40° C in the coldest season. Here, there are no bustling towns, nor tightly-packed villages to be seen, but only occasional tents and herds of yaks and sheep dotting the horizon, and everywhere peace and tranquility reign.

The birthplace of animal husbandry in Tibet, the Changtang has been a vital line of communication for northern Tibet ever since the Tang Dynasty. According to the *New Book of the Tang Geographical Records*, there were altogether twenty-three courier posts between Xining and Medro Gongka in Tubo territory, with Nakchu, the central town of the Changtang, located on this route between Gumang Post and Gechuan

Post. The route remained basically unaltered from the Tang Dynasty right up until Qing times. Owing to its vital position along the route, Nakchu had always been the centre of strategic focus, and became the target for punishment in every major expedition made by the Qing Dynasty. At the beginning of the Qing period, Goshri Khan responded to the call of the Gelugpa Sect for help and put an end to the Chogthu chiefs of Qinghai, before making his way via Nakchu to Lhasa where he consolidated the rule of the Fifth Dalai Lama. Later, he moved back north where he stationed troops in Damshung and Nakchu which thus became military bases for the defence of Lhasa. Today Mongolian blood is clearly discernible among the people of both Damshung and Nakchu as a result of this event.

Lakes Without Number

Deep within the Northern Grasslands lie numerous inland lakes. These are fed by snowmelt which flows through the grasslands, and finally accumulates in low-lying areas. The entire region of the Northern Grasslands consists of large basins separated by chains of hills. Each basin is studded with strings of sparkling crystal lakes. Mostly scattered throughout the north, the lakes on the Tibetan Plateau number about 1,500, more than anywhere else in China. Lake Byang Namtso in the Damshung Region, Lake Byang Namtso in the Damshung region, Lake Siling and Lake Palgon in the Palgon region are all huge lakes of one thousand square kilometres in area. Both salt lakes and freshwater lakes are to be found on the grasslands. The banks of the salt lakes are covered with a layer of caustic soda, mirabilite, and borax about thirty cm. in thickness, all important industrial chemicals. In addition, swans, wild ducks, and pigeons live by the lakes and on the isles.

Hot Springs and Geothermal Regions

Although the Changtang grassland is a high frigid zone frozen for eight or nine months in the year, yet it is well provided with geothermal heat and hot springs.

Nakchu town is cold enough for people to were furs all year round, but there is no need to waste kindling on heating water for a bath. A mere two kilometres from the town there is a hot spring where a delightful bath can be enjoyed throughout the year. The temperature of this hot spring reaches 60-70° C.

The cold, windswept grasslands around Yangpachen belie its rich geothermal resources. Yangpachen's well-known geothermal area, which extends over forty square kilometres, is enveloped by clouds of steam from the hot springs. Not far from here is a geyser which spurts boiling hot water all year round. You can place an egg in the spring and in two or three minutes it will be done.

The geothermal area of Yangpachen is undergoing trials to determine how best to exploit its potential, and wells are at present being drilled. Once the surface is dug up a magnificent hissing geyser of subterranean hot water shoots up one hundred metres into the air like a flood dragon shooting out from the sea, and can be heard up to five kilometres away.

More than three hundred geothermal spots have so far been discovered on the northern grassland, making up two-thirds of Tibet's geothermal resources. Besides the commonly seen hot and warm springs, there are steam geysers, steaming caves, boiling mud springs, steamy areas, and salt springs.

But what attract the most interest are the phenomena of hot streams and lakes.

Near the Yangpachen geothermal area, there is an amazing hot lake covering an area of seven thousand square metres with a temperature of above 50° C. In the morning and evening when the air temperature at ground level drops to about zero, a strange thing happens on the surface of this hot lake: Swathes of mist rise from the lake, thickening as they continue to rise to a height of ten metres or so. During the daytime, when the sun reaches the zenith and as the ground temperature rises, the lake becomes inviting as a spot for a refreshing swim.

The Changtang's geothermal areas are an extremely valuable resource just waiting to be utilised.

A Rich and Beautiful "No Man's Land"

To the west of Nakchu town where Nakchu borders on Ngari, there lies an extensive "no man's land" which occupies an area of 200,000 sq. km. Its remoteness and wildness have given it a fearsome reputation, and many past explorers who ventured into this wild region, if they did not die of hunger and scorching heat, lost their bearings and failed to find their way out, so that very few survived, man or beast.

Nowadays, if you venture into this wilderness you will find it not fearsome, but merely uninhabited. After all, nature has bestowed her favours here, too, with flowers, grass and murmuring streams. Driving through the "no man's land," the ground seems to be galloping along with you. Herds of wild asses, wild horses, and gazelles always race any passing car, and even rodents timidly dash to and fro in front of vehicles. Deer and wild yaks, too, stand imperturbably in the way, no matter how much you honks your horn, before leisurely moving on as if nothing was around.

In the "no man's land," not only are wild animals found, but also many plants and minerals which are awaiting exploration. Not long ago, more than five thousand nomads together with 520,000 head of yaks moved into the "no man's land," pitched their tents and set up camp ready to open up pastureland. The "no man's land" is no longer uninhabited.

Tanglha the Lengendary Mountain and China's Water Tank

The perennial snows of the Tanglha Range lie to the extreme west of the open grassland of the Changtang. At 5000 metres above sea level the Tanglha Range is not very high for a mountain range. If not snow-covered, the mountains are veiled in mist, and so from the distance, the mountain range seems to merge with the sky while clouds roll by at mid-level, which has given rise to this folk rhyme: "Tanglha! O Tanglha! Stretch out thy hand and seize the sky!"

The breathtaking scenery of the Tanghla Range amazes everyone who sees it. Peak after snowy peak and countless glaciers crisscross the far end of the Changtang, while the heart of the range presents dazzling wonderland of ice and snow, glittering like crystal amidst the clouds. Storms are sudden and violent, throwing all into confusion with dark scudding clouds, shrieking winds and biting hail and snow, but as the winds die down, tranquillity is soon restored.

Gallant nomads, heads swathed in fox-furs, clad in sheep skins, and armed with slings, roam the freezing Tanglha Range. Proud of their homeland, they often recount this age-old folk tale: once upon a time, the Jade Emperor drove a calf out to pasture on the Tanglha, and ordered it to eat up all the grass so as to leave the region a wild and stony waste. But seeing that the Tanglha was no haunt of ghosts and that the people were innocent of any misdeeds, the calf sent out two streams from its nostrils to moisten the pastures of the region, and the Tanglha flourished as never before. When the Jade Emperor discovered what the calf had done, he was filled with rage and turned the calf into a rock. Despite the calf's fate, two rivulets continued to flow from cracks in the rock, and swelling to become purling streams, formed the sources of the Yangtze River and Yellow River. Tanglha being the mother of the two greatest rivers in China is the nomads great pride.

No one can hope to gain a full understanding of the boundless Changtang grassland, but even a slight acquaintance with the region can change one's view and leave one with a fine impression of the Changtang. Just like the song says:

Once within her warm embrace
The grasslands soon become your home.

9

FESTIVALS

The Tibetan Calendar

Tibetan New Year

The Great Butter Festival

The Shoton Festival

Bathing Week

The Wangkor

Picnics

Horse Racing and Archery

Festivals in Tibet are a common occurrence, with one or two being celebrated every month. As well as traditional festivals there are numerous religious celebrations, while included under the name of "festival" are also a number of customary activities such as picnics, horse races and the like. Given here are brief descriptions of the major festivals, both regional and national. But first of all let us take a look at the Tibetan calendar according to which all major festivals are calculated.

The Tibetan Calendar

The Tibetan calendar formally came into use in the year 1027 and has continued to be used up to the present. Its establishment was largely connected with the people who introduced to Tibet the civilization of the Central Plains. Originally, the Tibetans used a different system of calculation. According to written records, Tibet possessed her own calendar from before the first century BC, although the method of calculation was very simple, based as it was on a system of lunar months decided according to the full moon, the new moon and the half moon. In this system of calculation, New Year's Day coincided with the first day of the eleventh month of the present Tibetan calendar. This was the calendar of the Bon religion. An almanac known as the *The Old Spinner's Calculation of the Moon* was discovered in the Lhoka region. This ancient calendar summarized in detail the Tibetans' rich knowledge of agriculture and astronomy at that time, and later influenced the Tibetan astronomical calendar.

Following cultural exchanges between the Tibetans and the people of the Central Plains, the present Tibetan calendar was developed and perfected. In the

Tang Dynasty period, Princess Wencheng brought with her many classical works when she came as a bride to Tibet, some of which concerned astronomy and the calendar and played a positive role in the development of the Tibetan calendar. By this time, the method of determining New Year's Day by looking at the phases of the moon, was improved by using the position of the stars as the major point of reference. Even so, New Year's Day still coincided with the first day of the eleventh month of the present Tibetan calendar. Certain areas in Shigatse observe New Year according to this method of calculation even to this day.

From the early ninth century, the Tibetan calendar took on similarities to the lunar calendar of the Hans, reaching its height of development while Pagpa's (1235 - 1280) Sakya Dynasty held sway over the whole of Tibet. During this period New Year's Day became fixed, and the year was divided into twelve months with thirty days in "big" months and twenty-nine days in "small" months. An intercalary month was added about every one-thousand days to maintain the balance of months and seasons. The Tibetans were acquainted with the use of the Ten Heavenly Stems and Twelve Earthly Branches in the lunar calendar of the Hans, but the Tibetan calendar groups the celestial bodies into twelve signs of the zodiac: Aries, Pisces, Taurus, Capricorn, Gemini, Leo, Cancer, Aquarius, Saggittarius, Virgo, Scorpio and Libra . The years are calculated by using the Twelve Earthly Branches: Rat, Ox, Tiger, Hare, Dragon, Serpent, Horse, Sheep, Monkey, Rooster, Dog and Pig combined with the Five Elements wood, fire, earth, metal and water. This creates five twelve-year cycles, forming a sixty-year cycle in entirety which is called the "rabchung," first introduced in

1027. To give an example of how the system works, the year 1980 corresponds to the fifty-fourth year of the sixteenth "rabchung" cycle. According to the calculation of the Ten Heavenly Stems and the Twelve Earthly Branches, the year 1982 coincides with the Earth Dog Year in the Han lunar calendar, which is the Water Dog Year in the Tibetan calendar.

Tibetan New Year

Tibetan New Year is a traditional festival of the Tibetans. On the first day of the Tibetan New Year (which falls in February or March), the entire populace greet one another with the words "tashi delek" (luck and happiness) and "losar sang" (happy New Year). Over the New Year's celebration, children let off fire crackers and everyone drinks "chang" (barley beer) and butter tea, toasting each other and wishing everybody well. Both in the town and countryside Tibetan opera, round dances and tap dances are performed, while in pastoral areas nomads sing and dance around blazing bonfires throughout the night. Various contests are held during the New Year's holiday such as wrestling, stone tossing, tug-of-war, horse races and archery.

Preparations for the greatest festival of the Tibetans start right from the beginning of the twelfth month, when everyone busies himself with getting food, costumes and entertainments ready for the occasion. Every household grows small pots of barley seedlings which, when they are one or two inches high, are placed on altars in front of the Buddha as an offering for a good harvest for the coming year. Midway through the twelfth month, every household starts deep-frying all types of doughnuts in butter, and it is the time for housewives to show off their skills. The doughnuts come in various shapes; there are the ear-shaped "ku-kog," strips called "mya-shak," "mug-tung" like hemp flowers, flat "bu-lug" and scoop-like "ping-tog." On New Year's Eve, every household prepares a "droso chemar." This consists of a grain dipper filled with a mixture of barley flour, butter, roasted wheat and wild "ginseng" (a common plant grown in Tibet), decorated with barley ears and cockscomb flowers, and with multi-coloured laths made of butter stuck upright in the mixture. The head of a sheep decorated with coloured butter is put on display, too. All these represent wishes for prosperity in farming and stock-raising for the coming year.

A couple of days before New Year's Day, a general spring-cleaning takes place in every home, new rugs are brought out and new pictures are hung on the walls. Before the supper on the twenty-ninth day of the twelfth month, the Eight Auspicious Symbols are drawn with flour in the centre of a wall in the newly-cleaned kitchen. A swastika, symbol of luck and eternity, is chalked on the front door, and some families chalk many white dots on the roof beam as a symbol of longevity and good harvests. That evening, the whole family sits down together to supper when a kind of dumpling, called "the dumpling of the twenty-ninth" is served. Some of the dumplings contain such strange things as a pebble, a pinch of chilli, a bit of charcoal, a twist of wool, and the like. Everyone watches carefully to see which member of the family gets a surprise dumpling, as the pebble means the recipient's heart is as hard as stone, charcoal means his heart is as black as charcoal, chilli means he is harsh in speech, and wool means his heart is soft as wool. Whoever happens to bite into one of these dumplings by mistake spits it out immediately with grimaces, which makes the whole family burst out laughing and increases the New Year's Eve jollity. On the evening of the thirtieth, families set out various kinds of food on the altar to Buddha, and new costumes are laid out for the next day. At daybreak on New Year's Day, the housewife serves "breakfast in bed" to the family in the form of a soup made of barley beer.

Traditionally, New Year's Day is celebrated in the following way. The housewife is the first to wake, and after fetching water from the well and feeding the livestock, she goes to wake the whole family by serving "breakfast in bed." When dressed in their festive attire, the family take their seats in order of seniority. The elder of the family then gets up and offers round the decorated grain dipper to each person. As each family member takes a few grains of "tsampa" (barley flour) and roasted wheat from the dipper, he or she tosses a little into the air as an offering to Heaven, and then eats the remainder. During this ceremony, the elder greets each person with the ceremonial words "tashi delek" to which the reply is "phunsum-tsog" (I wish you prosperity). Afterwards, a broth prepared from wheat flakes and ginseng is served which is followed by toasts in barley beer. On New Year's Day itself, each family stays at home, but from the second day onwards visits to friends and relatives and greetings of "tashi delek" continue for four or five days.

The Great Butter Festival

The fifteenth day of the first lunar month is an occasion of great celebration throughout China as people light up their homes and surroundings with lanterns for the Lantern Festival. In Tibet, too, a similar age-old custom persists, with the festival falling on the fifteenth day of the first lunar month according to the Tibetan calendar. But in the Land of Snows, the day takes on a whole new dimension in the form of butter sculptures.

On the night of the fifteenth of the first month, the whole of the Barkhor in Lhasa is filled with works executed in butter in the form of flowers, figurines, birds and animals. Townsfolk and countryfolk alike flock to the the Barkhor to see the sights. Monk artists from different monasteries and lay artists conjure up elegant flowers and dakinis in various poses out of the abundant local butter and dyes, displaying their works on finely made frames. The displays include fairy tales completing with figurines, flowers, birds and scenery sculpted out of butter, some unrolling like movies or three-dimensional picture-stories. Splendid views and lanterns in profusion draw thousands and thousands of spectators, and in front of these gigantic butter sculptures, people perform boisterous dances throughout the night.

The Great Butter Festival of Tibet first began in 1409, when the founder of the Gelugpa Sect instituted the Great Prayer Festival in Lhasa on the fifteenth day of the first month, and put offerings on display to solemnly commemorate the victory over demons after his enlightenment. People then maintained the tradition by making decorations out of butter and illuminating butter lamps every year on this day.

The Shoton Festival

At the end of the sixth month and the beginning of the seventh month, when summer is at its height, the annual opera performances of the Shoton (Yogurt

Bangquet) take place in the Norbu Lingka (the Summer Palace) to the southwest of Lhasa.

As day breaks over the mountain tops and while filmy mists still linger upon the poplar trees, people are ready and waiting outside the brass-studded gate of the Norbu Lingka. As the great gate swings open the crowd surges in, women in their sleeveless tunics, men in their long boots, and skipping children. Once the summer palace of the Dalai Lama, the Jewel Park's high surrounding walls used to keep the common folk out, and the meadows, ponds, rockeries and pavilions within the park were only thrown open to all during the Shoton when everyone gathered in the park to enjoy performances of Tibetan opera. Time has passed and now the Norbu Lingka has become the "jewel" of the people, open for the enjoyment of everyone.

During the Shoton, everyone gathers in the wide open meadows of the park, west of which is a building where the Dalai Lama used to sit and watch opera performances. With its brilliant golden roof and newly-varnished railings, it now provides an excellent view over the whole park. On special occasions and festivals, Tibetan opera troupes and other theatre troupes rush here to reserve the platform for their performances, while crowds of spectators jammed shoulder to shoulder feast their eyes on the show, now no longer the sole prerogative of a few.

The Shoton is one such festive occasion with a long tradition. "Sho" means "yogurt" and "ton," "banquet." So "Shoton" therefore translates as "Yogurt Banquet," which is what it originally was. Later the banquet part gradually gave way to Tibetan opera performances, so that the "Yogurt Banquet" in fact became an opera festival. This festival is held in

Shigatse as well where it is known as the "Sigmo Chenmo" (the Great Performance) and takes place slightly later.

Prior to the seventeenth century, the Shoton was a purely religious ritual. At that time, according to the religious law participants had to stay indoors for several weeks over the summer to fulfill three duties of purification, retreat and abstention. On the last day of the penance the participants left the monastery and came down to the plains where the lay folk offered them yogurt. After enjoying their feast of yogurt, the participants then gave themselves over to fun and merriment. This is how the Shoton Festival originated.

In the mid-seventeenth century, the Qing Dynasty gave formal recognition to the rule of the Fifth Dalai Lama and the Fourth Panchen Lama which led to the strengthening of the unification of state and church. By this time, the Shoton Festival activities had been expanded, performances of Tibetan opera were added, and the festival became fixed. Religious ritual had become combined with theatrical entertainment, but the festival was still confined to in and around the monasteries. At first, opera performances were held only in the Drepung Monastery, and the festival was known as "the Drepung Shoton." After the Fifth Dalai Lama moved his residence from the Drepung Monastery to the Potala Palace, the yearly Shoton which began on the thirtieth day of the sixth month, maintained the tradition with operas being performed first in the Drepung Monastery, and then for the Dalai Lama in the Potala Palace on the second day. When the Norbu Lingka was established in the early eighteenth century and became the summer palace for the Dalai Lama, the Shoton was moved from the Potala

Palace to the Norbu Lingka, and the townspeople of Lhasa were allowed into the park to attend the performances. From then on, activities held for the Shoton became more comprehensive and it took on a regular form, described below. The Shoton Festival followed this pattern for a long time right up to Liberation.

Every year on the twenty-ninth day of the sixth month, opera troupes from different regions registered at the Tsechag Lekung, a government office in the Potala Palace in charge of opera shows, and presented a short rehearsal in accordance with the custom. That evening the opera troupes left for the Drepung Monastery, and the next day, a day-long show was performed at the "Drepung Shoton." On the first day of the seventh month, four opera troupes, six "Tashi Sholpa" troupes (a special type of traditional dance), one Yak Dance troupe, and one Drum Dance troupe from the regions of Lhasa, Shigatse, Chong-gye, Toilung Dechen and Nyemo presented a joint show in the Norbu Lingka. Over the next four days, four opera troupes from Gyantse, Ngamring, Namling and Lhasa, presented a day-long performance by each troupe on the open platform in the Norbu Lingka. During the five-day-long Shoton, the Kasha (Cabinet) closed its offices and all the officials gathered in the Norbu Lingka to watch the performances with the Dalai Lama. Every afternoon a lunch party was given by the Kasha for all the nobles, during which yogurt was frequently served. With the development of the feudal-slave society of Tibet, the Shoton had undergone a change from a religious ritual to entertainment for the Three Ranks of Nobility.

During the Shoton, most of the townspeople and

nearby farmers stream into the Norbu Lingka to watch the operas, always dressed in their holiday best and carrying packed lunches.

Bathing Week

One intriguing local festival deeply rooted in Tibetan tradition is the Bathing Week, held when Venus appears in the night sky during the seventh lunar month. Outdoor bathing in a cold climate such as Tibet's seems a strange activity, but this custom has been passed down from generation to generation, and a suitable season selected in conformity with conditions in the Land of Snows.

At the close of the rainy season, when the weather is fine and daytime temperatures high, at the start of the seventh month, rivers and streams in town and countryside become filled with whole families, splashing and swimming as they wash off the grime accumulated over the year. Old and young, they gather in high spirits on the river banks to observe this age-old custom, first washing their hair as they squat by the water, then sponging the upper body before finally plunging into the water for a last rinse.

During Bathing Week it is believed that river water possesses special health-giving properties, and is more efficacious than the "sacred waters" themselves. Consequently everybody flocks outside to bathe with no fear of the cold. Some people even bring their laundry with them, together with a picnic and supplies of tea and "chang" (barley beer), and spend the whole day doing the annual wash of all their bedding. Their task over, it's time for a refreshing bathe before Venus appears to the north as evening falls, and they make their way homewards.

Bathing Week lasts for seven days as its name implies, and during this time everyone comes out to bathe. At any other time, bathing in public is strictly frowned upon especially in the countryside and particularly for women. It is considered an offence against public decency and highly inauspicious.

Bathing Week has at least seven or eight hundred years history in Tibet. As the Tibetan calendar was perfected following the introduction of astronomy into Tibet in the eleventh century, people learned to distinguish spring and autumn by the appearance of the planet Venus. In Lhasa, spring and autumn are heralded by the visibility of Venus to the naked eye, and it is this sign which signals the start of Bathing Week in the autumn.

Ancient Tibetan treatises on astronomy explain that in early autumn the water is at its most beneficial, being sweet, cool, soft, light, clear, odour-free, and harmless to the throat and digestion. In a word, the water in early autumn is the purest. And it seems that those ancient sages were not wrong. The Tibetan plateau has long winters and short summers, so that in the spring the icy snow-melt chills the bones, in the summer the rainy season creates torrents which muddy the rivers, in winter bathing is out of the question, and so therefore only in autumn does the water temperature rise sufficiently in the newly-scoured rivers to create the kind of conditions favourable to bathing mentioned in the ancient tests. A Tibetan folk rhyme sums it up vividly:

The sun beats down and warms the brook,
While moonlight clear the water cools.
When Venus rises in the sky,
We bathe in clear and limpid pools.

The Wangkor

In the Tibetan countryside, the Wangkor is considered the next most festive occasion after New Year. Celebrated in farming areas throughout Tibet, the Wangkor takes place when the crops ripen in the seventh month and expresses the countryfolk's wishes for a bumper harvest. "Wang" means "field" and "kor" means "round," so "Wangkor" literally means "making the rounds of the fields." In Lhoka, amidst the golden barley and wheat fields, rehearsals get under way for Tibetan opera performances, and families ready themselves to receive relatives and prepare new costumes. Even the boatmen of the rivers return to their villages during the Wangkor. Dressed in their holiday best, knots of people make their way towards the county seat, children and old people comfortably seated on horse carts, while the young people go together in groups, carrying pots of "chang," flasks of butter tea and containers of food ready for a picnic lunch. The Wangkor makes a delightful break for the farmers who are busy the whole year round. Apart from eating, drinking and merriment, some make use of this holiday to visit relatives, gather firewood, or do any other odd jobs.

There is no fixed day for the celebration of the Wangkor. In old Tibet, the festival was customarily held just before the wild geese, traditionally known as the "King of Birds," took their flight south. Now the date of the festival has differed from place to place, so for instance in the Lhasa region the Wangkor starts on August the first and carries on for three to five days. In the regions of Gyantse and Shigatse the Wangkor is held in mid-July, and when the festival is over, the harvesting and the seeding of winter wheat follows.

Originating in the region of Yarlung Shangpo (lower middle reaches of the Tsangpo River), the Wangkor dates back one thousand five hundred years or so. According to the *Bon Calendar* and other writings, it is said that as early as the end of the fifth century in King Pude Gongyal's time, agriculture was well developed, and the building of water conservancy projects and the use of wooden ploughs for cultivation were already in practice. Wanting to guarantee good harvests, Pude Gongyal begged the Bon priest for instruction. In accordance with the Bon belief, the farmers were instructed to walk around the fields so as to ask Heaven to bless them with good harvests. Such was the beginning of the Wangkor. The Wangkor at this time was not yet a regular festival, but merely a pre-harvest superstitious practice.

While the Bon religion held sway over Tibet, the celebration of the Wangkor generally followed this pattern. The villagers from each hamlet set off in a procession and made circuits of all their fields. One man holding a bundle of ritual incense and hoisting aloft a horoscope in the form of a banner walked at the front of the procession and led the way. Next came the Bon priest holding an arrow wrapped in a five-colour ceremonial scarf, known as the "da-dar" (arrow-and-scarf), and a leg of mutton. As he walked he rotated the "da-dar" unceasingly in an inward circular motion so as not to let the "luck of the earth" go astray and to guarantee a good harvest. After the priest came the procession of villagers, each holding ears of barley and wheat. At the completion of the ceremony , these ears of grain were stuck upright either in the granary or on the altar, and everybody prayed for a good harvest. A series of contests such as wrestling, fencing and spear flourishing followed next. Usually men of strength took part in these contests and the winners were awarded prizes. General singing and dancing lasting till evening brought the day's enjoyment to an end. Wangkor activities of this kind under the guidance of the Bon priests lasted up until the mid-eighth century during Trisung Detsan's reign.

The late eighth century was the period when the Nyingmapa Sect (the Red Sect or Old Mystic Order) founded by Padmasambhava, rose to its height, and the Wangkor celebrations took on Nyingmapa colouring. Spells were characteristic of the Nyingmapa Set, and at this time spells cast to protect the good harvest became a set part of the Wangkor.

In the fourteenth century, Tsongkapa, the founder of the Gelugpa Sect (the Yellow Sect or Order of Excellence), came to Tibet, and the Gelugpa Sect rose to prominence, becoming the dominant sect of Tibet. Once again activities held for the Wangkor underwent changes and more ritual practices were added. For example, a statue of the Buddha and sutras were carried at the head of the procession. By this time, the Wangkor had become a traditional festival, and entertainments had increased to include horse races, archery and Tibetan opera.

After 1950s, with the steady improvement in the lives of the people, the Tibetans spend celebrate the Wangkor in a different way. Today at the Wangkor people wave flags of many colours and clutch ears of barley, while festival activities have become rich and varied. Attired in their best, men and women, old and young alike, raising aloft a giant harvest sheaf and banners, proceed on their rounds of the fields with gonging and drumming and song. Apart from horse races, archery contests, Tibetan opera, folk songs and dances, people also enjoy themselves at sumptuous picnic parties.

Picnics

Each nationality has its own characteristics and likes, and the Tibetans are keen lovers of nature. During the summer holidays in Lhasa, good climate and environment with gentle breeze, radiant sun, clear skies, green trees and flower-bedecked meadows, draw groups of friends or whole families out into the parks and green spaces. Under the trees or out on the meadows you can find white tents or enclosures formed by bed sheets and plastic sheets, where groups of Tibetans are relaxing with barley beer and butter tea while strumming the six-stringed Tibetan banjo, singing folk songs or Tibetan opera. Some sit around and chat, others play cards or board games, while yet others dance to music played on cassette recorders. As the sun sets, grown-ups and children all make their way home, singing gaily after their day out in the open air. These are the picnics which are such a feature of Tibetan life.

Picnicking has become a custom among the Tibetans owing to the climate, environment and way of life on the tableland. The people of Lhasa have one particular picnic gathering called the "Zamling Chisang" or "World Prayer." In the past, for a fortnight at the beginning of the fifth month every year, people would leave their homes and go into densely shaded parks. In a region such as Tibet which has a long winter and a short summer, the bright sunshine and gentle breezes of summertime are a rarity to be treasured, and this has given rise to the Tibetan love of the blessings of nature. The fifteenth day of the fifth month marks the height of the picnic season and various religious rituals take place on this day.

The picnicking tradition of the Tibetans is popular not only in the capital Lhasa but in Shigatse and Chamdo as well. It is a springtime tradition for the men of Shigatse to set off on donkeys early in the morning on pilgrimage to an outlying spot to pay a visit to a statue of Padmasambhava kept in a hermitage. Later the women and children take foodstuffs to the outskirts of the town to await the return of their "blessed" husbands and fathers. Then everybody gathers in the Kyi-tsal Lubting Park. This custom was the earliest form of picnic, and later it grew to include donkey races, horse races, archery contests and so on. In eastern Tibet, characterized by its abundance of prime-val forests, the locals set off on a one or two day journey in the summertime either hiking or in horse carts, taking tents and enough provisions with them, and then set up camp in clearings in the forests (which are really natural parks), returning home only after several days. Hot springs make even more scenic camping spots, encouraging people to linger.

Horse Racing and Archery

Archery and horse racing are sports beloved by the Tibetans, and very popular in the vast rural areas. When autumn comes to the grasslands of northern Tibet, and when the crops are gathered in from the valleys of southern Tibet, the countryfolk gather for exciting horse racing and archery contests. The young men and women who take part dress up for the occasion in yellow satin jackets or close-fitting coats of red, green or blue together with striped archery breeches studded with gold. Quivers at their waists and bows slung across their backs, they gallop onto the race-course mounted on fine steeds adorned with silk sashes, feathers and bells. Crowds of spectators gather, drawn not only by the excitement of the contest but also by the opportunity to do a little business at the accompanying fair.

Originating in Gyantse in the region of Tsang, horse racing and archery have a history of more than five hundred years in Tibet. When Raptan Kunsang came to the throne of Gyantse in 1408, he restored the annual sacrifices to his grandfather which had lapsed in times of war. His grandfather, the highly-respected Pagpa Palsangpa, had been Internal Minister of the Sakya Dynasty as well as the religious-king of Gyantse. During the fourth month, Raptan Kunsang organized prayers and offered sacrifices, which were followed by horse racing, wrestling and weight lifting contests as well as the display of the Great Banner (a gigantic "tangka" with religious themes) and performances of religious dances. From then on, these entertainments became a fixed part of the annual grand sacrifice. When Tashi Raptanpal ascended the throne in 1447, more contests were added such as archery on horseback, and thus the Gyantse Damag (Gyantse Archery Contest and Horse Race) took shape.

With the establishment of a theocracy in the mid-seventeenth century and the recognition of the Fifth Dalai Lama as the ruler of the whole of Tibet, each Dzong was supplied with two law and order officials, one monk and one laymen. Subsequently, the Gyantse Damag came under the supervision of the Gyantse

Sakya Monastery

Yumbulagang, the first royal palace in Tibet

A complete view of Chamdo

The great thangka on display in Tashilhunpo

Tashilhunpo Monastery

Potala Palace

Gyantze

Mont. Qumolangma (Everrest)

Assembly Hall of
Drepung Monastery

Drepung Monastery, Lhasa

The renowned Chorten of Hundred-Thousand Buddhas at Gyantze

Norbu Lingka park in Lhasa

Ganden Monastery, Lhasa

A girl in opera costume

An opera mask

Tibetan opera performance
at the Shoton Festival

County Magistrate and the Abbot of Palchor Monastery. By then the ritual ceremony had become merely symbolic and the main stress was on the racing and archery contests, participants for which were provided by the three noble families of Gyantse. The period of entertainment was extended from one day to three. On the first day, after a brief ritual ceremony the racehorses were checked and branded to prevent last-minute changes. Races were held on the next day, followed by a day of archery contests. This was followed by three or four days of open-air feasting and partying.

Starting in the fifteenth century, horse races and archery were gradually introduced to Lhasa, Changtang and Kongpo, and each region developed its own characteristics.

Horse racing and archery contests began in Lhasa during the latter part of the Fifth Dalai Lama's rule, and followed on from the end of the Great Prayer Festival (Mon Lam C'en Mo). Two hundred noble families provided the men and horses for these four-day events, and so it was on a much larger scale than in Gyantse. The order of events was similar to that already described except that there were more archery contests. The third day was devoted to distance shooting, while a competition for height shooting was held on the fourth and final day.

In the Changtang, horse races are held at the end of the seventh month and beginning of the eighth month. The most famous is the Dam Chiren or Assembly of the Damshung people. It is similar to the Gyantse event but lasts for five to seven days, and its major highlight is the rural fair. Farmers and nomads from Lhasa and Lhoka come to the fair to sell their agricultural produce and livestock, and also to attend the races and archery contests. Damshung has an added attraction, the Yak Race. Decorated with red and green streamers, the sturdy yaks run riot on the race course much to the mirth of the crowd, bucking and galloping at the cries of their "jockeys" and quite oblivious to any rules of the race.

In the Kongpo region, racing and archery are even more popular. Due to the remoteness and distinctive terrain of the area, contests are solely village affairs. The natives are all excellent shots as theirs is a forest region and wild animals and birds frequently attack their crops. Young and old enthusiastically enter every competition, and in addition a rifle marksmanship contest is held.

The horse races and archery contests of Damshung are a county-wide attraction. Nomads come from hundreds of kilometres away to join visitors from the neighbouring areas of Nagchu and Lhasa at this annual event. Their tents cover a ten square kilometre area creating a scene like the battle camps of ancient legend. At the impressive opening ceremony, a squad of red flags heads the parade composed of phalanxes of people on horseback. As each spirited phalanx approaches the platform and executes a perfect "eyes right" salute, wild cheers break out from the audience. After the parade, exciting feats of horsemanship are performed which include picking up scarves from the ground, slashing posts in two, raising flags, jousting at flagpoles, as well as archery and rifle marksmanship contests, all performed on horseback at a full gallop. During the competition proper, there are one or two contests a day, including such feasts for the eye as races over long and short distances, pair shooting and trick riding.

During the horse races and archery events, the Dzong or County office moves into the camp to supervise the contests in detail. Between races, there's time for the nomads to barter at the general store and exchange their hides, cheese and butter for cotton cloth, tea and other daily necessities. As night falls, bonfires blaze under the starry sky and the nomads sing and dance throughout the night. It's also an excellent chance for sweethearts who may live far apart to get together and seek a secluded spot on the plains for a lovers' reunion.

10 ᘯᘓᘯᘓᘯᘓᘯᘓᘯᘓᘯᘓᘯᘓᘓ

TIBETAN SOCIAL CUSTOMS

Birth

Death and Funerals
Sky Burial

Water Burial

Cremation

Stupa Burial

Burial of Deceased Infants

Marriage
Proposal

Engagement

Wedding

Social Etiquette

BIRTH

The Tibetans have their own unique customs which have developed in the course of their long history and relative isolation, although there are traces of outside influence from the Han and other neighbouring cultures.

The customs and taboos surrounding childbirth in Tibet provide a fascinating glimpse into this culture. Traditionally, childbirth is considered "impure" and so in the past pregnant women were not well taken care of and had to give birth in appalling conditions; women in pastoral areas are not permitted to give birth within the tent, no matter what the season. In some places, women are even sent into cowsheds or sheepfolds to deliver their children. Fortunately, more and more women are today taking advantage of hospitals, clinics or the services of a midwife to deliver the child, and the new, hygienic ways are even penetrating into rural areas.

Nervertheless, the newborn infant, especially if it is a boy, enjoys better attention than its mother. When the child is three days old (four if it is a girl), close friends and relatives pay the family a visit. This occasion is known as "Bhang Seng," meaning "getting rid of impurity" or "Purification." Town dwellers usually present gifts of barley beer, butter tea and clothing, etc., for the child. First of all *hadas* are presented to the mother and child for luck, and then barley beer and tea is served to the mother. Then the visitors look the baby over, offer their congratulations on the successful delivery and wish the child luck and happiness. In rural areas, friends in addition present a sheepskin pouch used for kneading *tsampa*, filled to the brim with *tsampa* and a pat of butter. The countryfolk observe an old custom to wish the child healthy growth. Having offered barley beer and butter tea to the mother, the visitor takes a pinch of *tsampa* and smears it on the baby's forehead as a sign of best wishes. Then he or she highly praises the infant's good fortune and its five sense organs. Wealthy families usually give a party for the "Purification."

Older Tibetans say that the practice of "Purification" originated in the ancient Bon religion. Deep in the countryside today, people will still make a heap of pebbles at the family's door on "Purification" day, white if the baby is a boy, otherwise any colour stone will do. Near this heap of pebbles, fragrant juniper leaves are burnt. When visitors arrive to greet the newborn child, they add a little tsampa to the smouldering leaves before entering the house. This practice stems directly from the Bon religion, and is a 1,500 year old tradition.

When the baby is a month old, an auspicious date is selected for the child's first outing. All dressed in new clothes, mother and baby accompanied by a close relative set out to visit a temple or monastery (usually the Jokhang if the family are from Lhasa). The purpose of this visit is to receive blessings for a long and happy life for the child. From the temple or monastery, the child is taken to the home of a close friend or relative, preferably one where three generations live together so that the child, too, may share similar good fortune. Before this outing, parents smear the baby's nose with some soot from the cooking pot as a protection against being noticed by evil spirits.

After the first outing, the christening may take place. Christenings are important occasions, so the child's name is usually selected by a lama or family elder. During the naming ceremony, ceremonial scarves and gifts are presented to the name giver. If it is a lama who selects the name, it usually has a Buddhist meaning e.g. Tashi (Auspicious), Tsering Long Life), Dekyi (Happiness), Phuntsok (Prosperous) and so on. Otherwise a more mundane name is usually chosen. Examples include Phurbu (Thursday), Migmar (Tuesday), Tsechik (First Day), Tsegye (Eighth Day), Namgang (Thirtieth Day) and so on, according to the child's birth date. Some parents want their children's names to embody their wishes, resulting in such names as Gokye (Able Man), Samdup (Fulfillment of Wish), Bhuti (Followed by a Boy), Chokpa (the Last) and so on. Parents may even choose an inconsequential name such as Kyikyag (Dog's Dropping) to protect their child from the attentions of evil spirits. If the child frequently falls ill or meets with difficulties, the parents may return to the lama and ask for a new name for their child, as the old one was unlucky.

Death and Funerals

There are several different forms of funeral practised in Tibet: celestial burial, water funeral, cremation, interment and stupa burial. Which one is chosen depends on the wealth and social status of the deceased.

Celestial Burial

This form is practised by the vast majority of people. When a death occurs, the body is laid in a corner of a room and covered with a white sheet. The body may not be placed on a bedstead or elsewhere.

Buddhists believe that when a man dies, his soul leaves the body. In order to release the soul the body is placed on sundried bricks to which the soul adheres, and when the body is taken for the funeral, the bricks are tossed out at a crossroads together with the soul. This process takes three to five days and is assisted by the morning to night prayers of monks to release the soul of the deceased. During this time, relatives and friends come to offer condolences, bringing with them barley beer, ceremonial scarves, pats of butter, incense, and sometimes an envelope marked "Condolences" containing money. The scarves are intended for the deceased, while the other items are presents for the family in this time of need. When a death occurs in the family, noone is permitted to wash his face or comb his hair, or to wear any kind of ornamentation. Laughing, talking in loud voices, singing and dancing are all prohibited in order to allow the soul of the departed to enter heaven in peace.

A red earthern pot is suspended at the door of the home of the deceased, its brim surrounded by a twist of white wool or a ceremonial scarf. Inside the pot, "*tsampa* incense," a mixture of blood, meat, tallow, and cream, cheese and butter is kept burning and continually replenished. This is a substitute for meals offered to the soul of the dead person. Tibetans believe that when the soul departs from the body it loses its powers of thought and becomes unable to find its regular meals. Therefore, the living are required to "feed" the soul by keeping the "*tsampa* incense" burning.

Mourning is not restricted to the family alone; the whole neighbourhood also joins in. Wedding ceremonies and other amusements such as dancing and singing are postponed until the funeral rites are over. The

Tibetans have a common saying: "Even for the death of a cow, neighbours should observe three days mourning," so naturally they do so for a human being.

After a specific period of time, the family chooses an auspicious day for the funeral. The ceremony is usually held in the early hours of the morning, mostly before dawn. First the body is stripped, the limbs folded in and the whole body bound up like a ball and wrapped in white tweed. Next, a white line is drawn in *tsampa* from the corner where the body lies to the outer gate of the home. The younger members of the family shoulder the body and carry it out of the house along the white line as a sign of respect. At the outer gate the body is handed to a professional corpse carrier. A person of the same age as the deceased follows the corpse with a broom and a worn-out basket, and sweeps up the *tsampa*. This *tsampa*, the broom itself, and the sundried bricks on which the body has lain are all gathered together into the basket, and following the corpse carrier, the sweeper tosses these items out at a crossroads in order to release the soul of the deceased.

Early that morning, friends and relatives come to bid the dead man farewell. Bearing sticks of incense, they form a procession to escort the body as far as the crossroads, when the family turns back. Only one or two close acquaintances actually go to the burial place to ensure the ceremony is properly carried out. From the time when the corpse leaves the house, neither the corpse carrier nor his escorts are allowed to turn their gaze back towards the house, nor may they return there for two days or so. This is to prevent the soul from returning to its former home and bringing misfortune to the family.

On reaching the celestial burial spot, the body is

laid on the rocky platform. A pile of smouldering juniper leaves and "*tsampa* incense" burn up a huge cloud of smoke so as to inform the "sacred vultures" of the occasion. The vultures are accustomed to descend to feed whenever they see the smoke signal. The corpse carrier or undertaker then makes an incision in the back of the corpse. If the deceased was a monk, these first cuts are made in the shape of religious symbols. Next, the belly is slit open and the internal organs removed, the flesh is stripped from the bones, and the head is scalped and severed from the trunk. After being sliced into pieces, the flesh is set aside and then the bones are crushed, mixed with *tsampa* and rolled into a ball. The offering to the vultures commences with the ball of crushed bone followed by slices of flesh. Any bits of bone left over are burnt to ashes and then scattered to the winds. By and large, the corpse has to be disposed of in entirety in order to allow it to enter the "Realm of Heaven" with ease, which is the aim of celestial burial.

Once the celestial burial is over, the representatives of the family provide the corpse carrier or undertaker with barley beer and meat as a token of gratitude for his services.

Water Funerals

These are usually given to the lowest class of people such as beggars, widows, widowers, orphans and the childless. The body is taken to the river, torn limb from limb and thrown into the torrent. In some places, a simpler practice prevails where the whole body, wrapped in a white cloth, is thrown into the river. This method of burial is popular in the deep valleys of southern Tibet where there are no vultures.

Interment

Interment first appeared in about the 2nd Century BC when Pude Gongyal held funeral for his father, Drigum Tsanpo, the eighth king of the Tubo Dynasty. However, as Buddhism pentrated the whole of Tibet, interment gradually became a lower form of burial for those who have died of infectious diseases such as leprosy, anthrax and smallpox, and for robbers, murderers and those who have been killed by a dagger. Religious law does not permit such people to receive a celestial or water burial, but decrees that as punishment they must be buried under the earth in order to destroy their last vestige. Relatives regard such punishment as a great disgrace.

Cremation

This form of burial is permitted for lamas and those of noble birth. After cremation the ashes are taken to high mountains and scattered to the winds, or thrown into rivers.

Stupa Burial

This is a very distinguished form of burial reserved for famous lamas only. The body is painted with salt water and dried, and again smeared with precious ointments and perfumes, and then embalmed in a stupa. Such funerals are given to honour only great lamas like the Dalai Lama and Panchen Lama. After cremation ashes may also be placed within a stupa. Kept in monastery halls, stupas vary greatly depending on the rank of the occupant of each. Dalai Lamas and Panchen Lamas are given gold stupas, covered in sheets of solid gold, while the successor to Tsongkapa's religious throne in the Ganden Monastery is eligible only for a silver stupa. Other materials include bronze, wood and clay.

Burial of Deceased Infants

Another form of burial is that used when infants die, and consists of placing the body inside a clay pot, sealing the mouth and casting it into a river. Alternatively, the pot may be preserved inside a storehouse.

Generally speaking, no matter what kind of funeral was selected, in the past monks had to be invited to perform religious rites to release the soul from the body before the corpse could be disposed of.

The evolution of Tibetan funeral rites is largely connected with the development of religion. As far back as 1,500 years ago, in Drigum Tsanpo's time, interment was practised accompanied by funeral rites. Prior to this period, tombs were not erected for the deceased but a type of funeral known as "the result belongs to Heaven" was practised, according to accounts in the Tibetan history "The Mirror of the Genealogy of Tibetan Kings" and in later religious historical records. From the time of Lhato-Thori Nyantsan, tumuli were erected at the deaths of a Tsanpo (king), queen, royal concubine, prince or princess, and some of these survive as witnesses to history in present-day Chongye Dzong. It is recorded in the "Documents of Ancient Tibetan Language and History" excavated from Dunhuang that in those days a tumulus was erected even on the death of a minister, but no evidence of this has yet been uncovered. With the advent of Buddhism to Tibet, funeral rites began to be conducted according to Buddhist doctrine. Cremation, for example, is usually reserved for monks as it is believed that the cremated body becomes an offering to Heaven and so the soul is released directly to Heaven. This kind of funeral is practised in accordance with the "Three Paths of Sin" in the Buddhist scriptures. At celestial burials, the funeral procession should be headed by someone carrying burning incense for the whole way. Smoke from the incense is supposed to pave a five-coloured* road for the dakinis to descend to the place of disposal. The corpse is considered a sacrifice to the gods to expiate the sins committed by the deceased in his lifetime, and to request the Buddha to receive the soul into the realm of Heaven. Tibetans believe that as the vultures of celestial burial live solely off corpses and never harm a living creature, they are "sacred birds." They are totally protected and treated with special regard. Once gorged, the vultures fly back into the high mountains and deposit their droppings on lofty peaks. This means that the deceased will be reborn into a high and noble family. Water funerals also have some Buddhist significance. The poor and wretched may not be taken up into the mountains and offered to the vultures but must be thrown into the river to be devoured by the fishes. Even so, water funerals are still a form of sacrifice of one's own body and so the deceased may still be able to gain a better rebirth. In the past, fish, too, were considered "sacred creatures" and Buddhists did not eat them.

Funerals are followed by memorial ceremonies in Tibet. The family of the dead man performs religious

---

* Traditionally, rainbows are said to be five-coloured red, white, yellow, blue and green.

rites once a week for seven successive weeks in order to release his soul. Previously, these rites were conducted by monks. On the last day of the first week, friends and relatives visit the family of the deceased and help to wash the hair of each family member so as to mark the end of the mourning period. That afternoon, the earthenware pot hanging outside the front door is cast into the river. On the last day of each succeeding week, prayers are recited and butter lamps lit as offerings in the monasteries to release the dead man's soul. On the last day of the seventh week a grand memorial service is held when friends and relatives visit the family once again and are served with a meal in gratitude for their assistance. According to the "Ba-She" by Ba Salñang, memorial services were introduced by the Han Princess Jincheng when she came as a bride to Tibet. She felt that feelings towards the dead were not deep enough so she suggested to the Tsanpo that the people should mourn longer for the deceased. The custom of giving alms on behalf of the deceased also came into practice at this time. On the anniversary of the death, the family holds a great banquet for friends and relatives, and as well as holding commemorative activities, the family and guests enjoy themselves with singing and dancing for one or two days.

Marriage

Traditionally, marriage in Tibet is celebrated with highly elaborate ceremonies for the proposal, engagement and wedding. Nowadays most marriages are love matches contracted between the couple alone without parental interference, but the old traditions still persist when it comes to the nuptial celebrations. An account of a traditional Tibetan wedding follows.

Proposal

The first step is the formal proposal which is made by the groom's family only after the birth years of the prospective couple have been checked for compatability. The offer of marriage is followed by the presentation of a ceremonial scarf, or *hada*, symbolising luck.

If both parties agree to the proposal, an auspicious day is chosen for a representative of one family to visit the other and draw up a marriage contract. This is usually drafted by a gifted writer in verse form fit for recitation. In it wishes are expressed that the bride and groom may be united, have love, understanding and respect for one another, honour their elders, and be noble and lofty in character. Sometimes arrangements for the future inheritance of property are included in this contract.

Engagement

At the engagement ceremony, marked by the absence of both bride and groom, the bridegroom's family offers *hadas* to each member of the bride's family, and pays the "milk price" to the bride's parents as recompense for bringing her up since infancy. Food and drink are prepared by the bride's family to entertain the guests. Representatives of both families gather in the parlour and are seated according to seniority. The hosts then offer the "auspicious grain dipper of wheat and *tsampa*" after which butter tea and barley beer are served. The groom's representatives present gifts and are responsible for the day's expenses, and in addition they give the bride's mother an apron. The groom's family is seen as causing a lot of inconvenience to the bride's family, so this repayment is a kind of compensation and token of gratitude. The significance of the apron is that the bride is supposed to have reduced her mother's aprons to rags as a demanding child, so the new apron is to make up for past damage. After the ceremonial offering of butter tea and barley beer, two copies of the marriage contract are placed on a copper platter, read out by a witness from one family and checked by a witness from the other. Then the contract is sealed in the presence of all, and the two copies solemnly handed to the fathers of bride and groom. The witnesses are then presented with *hadas* as a token of gratitude from both sides. The ceremony is followed by entertainments for the rest of the day, and when the groom's family take their departure they are offered *hadas* and gifts in return.

Wedding

The day before the marriage ceremony, the groom's family sends the bride's family new clothes and ornaments, such as a headdress, amulet and bangles all wrapped in silk. These are to be worn by the bride when she leaves her home the next day.

On the day of the wedding, the bridal party from the groom's family arrives at the home of the bride. Headed by a respected elder, the bridal party leads with them a mare which has already foaled for the bride to ride upon. The colour of the horse has to be the colour of the element of the bride's birth year*. In addition they bring an arrow wrapped in a five-colour

---

* Each of the twelve animals of the Tibetan calendrical cycle is associated with one of the five elements earth, water, fire, wood and iron.

215

silk scarf, on top of which are attached a bronze mirror, turquoise and pearls. Before the bridal party arrives, the bride's family completes the customary farewell offering of the "auspicious grain dipper of wheat and *tsampa'* to the bride. The moment the bridal party enters the bride's home, they slide the arrow down the back of the bride's dress to show that she has become part of the groom's family. At the same time the turquoise, customarily representing the groom's soul, is attached to the bride's head-dress to symbolise the cleaving of the bridegroom's soul to his bride. As the bride takes her departure, usually accompanied by a maid, a member of the bride's family holding another arrow wrapped in a five-colour silk scarf and a leg of mutton, stands on the rooftop and shouts again and again, "May fortune remain with us" until the bride is far away.

The bridal party leaves the bride's home led by an astrologer born in the year of an auspicious animal, dressed in white and mounted on a white horse, and with a horoscope in his hand. Behind him come the bridegroom's relatives, the bride and the bride's maid, with a whole retinue of horsemen bringing up the rear. On the way, the groom's family offer three ceremonial toasts to the bridal party. It is considered lucky for the bridal party to come across anyone carrying water or cow dung, and a member of the bridal party will dismount and offer a *hada.* Conversely, if the procession meets a sick person, anyone discarding refuse or carrying an empty container, this augurs bad luck, and in this case monks are invited to perform religious rites against misfortune after the wedding ceremony. As the bridal party processes towards the groom's home, the retinue sings the wedding song while the bride weeps with grief at leaving her family.

During this time, the groom's family have decorated the front door and prepared a mounting block for the bride to dismount. This is made out of sacks of barley and wheat covered in brocades of five different colours on which the symbol of eternity is formed with grain. The bride is greeted with the "auspicious grain dipper of wheat and *tsampa*" and barley beer, and then an elaborate ceremony is performed for the bride to enter the new home. Beginning with dismounting, entering the front door, climbing the stairs, up to entering the audience hall where the wedding ceremony is to be held, each stage is followed by a song of praise and the presentation of *hadas*.

Inside the audience hall the bride takes her seat next to the bridegroom and all the other guests seat themselves according to seniority. Toasts are offered in barley beer and the "auspicious grain dipper of wheat and *tsampa*" is also presented. *Hadas* are offered to the statues of Buddha and to the groom's parents, and another is hung from the main pillar. Everyone performs the traditional wedding song and dance, and are rewarded with *hadas* by the hosts. Then the bride and groom retire to the nuptial chamber, and the feasting and entertainment starts for the guests. Wedding celebrations usually last for three days, and during this time friends and relatives visit to present *hadas* and wedding gifts, and in turn are entertained with barley beer and butter tea. The bride stays apart from the company at this time.

Before the wedding, an auspicious day is selected for the bride's family to visit the groom's family to extend greetings and hand over the dowry. This ceremony is performed by representatives of both sides: one person reads out the list of dowry articles in a loud voice as the representative of the bride's family hands over each item to the groom's representative. Dowries vary in size depending on the family's wealth, but must include a small bronze statuette of the Buddha, a volume of sacred texts and a small stupa. This custom dates from the time of Princess Wencheng, as this ritual objects were reputedly part of her dowry. When the dowry has been checked, the list is carried in to the bridegroom on a copper platter as a sign that he has received the dowry. Only when the wedding feast and checking of the dowry is over may the bride descend from her chamber and join the family in the festivities.

Although many traditional features of Tibetan weddings have been retained there have been changes too. In old Tibet marriages were mostly arranged by the parents, and girls might sometimes be married off to complete strangers. Nowadays young people decide for themselves and then inform the parents, when the customary formalities are carried out and the marriage eventually takes place.

In the past many restrictions were laid on marriage. For example, a member of the nobility was not allowed to marry a commoner. Strict attention was paid to matching social status and wealth, while conduct and appearance were secondary. Naturally it was out of the question for a serf to marry a feudal landlord.

Another restriction was that the birth years of the couple had to be compatible. Before the formal proposal, a representative went with a *hada* to find out which year the prospective partner was born in. This information was examined by a lama or astrologer to see whether the birth signs of the two were suited for marriage. Only if the outcome of this comparison was satisfactory could the proposal and eventual marriage proceed.

For serfs there were even more restrictions. Before even asking the parents, permission had to be sought from the feudal master if a serf wished to get married. It was easier for serfs under one master to get approval, but in cases where the couple were bound to different masters, a marriage would result in the loss of a serf, and so both masters had to agree.

Tibet's old social system was strictly stratified. Butchers, blacksmiths and beggars were considered the lowest class, and so marriages could only be arranged amongst themselves. Restrictions also existed among blood relatives. Paternal relatives were forbidden to marry while maternal relatives could only marry in the fourth generation or after. Of course these taboos did not hold in remote mountain areas such as Nyingtri and Minling where as a result of consanguinous marriages there was a high incidence of idiocy.

Thwarted in marriage, some shaved their heads and became monks or nuns, some ran away and others even committed suicide. There are a number of Tibetan folk songs which chronicle the wrongs of the unfair marriage system, and express the despair felt by many ill-starred young lovers:

Let me brave every danger
For the one in my heart;
Should our love meet with failure,
Shave my head for a monk.

Let me stroll with my lover,
I care naught for torn feet;

Cutting bramble and thornbush,
I walk through unshod.

Is it true that we two
Are to ever be parted?
What have we to live for?
Fare thee well, let me die.

Social Etiquette

Tibetans express courtesy in a number of characteristic ways which again are closely connected with
Buddhism. A brief description of major forms of courtesy follows.

The presentation of ceremonial scarves or *hadas*
is the most usual form of courtesy. *Hadas* are offered
at weddings, funerals, festivals, audiences with elders,
when on pilgrimage, when sending or receiving tidings,
seeing people off on long journeys, and so forth. The
scarves are made of loosely woven raw silk with finer
quality *hadas* made from silk cloth. Scarves vary in
length; the longer ones are ten to twenty feet while
shorter scarves may be only three to five feet long. The
presentation of scarves expresses honesty, sincerity
and loyalty. From ancient times, Tibetans have considered white to be the symbol of purity, and so *hadas* are
usually white in colour. Scarves may also be multicol-
oured in green, white, yellow, blue and red. Blue
symbolises the sky, white signifies cloud, green symbolises water, red stands for fire and yellow for the earth.
The five-coloured scarf is the highest of courtesies,
reserved only for offerings to Buddhist images and for
wrapping arrows for marriage ceremonies. According
to Buddhist belief, the five colours of these scarves are
said to be the colours of the Buddha's garments, and

therefore they are presented only on special occasions.

The presentation of *hadas* was introduced to Tibet at the time of the Yuan Dynasty. When Pagpa, the religious-king of Sakya, returned to Tibet after his meeting with Kublai Khan, the first emperor of the Yuan Dynasty, he brought with him the first ceremonial scarf. The *hadas* of those days had pictures of the Great Wall of China at either end and were inscribed with the word "auspicious." From this, we can deduce that the scarves were introduced to Tibet from Mongolia. Later, religious explanations were added which claimed that the scarves were the streamers of dakinis.

Another form of courtesy often seen in Tibet is prostration which is usually performed before Buddhist images, stupas and lamas (living Buddhas) and sometimes even before elders. At the Jokhang Temple and Potala Palace or in other monasteries which are still religiously active, there are always crowds of people performing full prostrations. A full prostration is performed as follows: first, the arms are stretched overhead with palms together, then the palms are lowered to the forehead and then to the breast. Next, the whole body is prostrated flat on the ground with arms stretching straight in front, and then the prostrator returns to his or her original position ready to begin again. In the past, certain pious Buddhists from Sichuan, Qinghai and other regions made their way to Lhasa on pilgrimage by prostrating themselves throughout the entire journey of thousands of kilometres. As one prostration covers only three paces, it would take several years of continuous prostration to complete the pilgrimage. Many lost their lives on the way, but satisfied to the heart without a word of complaint. The rough slabs in front of the Jokhang have been smoothed in this way by perpetual prostrations over the ages.

In monasteries and temples it is the custom to touch one's forehead against the feet of images. Men and women, old and young, all place their palms together at the breast, bow and touch their foreheads lightly against the feet of the image to express sincere repentance.

In the past in the presence of officers, headmen or respected personages, people made deep bows and almost swept the ground with their hats as they doffed them in courtesy. People of the same generation and ordinary people now bow to each other in respect with their heads slightly inclined, and remove their hats to breast level. Some place their palms together in mutual respect. People of the same standing exchange courtesies by placing their palms together and bowing slightly at the waist with inclined heads.

At the New Year Festival or on other special occasions, guests are entertained with barley beer, while in the countryside it is quite customary to offer barley beer at all times. Not distilled, barley beer is a watery alcoholic drink with an alcoholic content of 15 to 20 per cent. In Tibet, people of all ages drink this beverage. When a guest is offered barley beer, he or she should take three sips first, and then drain the whole cup. Observance of this rule satisfies the host and is a sign of respect. Butter tea is also offered as a common courtesy. When the guest is seated, the mistress of the house or a younger person approaches him or her and pours a cup of tea. According to etiquette, the guest should not pick up the cup but wait for the host to hand it to him or her.

Courtesy is also observed in forms of address, and when addressing a person the honorific suffix -la is added after the person's name to show respect. Certain manners are observed when eating, too. Mouthfuls should not be too large, sounds should be avoided while eating and drinking, and one's hand should not pass over another's plate when reaching for food. Other good manners include not pushing in front of someone ahead, and giving way respectfully to someone approaching from the opposite direction. When taking a seat, one should not rush for the seat of honour, one should sit up straight and avoid casually stretching out the feet. These are accepted good manners that elders inculcate into the young.

11

WOMEN, MARRIAGE AND THE FAMILY IN TIBET

In pre-liberation days, Tibetan women, and labouring women in particular, were subject to four kinds of oppression, in the form of religious and political authority, the authority of the clan and of her husband. Women had the lowest social status both within the family and in society as a whole.

Women were discriminated against as the "low-born" of humanity in old Tibet under the feudal-slave system. In the written law of the old local government of Tibet, it was stipulated in explicit terms: "Women have no right to discuss state affairs" and "Slaves and women may not take part in military and state affairs." Women were not even allowed to touch a man's amulet or dagger. And amazingly enough, if a man raped a woman, the latter was fined. The reasons behind this prejudice were simple. In old Tibet, people believed women to be "witches," "demi-demons," "unlucky creatures" and "incarnations of catastrophe." In summer, women were not permitted to shout or play while labouring in the fields for fear of causing a natural calamity such as a hailstorm or frost which would damage the crops. Numerous sayings despising women ran as such: "Dogs, women and children are the three sources of quarrels," "Believing women's words is like growing weeds on your roof-top," "A woman's word is like a galloping mare'" and "A woman who engages in social affairs is as strange as a girl bow-man." Judging from these proverbs passed down for generations, we can well imagine what kind of social status women enjoyed during the long period of the feudal-slave society.

Since ancient times Tibet had been paralysed by

' This means: mares do not gallop well and women do not speak well of others.

such beliefs as "men are born superior and women inferior," and so from infancy boys and girls were differentiated. For example, in well-to-do families a boy was sent to school as soon as he reached the age of eight. Even boys born into a poor family were made monks so as to gain an elementary education in the monastery. However, this was not the case for girls as it was considered extra trouble for a girl to receive an education. As a result, in old Tibet over ninety-five percent of women remained illiterate, and even to this day many elderly women in the countryside and pastoral areas do not know their own age. Even the daughters of the nobility and merchants were taught only to write simple letters and keep accounts, while study of the holy texts was deemed unnecessary. From the age of eighteen, a boy was trained in the management of the household and how to deal with business and legal matters, while after she was fifteen, a girl was taught only to milk cows, brew barley beer and wait on guests. There is a Tibetan saying which runs: "Boys should run as wild as madmen, girls should be as silent as mutes." The requirements and aims of society in educating boys and girls were completely different. According to unwritten law, when a family took on a daughter-in-law it was the same as getting one more slave. The following proverb explains further: "When a girl is married into another family, she has to serve as a slave for three years." When a girl was given to another family in marriage she had no property or inheritance rights; conversely, when a boy married into a girl's family, he took over the family's property and enjoyed the right of inheritance.

In monasteries, women were forbidden to enter certain shrines and they had to do their prostrations outside the door. Neither were they allowed into the shrines and scripture halls of noble families. In settling disputes in the law courts, if there was no man in the family, another man was hired and sent as a substitute. Within the family itself, women were also despised. In some regions women's freedom was restricted by ten prohibitions, and women's names were not even permitted to appear on the list of forced labourers. While guests were being entertained at home, women were forbidden to look on openly.

Despite the downtrodden status of Tibetan women in the old society, the social burden they shouldered was far from light. In rural areas, apart from the three kinds of jobs reserved for men, namely ploughing, field irrigation and construction work, all other work such as harrowing, seed broadcasting, weeding, reaping, grain threshing, filling the granary, roasting barley and grinding barley flour, gathering firewood in the mountains, etc., was performed by women. In pastoral areas, the amount of women's labour was astounding. In spring they delivered lambs and took care of them, in summer they milked livestock, sheared sheep, made cheese, churned butter, collected and stored fodder, etc. They were kept so busy that often they did not even take off their sheepskin cloaks at night. In winter, they were again busily engaged in spinning wool and weaving striped aprons and tweed.

More proof of women's low status in old Tibet can be found if we examine marital and family relationships. As chattels of their masters in the feudal-slave society, serfs' and slaves' marriages were decided first and foremost by the feudal lord, and parents had only second say in the matter. The couple themselves, of course, had no choice. Marriage between serfs had to be approved by the master, and agreement was usually obtained through bribery. As many as twenty head of sheep might be offered to the feudal lord in order to win permission. If the man and woman belonged to separate masters, the problem of marriage was even harder to solve. For example, if a woman serf was given in marriage to a man serf, the owner of the man had to be bribed to offer the woman's feudal master a replacement serf. Serf owners sometimes even withheld permission for their serfs to get married for their whole lives, while others forced them into unwanted marriages, and a female serf of eighteen or nineteen might be given to an old man of sixty or seventy.

In the past, marriages among ordinary people were mostly arranged by the parents alone, and kidnap marriages and marriages by deception were often the result. When it was decided to give a daughter in marriage, the occasion was kept secret from the girl. Under pretexts such as visiting a relative, doing business, or visiting a friend in the boy's village, the unsuspecting girl was sent out and as she approached the appointed village, she was forcibly taken to the groom's house. Such marriages were common in the Kongpo region and Shigatse, and the custom of kidnap marriage is still practised among the Sherpas to this day. Mercenary marriages were also a feature of old Tibet. The nomads of Northern Tibet would pay twenty head of yak for a bride under the fine-sounding name of "milk price."

Marriages in old Tibet were mostly monogamous, but other primitive forms were still widespread, such as communal marriage. Remnants of communal marriage are discernible in the practice of polyandry, polygamy and casual sex. According to investigations made by relevant departments, in the past twenty-four percent of all marriages were polyandrous and five percent polygamous.

Families practising polyandry were generally cases of two or three brothers sharing one wife in common. As far as the poor were concerned, polyandry lightened the load of corvee labour, while for the parents it served to keep their sons together. Moreover, public opinion praised and respected a polyandrous wife. As for the nobility and wealthy families, the purpose of polyandry was to keep the family property together.

Polygamy was mainly practised among officials and nobility, and was similar to the concubinage practised in other regions of China in the past. Polygamy served to strengthen the family lines of nobles and officials for if the first or second wife failed to produce a son, a third was taken in the hope of getting an heir. In some poor households, polygamy was practised by sisters taking one husband into their family, and cases of a mother and daughter sharing a husband also occurred. This mainly happened when the mother was widowed while the daughter was still young, and then remarried a young man so as to let him shoulder the family burden. When she grew up, the daughter became the wife of her step-father.

The male-female ratio in Tibet is approximately forty-eight to fifty-two. In addition, owing to the popularity of religion, a great number of men became monks and remained celibate. Moreover, polyandry meant that even more women were left without partners, and so formed casual attachments when and where they could. In rural areas and among nomads, cases of unmarried women with two or three children were common, and it was considered the woman's duty to bring up the children while the man took no responsibility. This, too, showed the unfair position of women.

Communal marriage has been basically eliminated since the democratic reforms of 1959, and existing cases are mostly remnants of the past. At present monogamy and marriage based on love is gradually replacing the old, unfair forms of the past. However, rural areas and remote regions still lag behind the towns.

After the peaceful liberation of Tibet in 1951 and especially since the democratic reforms of 1959, the Tibetan people have achieved liberation and the status of women has undergone a fundamental change.

First and foremost, women have their own organization. On March 8, 1953, a preparatory committee for the Women's Friendship League was set up in Lhasa. It was Tibet's first organization for women and brought together women from various strata of society, safeguarded women's interests, and worked hard for the defence of equality between the sexes. This was a step forward of great historical significance. In the past, Tibetan women had no right to take part in political affairs. Even the upper-class ladies of officials and the nobility were allowed only to accompany their menfolk to social occasions and had no right to interfere in social or political affairs. In August 1959, the Patriotic Women's Friendship Federation was formally established, and in June 1960 Tibet held its first women's congress and set up the Patriotic Democratic Women's Federation of the Tibet Autonomous Region. The founding of the Women's Federation aroused women, making up over half the population of Tibet, to join the work and construction of Tibet.

Tibetan women are able workers too. On the

Tibetan plateau today, women who were once treated as half-human are now doing battle in agriculture, animal husbandry, industry, transportation, geology and hydroelectric power projects.

Tibetan women are furthermore to be found in such fields as science research, elementary education, sports and health work, literary and artistic creation etc., and have achieved remarkable results. One example is the Tibetan woman mountaineer Madame Phantok, vice-chairman of the All-China Mountaineering Association, who became the first woman in the world to conquer the summit of Mt. Jomo Langma (Mt. Everest) not long ago. The famous Tibetan singer Madame Tsetan Dolma is another who has attained considerable popularity both at home and abroad.

Today the state and society pays great attention and care to women's education, labour protection, maternity and child health care. Along with the realization of social advancement and equality of the sexes, Tibetan women have not only been promoted in terms of political status but also enjoy equal pay for equal work, while their progress in education has been unprecedented. In schooling, girls enjoy similar privileges to boys. Since liberation, many young women of Tibetan, Moinba and Lhoba origins have passed through the Central Institute of Nationalities, the SouthWest China Institute of Nationalities, the North-West China Institute of Nationalities, the Tibet Institute of Nationalities, the Tibet Medical College, the Tibet Teachers College, and the College of Agriculture and Animal Husbandry.

In order to protect the physical and mental health of women and children, the government have taken a series of measures to meet women's special needs during menstruation, pregnancy and childbirth. They enjoy maternity leave on full pay and are given consideration in the form of material previleges.

Since liberation, health care for mothers and children in Tibet has shown a speedy development. The state now guarantees health care for mothers and children. Hospitals above county level have set up gynecological and obstetrics departments, and health departments in some areas have arranged fixed times for gynecological examinations in order to provide timely treatment. Below district level, there are infirmaries and midwives who work to lower the infant mortality rate and to guarantee the safety of the mother.

In order to further emancipate women and bring their talents fully into play, counties and districts of the Tibet Autonomous Region have set up plentiful day nurseries, seasonal nurseries and kindergartens. These nurseries and kindergartens concern themselves with the good upbringing and health of the children while freeing women from household and family duties.

With the changes in the social system, marriage and the family have undergone great changes too. The emancipation of women has become a reality, and the nuclear family, the basic cell of society, has been enriched with many new ingredients.

12 ⎣⎧⎣⎧⎣⎧⎣⎧⎣⎧⎣⎧⎣⎧⎣⎧⎣⎧⎣⎧⎣

THE TIBETAN WAY OF LIFE

Typical Fare
Yak Butter, Butter Tea, Tsampa
Barley Beer, Dried Meat

Costumes and Adornments
Costumes, Brocade Fur Hats, Aprons
Boots, Jewellery

Architecture and Typical Dwellings
Simple Dwellings, Houses, Mansions
Monasteries, Tents

Local Transport
Horses and Donkeys, Yak Caravans
Porters, Yakskin Coracles

Handicrafts
Churns, Wooden Bowls, Jade Bowls
Pottery, Knives, Gold and Silver Ware
Carpets, Wool Rugs, Blankets
Stuffed Mattresses, Wooden Furniture
Bamboo Articles, Bellows, Slings

Cut off from surrounding areas by high mountains and deep gorges, Tibet and her people have for centuries existed in splendid isolation which has resulted in a unique way of life found nowhere else. Tibetans have a strong sense of identity, and those living in the Tibetan-inhabited regions of Qinghai, Gansu, Sichuan and Yunnan too have retained their typically Tibetan customs and traditions. In this section we present a brief account of the major aspects of the Tibetan way of life, although such a survey necessarily only touches the surface of the age-long history and tradition behind its present form.

Typical Fare

Yak Butter

Tibet is famed for its yak butter which is a basic necessity for the local people. In Lhasa's Bharkor Street the visitor will see a line of stalls laden with huge rounds of yak butter, thronged with countless customers making their daily purchases. In town or country, butter supplies are never allowed to run out as for nomads and city folk alike yak butter is an indispensible part of their diet.

Yak butter is, naturally, made from yak milk. In pastoral regions where milk separators are not commonly used, the nomad women churn the scalded milk themselves until the specks of butter coalesce when they are skimmed off, packed into a yakskin bag and left to cool.

Yak butter has a high nutritional value which is important for the Tibetans, especially the nomads, as fruit and vegetables are scarce in their diet. Yak butter is used in a number of ways, mainly in butter tea but also eaten mixed with *tsampa* (barley flour) and used for deep frying New Year doughnuts.

Butter Tea

Butter tea is an indispensible part of Tibetan life. Before work, a Tibetan will down several bowlfuls of this tangy beverage, and it is always served to guests.

To prepare butter tea, a little freshly-brewed brick tea with the tea leaves removed, a lump of butter and a pinch of salt are put into the wooden "tea churn" with some boiling water and then churned for a minute or so until the tea is well mixed. The resulting liquid is poured into a kettle, heated and then served. Since butter is the main ingredient butter tea is a vary warming drink and a good antidote to the cold, so it is especially suited to high altitudes.

According to the Tibetan custom, butter tea is drunk in separate sips, and after each sip the host refills the bowl to the brim. Thus the guest never drains his bowl yet it is constantly topped up. If the visitor does not wish to drink, the best thing to do is leave the tea untouched until the time comes to leave and then drain the bowl. In this way etiquette is observed and the host will not be offended.

Tsampa

Tsampa, or barley flour, is the staple food of the Tibetans. *Tsampa* is made from sun-dried barley which has been roasted and ground into flour. It is eaten by adding a little of the flour to some butter tea in a bowl, kneading the mixture into a dough with the fingers, and then breaking off a tiny portion, rolling it into a ball and eating it. Another way to serve *tsampa* involves cooking a kind of *tsampa* broth to which meat and vegetables is added.

Tsampa has a higher nutritional value than wheat flour and is more convenient when away from home, as all one needs for a meal is a wooden bowl and leather pouch filled with *tsampa,* plus a dash of tea; there's no complicated cooking involved.

Barley Beer

Barley beer, known as *chang* in Tibetan, is a low-alcohol beverage which could be said to be the national drink of Tibet. Men and women, young and old all enjoy barley beer and it is indispensible on festive occasions. Barley beer is a slightly milky liquid with a sweetish tangy taste. Only 15 to 20 proof, it comes in once-brewed, twice-brewed and thrice-brewed strengths.

The brewing process is a simple one: first the barley is washed and boiled, and then when it has cooled to a certain temperature yeast is added and the mixture left to ferment. After two or three days, water is added and then covered for another couple of days after which the barley beer is ready to drink.

When visiting a Tibetan family, a guest will be served with a glass of barley beer. According to custom, the guest takes one sip and host fills his glass to the brim. This is repeated twice more, after which the guest drains the glass. Thereafter the guest is free to drink as much or as little as he likes.

Yoghurt, Curd and Cheese

Yak and sheep dairy products are produced in

quantity in Tibetan-inhabited regions. Popular because of their convenience, the most common items are yoghurt, curd and cheese. Delicious cream too is produced.

Yoghurt and curd differ only in that yoghurt is made from full-cream milk and curd from skimmed milk. Easy to digest, these products are ideal for infants and the elderly. Cheese is made by boiling the curd until the whey evaporates, and comes in rounds or blocks. It is often given to children as a treat.

Dried Meat

Dried raw meat is viewed with suspicion and distaste by most people, but the Tibetans love it. Mutton and beef are dried during the winter, usually at the end of the eleventh lunar month when the temperature drops way below zero. Then the meat is cut into chunks and hung up in the coldest rooms so as to become thoroughly "freeze-dried." In this way the moisture evaporates while the flavour of the fresh meat is preserved. By the second or third lunar month, the meat is ready and it is taken down to be roasted or eaten as it is; both are delicious.

Costumes and Adornments

The rich and colourful costumes of Tibet have a long history and distinct characteristics which show the influence of the way of life on the high plateau and display the characteristic Tibetan love of beauty.

Costumes

The main feature of Tibetan clothing is that it

envelops the wearer in huge, loose-fitting, long-sleeved garments, loosely tied at the waist. Styles and material vary from agricultural to pastoral regions.

People in rural areas usually dress in the traditional Tibetan gown or *tuba* and outer garment with an undershirt. Simple, loose-fitting garments, *tubas* are chiefly made from Tibetan tweed although some are made from serge. The gowns have a wide left lapel which fastens under the right sleeve with either buttons or cloth ties. *Tubas* are worn by both men and women.

Men's *tubas* are usually made of black or white tweed edged with a narrow cotton or silk border in a contrasting colour around the collar, sleeves, lapel and hem. Tibetan gowns are outer garments and a white, red or green undershirt is usually worn underneath. In summer or while working, the right sleeve is pulled off, and sometimes both arms are freed and the sleeves tied at the waist. In cold weather, however, the long sleeves keep the hands and arms warm. *Tubas* are made extra-long, and so when dressing the gown is raised to knee-level and tied in place at the waist with a sash, which is usually red or blue.

Beautiful *tubas* for women are mostly made from tweed, serge or other woollen suitings. In summer and autumn, a sleeveless gown is worn over a bright, colourful blouse of red or green. With or without sleeves, the *tuba* is tied at the waist with a red, purple or green sash. Women's costumes are usually more colourful than men's in any nationality, and Tibetan women are no exception with their striped multi-coloured aprons worn over their gowns.

Shirts and blouses also differ for the sexes. Women's blouses are usually made from silk print and have fold-over collars. Their main feature though is their extra-long sleeves which are usually rolled up but can be let down for dancing to add grace and elegance. Men's shirts have high mandarin collars and are made from white silk as a rule.

Tibetan nomads dress in their own distinctive style. Living as they do in cold, high-altitude regions, their *tubas* are made from sheepskins. Men's gowns are edged along the collar, sleeves and hem with a black velvet, corduroy or woven wool band, ten to fifteen centimetres wide, while *tubas* for women are bordered along the sleeves and hem with a five-colour striped band on the outer edge, and three to ten additional four-centimetre strips in red, green and blue within, which creates a beautiful rainbow effect.

Nomad *tubas* are large and loose-fitting with wide-cut sleeves to allow ease of movement. They are all-purpose garments and may be used as a blanket when sleeping, while during the day the arms can be slipped out and the sleeves tied at the waist. A sash is indispensible when wearing a *tuba*, and before tying it, the front of the *tuba* is raised well above the knee, thus creating a huge pouch which is used to store all kinds of useful articles.

In both pastoral and agricultural regions, a flint, small dagger, snuff box and strings of silver coins are tied to the waist sash as ornaments.

Brocade Fur Hats

Tibetans have a wide variety of hats for both men and women which differ from region to region in style. Mostly found in Lhasa and Shigatse, brocade fur hats are made with a glittering gold and silver brocade crown, a locally hand-woven tweed brim and are lined with fur. These hats are very popular with Tibetans, men and women, young and old alike, although they are worn in different ways and come in a number of styles.

Aprons

Symbolic of Tibetan women, aprons are a popular adornment. With their distinct hues, beautiful designs and precise weaving, Tibetan aprons show unique craftsmanship. Aprons are made from hand-spun wool which is then dyed and woven into a long narrow strip. This is then cut into three and stitched into a square, which is used as an apron. The best quality aprons are known as *shad-ma* and are neatly woven in fourteen to twenty different colours. More commonly found are the *pu-tag* aprons which are of a lower quality.

One of the most famous places for aprons in Tibet is the Apron Handicraft Workshop, situated in Chi-de-shol District, Lhoka Prefecture. Known as the "apron village," apron weaving in the village goes back five or six centuries, and its products, sold far and wide, are greatly prized as ornaments.

Boots

Tibetan boots bear a curious resemblance to the built-up boots worn for Peking Opera in central China. With two-inch thick soles, these knee-high boots have red and green woollen tweed uppers embroidered with flowers and other designs. To the untutored eye they look just like costume boots for the stage. The two major types are *som-pa-lham* boots and *ga-lo* boots.

Som-pa-lham boots come in a variety of styles. Those with "double-leather" soles and worked with exquisite fineness are highly thought of and worn on

242

festive occasions. These boots have firmly stitched yakskin soles about one inch thick while the uppers sport a decorative border of flowers embroidered in silk in eight colours. The leggings are made of black tweed and joined to the uppers by two nicely contrasting strips of red and green woollen cloth. A ten-centimetre slit at the back of the leggings makes the boots easy to put on. These boots are ideal for the Tibetan plateau. Other *som-pa-lham* boots have two-inch thick soles stitched with leather which makes them well suited to seasonal wear. In addition there are winter boots called *ko-sum* which have yakskin-wrapped soles and are popular with nomads.

Ga-lo boots are the customary footwear of women in the valleys of Nyingtri and Lhoka. Soled with yakskin, the uppers are made of three layers of tweed stitched together, while the heel and toe are made of black yakskin. The leggings of the boots are made of black tweed with a two-inch strip of vertically-striped tweed at the top. An edging of black tanned leather strips with yellow silk stitching makes them durable and attractive, while the back slit is strongly bound with a trip of red leather. *Ga-lo* boots are characterised by their upturned toes which give the wearer a tough, manly air.

Of course, Tibetan costumes show distinct variations from region to region. So many styles cannot possibly all be described here but for example, each area has its own style of hat or headdresses, while the people of Kongpo dress in a special type of tunic, and in Lhoka men wear a kind of striped loose gown.

Jewellery

The widespread use of jewellery is proof enough

of the typical Tibetan love of ornament among men and women alike. Tibetans wear jewellery all over the body; in their hair, as headdresses, at their ears, around their necks, wrists and fingers and at their waists. Consequently a wide range of ornaments are to be found, such as rings, bracelets, earrings, necklaces, hair ornaments, snuff boxes, amulets of gold, silver and brass, together with sharp, finely crafted daggers, pouches and flints, and even strings of silver and copper coins worn at the waist or down the back. Gold, silver, ivory, coral, jade and turquoise are the most popular materials for fashioning jewellery, and even prayerbeads are sometimes strung with turquoises, agates, amber and so forth.

Architecture and Typical Dwellings

In the course of time Tibet has developed a number of unique styles of local architecture, examples of which dot the towns and countryside in profusion. Flat-roofed Tibetan houses are usually built of sun-dried bricks and stone, while monasteries and the former estates of the nobility are fortified by high perimeter walls. A brief introduction to the major architectural styles follows.

Simple Dwelling

The simplest dwellings are the single-storeyed houses of ordinary people. Built out of stone and sun-dried bricks, the beams and rafters of these simple structures are placed flat across the walls and covered with mortar. The roof is levelled with a kind of local concrete call *ar-ka* stone. The family usually lives in the inner rooms while the livestock are kept in the outer yard.

Houses

Built on a stone foundation, these brick houses are usually two-storeyed. The upper floor serves as living quarters, while the ground floor houses the kitchen, storage space and livestock.

Mansions

In the past the nobility, feudal landlords and wealthy merchants lived in stone-walled mansions of three to five storeys. Inside the mansion, each room contained numerous wooden pillars, with approximately one pillar every four square metres. The square rafters were covered by planks which served as a ceiling. An additional feature was that second and third floor rooms which faced the sun were fitted with full-length windows. The rooms were not heated in winter, but the rooftop terrace served as a place to lay things out in the sun, take a stroll and to admire the view. Mansions were fortified with a two-foot thick perimeter wall enclosing a courtyard and could be defended in battle. Most of the windows faced onto the courtyard, and those facing outwards were mere slits to keep out the wind and cold. The family usually lived in the upper storeys, and the ground floor was used for storage. Tibetan mansions are notable for their beautifully carved beams and brackets.

Monasteries

Huge in size and sumptuously decorated, monasteries exhibit the most typical Tibetan architectural style. Monasteries are built around a Central Assembly Hall which towers majestically above the other buildings. Dazzling golden roofs and clustered buildings create a magnificent sight, like that of a city. As for the interior of the monastery, beautiful murals, corridors threading through statuesque pillars, exquisitely carved and painted beams and brackets produce an effect of unusual magnificence.

Tents

The homes of nomads throughout Tibet, tents are made out of a coarse yak wool tweed, shaped and stitched into a rectangular tent. After erecting the central tent pole, the four corners of the tent are pegged out taut, and a three-sided, low wall of sods and yak dung built around it. During the day the entrance flap is tied up for ease of entry, and let down when evening falls and fastened by a rope. Inside the tent at the centre stands a clay oven situated directly under the ventilation opening, the size of which can be controlled by ropes. The coarse thick tweed of the tents can withstand fierce winds, rain and snow, and the simple structures are easy to erect and dismantle when shifting from pasture to pasture. Nowadays, the elderly and young children spend the winter in permanent dwellings built out of clay and wood similar to those in rural areas.

Local Transport

A vast land, Tibet has an extensive but sparsely populated grassland to the north while to the south lie valleys of barley surrounded by great mountain ranges and deep rivers, where winding tracks are most in evidence. Transport and communications were very poor in the past, but since liberation highways have been built year after year, and motorised traffic is becoming more and more common. Nevertheless, traditional local transport is still widely used in the vast rural, pastoral and forest regions of Tibet.

Horses and Donkeys

Tibet's high-altitude rarefied air makes travelling on foot for any distance highly exhausting. Consequently, people ride everywhere to save their breath, while loads are carried on pack donkeys and horses.

Yak Caravans

A caravan of tens to hundreds of pack yaks will be loaded up with salt, wool or hides when the nomads decide to set off on a bartering trip. Pack yaks truly deserve their name of "ships of the plateau" for they are able to cross towering passes four to five thousand metres high and withstand temperatures of -20 to 30°C while carrying loads of over fifty kilograms. Yaks may be slow but they are indefatigable and can undertake journeys of a week or more. Nomads when accompanying their caravans are accustomed to camping out in all weathers, tethering the animals and building a cooking fire when night approaches. When they reach the agricultural areas, they barter their salt for grain and then slaughter most of their pack yaks, selling their meat and hides on the spot, only sparing a few for the return journey.

Porters

The strategically situated border regions of Legpo, Dam and Minling are notoriously difficult terrain where traffic is often blocked and even pack animal caravans find the going difficult. But vital trade routes pass through these regions to neighbouring countries such as India, Nepal and Bhutan, and so traders mostly employ porters to carry their goods. Porters can carry a thirty to forty kilogram load each with the support of a staff, and make their way over high passes seeking their own paths. For many, portering is a way of life and a means of earning their livelihood.

Yakskin Coracles

Yakskin coracles are a commonly seen method of water transportation in Tibet. The Tibetan plateau is crisscrossed with fast-flowing rivers and rapids, and to suit their environment the Tibetans have devised the yakskin coracle. Made of a frame of tough boughs enveloped in well-stitched yakskins, these coracles can carry from three to ten people, depending on their size. They only require a single steersman. Yakskin becomes flexible when wet and so does not tear or break when the coracle runs up on shoals. Its small size and light loading capacity means that a coracle can be used in both deep and shallow waters. Coracles are light enough to be carried by one person, which makes them a very convenient mode of transport. Along the Tsangpo River fishermen can be seen casting their nets from yakskin coracles, while they are also used for transporting grain and other goods down the Nyangchu River, and ferry boatmen ply their trade from bank to bank in coracles large and small.

Handicrafts and Articles of Daily Use

Churns

For a Tibetan household, a churn is an absolute necessity as it sees day in day out usage. There are two types of churns used in Tibet. The larger kind is over a metre in height and thirty centimetres in diameter, and is commonly found in pastoral areas where it is used to churn butter. Then there is a smaller churn, about sixty centimetres in height and fifteen centimetres across, which is used for making yak butter tea. Tiny thrity-centimetre-high travel-size yak butter tea churns are often carried on journeys.Both kinds of churn work in the same way, and consist of an outer cylinder and an inner "piston." The cylinder is made of wooden planks tightly bound together with brass hoops, while the top and bottom brass plates are decorated with various designs. The square "piston" is also made of wood cut slightly smaller than the diameter of the cylinder, and is drilled with four four centimetre holes. The function of the holes is to allow the liquid and air to pass through the "piston" during churning. The "piston"s handle extends fifteen centimetres above the churn and is fitted with a decorative brass knob.

Yak butter tea churns are usually made of Korean pine which is knot-free, especially that grown in the middle and lower reaches of the Tsangpo River. Quick and simple churns are also made by cutting joints of the huge bamboos grown in Metok.

Wooden Bowls

Tibetans, Moinbas and Lhobas always carry a

small wooden bowl with them wherever they go, tucked into the front of their *tuba* or gown. Thus it is always at hand for a bowl of tea or kneading *tsampa* when up in the mountains cutting firewood or out in the fields. And nobody thinks it is at all impolite when a visitor reaches into his *tuba* and brings out his wooden bowl for the host to fill with tea or a handful of *tsampa*.

These wooden bowls are made from birchwood or *zab-ya,* a rare wood grown only in Tibet. *Zab-ya* bowls are the best kind of wooden bowl as they do not crack easily and display the beautiful natural grain of the wood. Making wooden bowls is quite a craft. First, the right kind of wood has to be selected as only trees with huge nodes are suitable. Next, the pieces of nodal wood are left to dry in the air for about ten days to season the wood so it does not crack. Then the nodes are shaped into bowls on a lathe, sanded to an even thickness and diameter, and adjusted to stand level. Finally the bowls are polished to a glossy orange using a vegetable dye.

There is a wide variety of Tibetan bowls and they range in size from large *tsampa* kneading bowls to smaller ones used for drinking yak butter tea. The very largest bowls are used as containers and are provided with covers. Wooden bowls are durable, glossy and attractive; moreover they leave no aftertaste and do not burn the lips when filled with hot liquid. Bowls made of *zab-ya* wood can even detect poison.

Jade Bowls

Tibet's most famous jade deposits are found at Rinpung Dzong in the Shigatse region. There, rich deposits of jade in a number of shades from yellow to green have been found, and so it is hardly surprising that Rinpung is the home of jade bowls. Through processes of cutting, smoothing and carving, Rinpung jade is fashioned into durable translucent bowls of unique style. The beautiful carved designs on the outside add to the value of the jade bowls.

Jade bowls are precious works of art, and apart from their practical use they make beautiful ornaments. Besides bowls, Rinpung also produces barley beer pots, wine cups, snuff boxes, *tsampa* containers and other items all out of jade. Farmer and nomads greatly appreciate the fine jade bowls of Rinpung, and the prospects for a wider market look most favourable.

Pottery

Pottery in Tibet has a long history. Neolithic pottery fragments unearthed at the Karo site in Chamdo date back more than four thousand years, but local techniques have not shown a high level of development up to this day. Pottery still remains at the handicraft stage in Tibet.

The kinds of pottery in daily use in Tibet include soup and dumplings pots, deep casseroles, flat baking pans, pickle jars, charcoal trays used to keep butter tea hot and also to heat up food, beer brewing jars, tea pots, flower pots, barley beer containers in various shapes and sizes, and so on.

Knives

It is quite common to see Tibetans carrying knives, daggers or swords at their waists, and nomads and Khampas (people from the Kham region of eastern Tibet) in particular always carry a weapon on them. Some even attach a dagger at their waist and tuck a sword into their sash or belt.

Nomads need swords to defend themselves from wild beasts while farmers and forest dwellers use long knives to hack through undergrowth and open up new cropland, and also to split firewood and to prune fruit trees. Daggers, too, are indispensible to the nomads who use them for slaughtering and skinning livestock, and slicing up meat and vegetables. As well as being vital tools, daggers and knives are also ornamental.

The forging of blades dates back a thousand years in Tibet, and knives have always been essential items for the Tibetans. Records show that as early as 1,600 years ago the Tubo tribes had already discovered copper, iron and silver and had mastered the art of smelting.

Daggers are produced in many parts of Tibet but the most famous are those from Lhasa, Lhatse, Damshung, Tongchen, Yigong and Gangtse. Daggers made in these places have keen blades, bone handles or brass and silver covered wooden hilts, while the scabbards are decorated with dragons, garudas, tigers, snow lions and flowers, or even inlaid with precious stones, creating an exquisite and unique ornamental dagger.

Gold and Silver Ware

Gold and silver ware is a traditional craft among the Tibetans and exhibits the colourful style of the nationality. As well as jewellery, all kinds of other items are made out of gold and silver. In the Potala Palace there are gold and silver tea pots, cup stands and lids on display, while silver spoons, bowls and chopsticks are commonly found in ordinary households. Tibetan gold and silver ware shows exquisite detail and is beautifully engraved with life-like dragons, tigers, snow lions, elephants, garudas, peacocks and the Eight Auspicious Symbols, creating precious art souveniers. Gold and silver working techniques have been passed down from generation to generation of smiths who have now reached a superb level of craftsmanship, although their numbers are small.

Carpets

The coarse, springy wool of the Tibetan plateau is ideal for carpet weaving, the centre of which is to be found in Gyantse. The tradition of carpet weaving in Gyantse goes back six hundred years. Carpets were first introduced to Gyantse from Ghampa Dzong, and later the region's weaving techniques spread to the whole of Tibet. The durable and colourful Gyantse carpets are closely woven in traditional designs and are much appreciated by customers at home and abroad.

Gyantse carpets come in two basic sizes: the larger ones which measure around two square metres are used as floor coverings, while the smaller size makes up into small stuffed mattresses. In Gyantse cotton thread is used for the warp and woollen yarn for the woof. As well as chemical dyes, thirty-six different colours are prepared from natural pigments found in vegetable dyes, ores and coloured earths. The bright colours are fast and do not fade with washing. Patterns on the earliest Gyantse carpets mainly depict ancient monastery murals with such designs as dragons, flowers, birds, animals, hills and rivers, but in recent years the range of designs has expanded to include large-scale pictures of the Potala Palace, Mt. Jomo langma (Mt. Everest), the Great Wall, and the Yangtze River Bridge.

Wool Rugs

A typical Tibetan product, these soft wool rugs are woven from sheep's wool, abundantly available on the high plateau. There are four kinds of rug, ranging in quality from two-ply, three-ply, four-ply to luxury rugs. A lightweight wool rug weighs about five kilograms, while heavier versions may weigh up to 12.5 kilograms. Soft, smooth, thick and warm, the rugs are used as bed coverings and last for years.

Blankets

Generally speaking, Tibetan blankets can be divided into three types. The best blankets are woven from fine yak or sheep's wool in a variety of designs. Smooth, colourful and light, they are ideal for the comparatively warm regions of southern Tibet. The second type is also woven from wool, and comes in both plain and colourful striped designs. These lightweight blankets are generally used by town dwellers. The third kind of blanket is woven from a mixture of undyed yak and sheep's wool, creating an attractive black and white plaid design. Popular among farmers and nomads, these coarse, thick blankets can stand up to wear and tear and filth, and are suitable for long journeys. In addition, nomads use smooth, thick, warm blankets as bedclothes or mattresses. They are durable and long-lasting.

Stuffed Mattresses

As a rule, Tibetans do not sit on chairs or stools but use a kind of small stuffed mattress instead. About seventy-five centimetres square and thirty centimetres thick, the ticking-covered mattresses are stuffed with musk deer hair, soft hay or wheat stalks. The best mattresses have a musk deer hair stuffing and a satin cover.

Stuffed mattresses can be laid together to form a couch or bed, while a thinner version can double as a saddle cloth and a sleeping mat when travelling. Soft, durable and warm, stuffed mattresses keep out the wet and are ideal for the high plateau. Even in the forest regions where wood is readily available, people prefer to use mattresses instead of chairs.

Wooden Furniture

Furniture making is a traditional Tibetan craft and has a long history. Wooden furniture generally consists of cupboards and tables.

One style is a sort of bookcase consisting of two shelves, the lower one of which may be used to store clothes. There are also cupboards measuring 1.3 by 0.5 metres, standing about one metre high, which are used for storing food and butter tea utensils. Cupboards are decorated with carved designs, beautifully painted and varnished, and are usually bought in pairs and placed together in the room.

There are several types of Tibetan table: a small rectangular table used for meals and drinking tea, a square table used for meals only, folding tables for outdoor use, and a square mahjong and domino table. Tibetan tables are very like square cupboards in appearance. They are usually about sixty-five centimetres high and are panelled on three sides, with a pair of doors without handles on the remaining side.

The typical characteristic of Tibetan furniture is its decoration. Panels are brightly painted with flowers and plants, human figures, animals, birds, red-crowned cranes and the god of longevity, while the corners are decorated with a flower and bamboo joint design. The effect is colourful and attractive.

Bamboo Articles

Bamboo grows in abundance in Nyingtri, Miling, Legpo, Metok and Zayul, and weaving bamboo articles is quite a craft among the Tibetans, Moinbas, Lhobas and Sherpas. A wide variety of bamboo articles are produced including small containers for delicacies, scabbards, baskets and creels of all shapes and sizes, sieves, birdcages, etc. The Lhobas even make bows out of bamboo. Bamboo articles for household use are finely woven, especially the containers for delicacies which are decorated with various designs.

Bellows

Tibetan bellows have their own unique syle. Small and round, they are made of a sheepskin bag with a metal tube. One or both hands are used to work the bellows, forcing the air along the metal tube into the charcoal or yak dung fire. Durable, light and easy to use, these bellows are commonly found all over Tibet.

Slings

Other nationalities use whips when herding sheep or cattle but the Tibetan nomads use slings instead. Plainted from yak hair twine, the sling has a ten centimetre loop at one end for the forefinger, while in the middle there is an oblong-shaped seat for the stone and at the other end a woollen lash.

When out herding their livestock, the nomads use their slings by inserting the forefinger into the loop and grasping both ends of the sling in one hand, fitting a stone into the seat, whirling the sling around the head, and then releasing the lash to send the stone flying hundreds of metres. In this way they direct their yaks and sheep. Nomads are very skilled with the slingshot and some are able to hit a target with accuracy from a distance of over three hundred metres. Slings are used also for fending off wild beasts.

13

TIBETAN
NAMES

If on meeting a Tibetan you were to ask, "What is your surname, please?," the Tibetan would have no way of replying as the natives of The Land of Snows have no surnames, although they may have a clan name. In fact there is no simple way to classify Tibetan names, but the story of their various origins is a fascinating one.

Generally speaking, Tibetan names are composed of four syllables, e.g. Tashi Dorje, Tsering Wangdu, etc. The descendants of the first king Nyatri Tsanpo (137 BC), the first of The Seven Heavenly Tris, Mugtri Tsanpo, Dhingtri Tsanpo, Sotri Tsanpo, Mertri Tsanpo, Dagtri Tsanpo, and Siptri Tsanpo each took the first syllable of his mother's name as a component part of his own. Thus Mugtri Tsanpo's "Mug" was derived from his mother's name Nam Mug-mug, Sotri Tsanpo's "So" was derived from his mother's name So Thamtham, the "Dag" of Dagtri Tsanpo came from his mother Daglha Karmo, and so on. This proves that in Tubo society at that time there were still remnants of matriarchal society, which did not use surnames.

Later, with the emergence of classes, people became differentiated by their social status, and people of position in order to preserve the inheritance of their clan from one generation to the next took clan names as their surnames, and it was at this time that surnames actually came into existence. One example is the famous Khon family:

Khon Kunchog Gyalpo
Khon Kunka Nyingpo
Khon Sonam Tsemo
Khon Dagpa Gyaltsan

This adoption of clan names for surnames is just like our way of referring to a family by its surname, such as "the Brown family" or "the Li family."

Following Songtsan Gampo's founding of the Tubo Dynasty in the seventh century, nobles who had rendered outstanding services were rewarded with estates and titles, and the name of the estate was added in front of one's personal name so as to indicated that the clan was of high status. For example:

Nie Trisang Yangton
Dri Siru Gongdu
Thonmi Sambhota

This way of adopting a surname has remained up until today. Examples include:

Yuthok Yontan Gonpe
Doring Tenzin Paljor
Dokhar Tsering Wangyal
Tengchen Tsering Wangdu
Dege Kalsang Wangdu

Since estates were hereditary properties, the names of these estates were handed down for generations. Thus Dokhar Tsering Wangyal's son was named Dokhar Tashi Gonpo.

As Buddhism became more and more influential in Tibet in the seventh century, people began to seek christening from the lamas. If a child was of noble birth, special care was taken. The child was taken to a lama where it was received with a simple naming ceremony; the parents offered *hadas* for luck and other gifts to the lama, the lama recited prayers and chanted some words of praise and good wishes for the child, and finally the name was bestowed.

Whenever anyone of any age became a monk, he was tonsured by the abbot of the monastery and given a religious name, after which the lay name was abandoned. The new monk took part of the abbot or lama's name, so that supposing the name of the abbot was Jampal Trinle, then the name given to the new monk would be something to do with Jampal, e.g., Jampal Dorji, Jampal Wangdu, Jampal Phuntsok or Jampal Geleg. The popularity of Buddhism can be detected in personal names too, as many names show the strong influence of religion. For example:

> Tenpa - religion
> Dhargye - prosperity
> Jamyang - celestial sound
> Dorje - Vajra or thunderbolt
> Geleg - auspicious
> Chopel - prosperity in religion
> Tenzin - supporter of religion
> Lhamo - dakini
> Dolma - Tara

If a monk or lama was promoted to a higher rank, his new title was added to his personal name. Let us take Abbot Lhundup Thabke for example: Abbot is a title, and Lhundup Thabke is his own name. Or, if we look at Panchen Lama Chokyi-Gyaltsen for example, Chokyi-Gyaltsen is his own name and Panchen Lama is the title which was first conferred on the Fifth Panchen Lama, Lobsang Yeshe, by the Emperor Kangxi in 1713.

In front of a lama's personal name, the name of his monastery or the name of his seat is generally added. If we take Lobsang Trinle, the head lama of the Tungkar Monastery, as an example, by adding the name of

The opera troupe comes to a village

Typical headdress of women from the Tsang area

Two young lamas in their traditional rope

A Lhasa woman in typical local costume

girl from the Kongpo area

Familiar faces on pastoral areas

Deputies from various localities chatting during a break

An opera actor

A crowd in front of Jokhang Monastery, Lhasa

he colorful costume of the Tsang women

Another point of view

Tibetan children in their holiday best

his seat his full name Tungkar Lobsang-Trinle is formed. Again, when Dorje Tsering became the head lama at the Rating Monastery, he took the name Rating Dorje Tsering. When people address lamas who have monastic titles, they usually use just the titles as a short form, plus an honorific, e.g., Tungkar Rinpoche* or Rating Rinpoche, and so on. There are also lamas without monasteries but with seats, in such cases the names of their seats are added in front of their personal names. There are also famous lamas born in certain regions or to certain families, and in such cases the corresponding names of these regions or families are used in front of the names of their reincarnations.

Common people generally do not have surnames, and so they usually use their four-syllable personal names alone, e.g., Dorje Tseten, Sonam Wangdu, Gedun Chopel, etc. These names can be abbreviated to two syllables when calling. Usually the first and the third syllables are used for the short form, so that Gedun Chopel becomes Gecho, and Tenzin Chodrag becomes Tencho. Some names can be abbreviated by using either the first or second part, e.g., Dorje Tsetan can be shortened to Dorje or Sonam Wangdu to Wangdu. Short forms of names composed by using the first and third syllables or the first two syllables or the last two syllables are frequently seen, but no short form exists combining the second and fourth syllables. There are also many people who have names of only two syllables, e.g., Tenzin, Nyima, Tsering, Dawa and so forth.

The names of ordinary people all have meanings, which might express a wish or simply be chosen for

---

* Rinpoche, meaning "precious" is used for addressing incarnated lamas.

colour and variety. Some names are taken from nature:

>Dawa - the moon
>Nyima - the sun
>Pema - lotus
>Metok - flower

Some adopt the gate of birth:

>Namgang - the thirtieth
>Tsegum - the third
>Tse-gye - the eighth
>Tsechig - the first

Others use the days of the week for names:

>Nyima - Sunday (also the sun)
>Dawa - Monday (also the moon)
>Migmar - Tuesday
>Lhakpa - Wednesday
>Phurpu - Thursday
>Pasang - Friday (also Venus)
>Penpa - Saturday

Many parents express their wishes in the names given to their children. If the parents have too many children and hope that this one will be the last, the child may be named Tsamcho (cut off) or Chungtag (the youngest). If the parents are in want of a boy, the last born girl is named Phutri (followed by a boy). Sometimes a boy is given a girl's name such as Kalsang Dekyi in the belief that such a name may safeguard the boy's life. If the parents wish a child long life, the name Tsering or Tsetan (long life) is given, but this usually happens only when the previous children have died young. In cases where the parents are elderly or where a child is precious as in families where children have died young, the name Lhanze (beauty of a goddess) or Norbu (jewel) or Lhamo (dakini) is given. Some parents, frightened by too many deaths of their children, purposely give new babies humble names like Kyigyag (droppings of the dog), Phag-kyag (droppings of the pig) and Kyitruk (puppy) in the hope that they will survive to adulthood.

Among wandering nomads and in remote regions where education is poor, the inhabitants give their children very prosaic names. For example:

Marchung - a pat of butter
Nagril - Blacky
Nagsang - good hair
Balpa - frog
Goril - round head
Gaga - happy
Khogtir - teapot

There are a number of very common Tibetan names such as Tsering, Tenpa and Pasang, so that there may well be three or four people with the same name, and sometimes more than ten, in a single department or village. Distinguishing descriptions or nicknames are then added in front of the names. One way is to add "Senior," "Middle" or "Junior" in front of names, for example: Senior Pasang, Middle Pasang and Junior Pasang. Another way is to put the name of the person's native place in front, as in Duchung Wangdu and Yatung Wangdu, meaning Wangdu from Duchung and Wangdu from Yatung. Nicknames referring to the person's appearance may also be used, but these occur after the personal name. For example:

Kalsang Subkyog - Lame Kalsang

Tashi Bartsag - Pock-marked Tashi
Tenpa Gochen - Bighead Tenpa
Dorje Sharkog - Blind Dorje
Pasang Gyagpa - Fatty Pasang
Wangchen Terpo - Shorty Wangchen
Tseten Togur - Hunchback Tsetan

Or the person's occupation may be set in front as in:

Machen Tsetan - Cook Tsetan
Shepon Chimmi - Plasterer Chimmi
Shingsog Champa - Carpenter Champa
Amchi Kalsag - Doctor Kalsang

Sex and age differences are also used to distinguish people who have the same name. For example, there may be a "Male" Dawa and a "Female" Dawa, or if an older and a younger person both share the name Tashi, they can be distinguished by calling one Po Tashi (Grandpa Tashi) and the other Pu Tashi (Boy Tashi), or Mo Yangchen (Granny Yangchen) and Pumo Yangchen (Girl Yangchen).

Since Liberation, some new names have appeared such as:

Chingtol - Liberation
Dharmar - Red Flag
Dekyi Metok - Happy Flower

Some, in order to keep up with changes in society, give their children names like Sarkye (new life). Such names are mostly derived from meanings in the Han language.

In regions such as Sichuan, Qinghai and southern Gansu where the Han and Tibetan nationalities live intermingled, or in places like Chamdo, which was liberated slightly earlier, names composed of Han surnames and Tibetan personal names have emerged, owing to intermarriage between Hans and Tibetans, or through Han influence. Examples include Zhang Wangdu, Li Tsegyal, Chen Gonpo and Zhao Rinchen. In Tibetan-inhabited regions which neighbour on Han-inhabited regions, some people imitate the Han naming practices and adopt surnames for themselves. For example, if a person's family name is Mai Jia (granary) he might choose the Han surname Mei (plum) which is close to Mai in pronunciation, and thus create a full name such as Mei Dorje or Mei Tokme, and so forth.

Many Tibetan names are common for both sexes, e.g., Dawa, Nyima, Pasang, Tashi, Kalsang, and so on, but some are strictly for women and girls only. Examples include Wangmo, Dolma, Dolkar, Yangchen, Zangmo, Chodon, Lhadon, Lhamo, Tsamcho, etc. Other names such as Gonpo, Bakdro, Dondup, Dorje, Jigme, Wangdu, Drugge, Lodro, Damdul, etc., are solely used for men and boys.

In the regions of northern Tibet, four-syllable names become three-syllable names in the local dialect. Thus, Tsering Dekyi is pronounced Tsering-Kyi, omitting the third syllable. Another example is Yangchen Tashi which is habitually shortened to Yang Tashi by omitting the second syllable. But Tibetans living in Qinghai Province also have names of three syllables such as Sangye Gya and Dolma Tso.

Tibetan kinship terms, like English, make no distinction between paternal and maternal grandparents who are called "Pola" (grandfather) and "Mola" (grandmother). Neither do Tibetans differentiate in terms of address for older or younger brothers and sisters, so for example the father's brothers are all called "A-ku" (uncle) and his sisters are all called "A-mi" (aunt).

Terms of address for paternal relatives are fairly loose, distant relatives being addressed in the same way as close relatives. But kinship terms for the maternal lineage are stricter, so that a man addresses his relatives on his wife's side as "Gyo-po" (father-in-law), "Gyo-mo" (mother-in-law), "Gyuk-po" (brother-in-law) and "Gyuk-mo" (sister-in-law).

14

TIBETANS AND TEA

Visitors to the Tibetan plateau are greeted with the sight and smell of tea everywhere they go. From the tents of the nomads in far-flung corners of the grassland and from homes in bustling towns and cities wafts the delicious aroma of butter tea, while in the early mornings the tea houses in the towns are packed with Tibetans of all ages who like to start off the day with a few bowls of steaming hot tea.

As part of traditional Tibetan hospitality, tea is served as a natural courtesy in countless situations. At bus stations, at airport departure lounges or at ferry docking points, you may see aged grandparents in sleeveless tunics and boots carrying vacuum flasks of butter tea or shiny kettles of boiling hot sweet tea who are waiting to greet their arriving friends or giving loved ones a warm send-off. Tea is both a form of welcome and a wish for a safe journey. When visiting friends in hospital, Tibetans forget the flowers and fruit and bring with them instead a flask of strong butter tea as a compliment and a wish for a speedy recovery. Together with barley beer, the serving of butter tea is an old-established Tibetan courtesy. Any time a Tibetan receives guests, he will warmly welcome them with a bowl of butter tea proffered with both hands before moving onto the customary greetings and inquiries.

But it is not only out of politeness that the Tibetans drink tea. Seeing as they are items of daily consumption, tea and butter are important parts of the family budget. Tibetans themselves say that although they can go without food, they cannot do without tea. In pastoral areas, when the herdspeople set off for a day's work out on the grasslands, they never forget to carry with them their kettles and tea so they can brew up a bowl of tea even when far from home. The nomads also firmly believe that tea makes horses sturdier and increases the milk yield in cows as well.

Whether you are cold, hungry, tired or sick, a Tibetan will urge you to have some tea. And it is true that tea is a pick-me-up as it contains the stimulants caffeine and tannin. Moreover as well as being a source of vitamins, butter tea acts as an aid to the digestion; very useful for the usual Tibetan diet of mainly meat with very little fresh fruit and vegetables. Tea is also credited with promoting longevity, and Tibetans claim that the symptoms of altitude sickness - breathlessness, dizziness, irritability - can be eased with a good, strong bowl of tea.

Tibetans drink tea in three different ways, black, with sugar or with the addition of butter or milk. To make tea Tibetan-style, water and tea leaves are boiled together and then each person adds salt or sugar to their bowlful to taste and stirs to make a delicious, warming and aromatic brew.

As well as being a favourite beverage in the Land of Snows, tea has played an important role in Tibet's history.

Tea-drinking in Tibet dates back more than a thousand years or so. Before that, in the third and fourth centuries the Tubo people of Tibet drank a kind of bark tea made from a certain type of tree. As the Tubos became stronger and extended their territory, they captured quantities of an unknown substance, tea, at the borders of the Tang Empire. At first the Tubos did not know what this strange stuff was, still less what to do with it. A legendary tale explains how tea-drinking was introduced to the Tubos. Chang Lugong, a ministerial envoy sent to Tibet from the imperial court, was once brewing himself some tea behind a curtain when the Tubo Tsampo out of curiosity asked him what this strange stuff was. Chang Lugong replied that it was a thirst-quenching substance called tea. At this, the Tsanpo suddenly realised that it was one and the same thing as he had stored in the palace. He sent for seven or eight different kinds of tea and laid them before the envoy who identified where in Central China each came from. From this story it is clear that although the Tubos had tea they had no idea what it was.

With the arrival of Princes Wencheng in the seventh century, and then Princess Jincheng in the eighth century, tea gradually began to gain popularity as a drink when the two Han princesses introduced the habit from the Tang court. The historical account *The New Tang Annals* states: "During the latter part of the Tang Dynasty, of Tang products available in Tubo territory, tea alone could be found in abundance."

Tea-drinking became more and more widespread in Tibet and large quantities of tea began to be regularly imported from the Central Plains, where it was known as "border tea" or "Tibetan tea." This dependance on central China for tea supplies was to prove dangerous to minority nationality autonomy as Han chauvinists strove to impose their will over them.

The first to see the uses to which the border tea trade could be put to was a Song general named Wang Shao. At that time the Song Dynasty (960-1279) was engaged in a sharp struggle with the Khitan of the north and was in dire need of warhorses. General Wang Shao sent a memorial to the emperor while on an expedition westwards noting that the Tibetans came to the border to trade with huge cavalcades of horses. Pointing out the insatiable Tibetan demand for tea, he suggested that tea markets be set up to exchange Chinese tea for Tibetan horse. Emperor Shenzong (1068-1085) approved of this suggestion and a special office was set up to run this trade in tea and horses.

The founder of the Ming Dynasty (1368-1644), Zhu Yuanzhang (the Taizu Emperor) maintained this control of tea exports to minority regions. Tea was used to bribe Tibetan officials into compliance with Ming designs, while at the same time the tax on tea was raised. A certain Liu Liangqing then made a suggestion to the emperor that the supply of tea, the Tibetan's lifeline, should be cut in order to bring Tibet more into line. This move was tantamount to disaster for the Tibetans. Their source of tea cut off, they nevertheless remained steadfast and refused to bend under Ming pressure. During this period, the people ground their precious remaining tea into a fine powder and sewed it into little pouches to wear round their necks. Whenever the craving for tea became unbearable, they would inhale the aroma or lick the pouch.

In later years the Kuomintang regime made use of this same policy of ruling the border regions through tea. The tea-trade was in the hands of a manager appointed by the nobility and was strictly controlled. Nevertheless, mule-trains loaded with tea still poured into Tibet from Sichuan and Yunnan, and folk songs from that time tell of the difficulties faced by these brave muleteers as they brought tea in through Chamdo.

Given the Tibetan craving for tea, it is strange that they never tried to grow it themselves. It seems unlikely that all areas of Tibet are completely unsuited to tea-growing, and in fact, since liberation, this has proved not to be the case. The mild climate and adequate rainfall of the "rongyul" or deep valleys of Southern Tibet have been found suitable for tea, and nowadays in Zayul, by the shores of Lake Yigong, in Kongpo and Metok, tea plantations have been set up.

15

TIBETAN FOLK TALES

The Four Genres
The Great Deeds of King Gesar

Art and literature are deeply rooted in the history of Tibet, and in the splendid isolation of the Tibetan plateau folk tales, songs, dances and opera have developed their own unique form and local flavour.

Tibetan folk tales are many and diverse, and form an important part of Tibet's rich age-old culture. Folk tales are preserved both in the oral tradition and in written form. Examples of the latter include "Explanations of the Mottoes of Sakya" consisting of fifty-one stories collected by Rinchen-pal and later revised and supplemented by Maston Paldan Chogyal. Another similar collection is the "Explanations of the Mottoes of Ganden" which contains seventy-one stories. Tales from the oral tradition also found their way into historical works, and examples abound in such records as *A Mirror of the Genealogy of Kings, A Happy Feast of Sages, The Blue Annals* and *The Red Annals*. These written versions were revised and supplemented by succeeding generations resulting in the crystallisation of artistry reflected in the tales we know today.

Coming directly from the people, Tibetan folk tales are rich in content and describe the reality of Tibetan society at the time. Reflecting the aspirations and struggles of the Tibetan people, they have always commanded a wide audience and maintained their rich vitality.

The Four Genres

Tibetan folk tales fall into four categories: tales of outwitting those in power, fairy tales containing elements of fantasy, love stories depicting the strength of true love, and animal fables.

Many Tibetan folk tales recount how the clever hero outwits his oppressors and exploiters. Every

Tibetan knows the names A-Ku Tonpa and Nyicho Sangpo, the resourceful, intelligent and quick-witted serf-heroes who outwit their cruel, greedy, stupid masters every time. The story "The Three Tasks the Hired Hand Could Not Do" is a case in point. Briefly, A-Ku Tonpa reached an agreement with a feudal serf-owner that he would work for him for one year providing that the master did not ask him to do three specific things. The first was that he would not cut the mountain's hair, the second was that he would not carry the ocean, and the third was that he would not do in the space of one day what had taken a year to accumulate. Moreover, if the serf-owner dismissed him before the year was up, he would have to give him the whole year's wages. Thinking that these were unlikely tasks, the foolish serf-owner agreed to the conditions. When A-Ku Tonpa reported for work the next day, the master told him to go to the mountains to cut firewood but A-Ku Tonpa refused saying that it would be "cutting the mountain's hair." Next, he was ordered to fetch water, but once again he refused, as that would be "carrying the ocean." Finally he was told to carry manure to the fields, but that too was impossible as it was "doing in the space of one day what had taken a year to accumulate." Realising that there was nothing he could order A-Ku Tonpa to do, the serf-owner fired him in a fit of temper, and then had no alternative but to pay out a whole year's wages to the clever hired hand.

Another tale of this type is "The Clever Butter Tax Evader." The story goes that the people of Lhoka, having handed over all their butter in tax to the king, had nothing left to eat. One day, the king was taking the air on his balcony when he heard a donkey-driver shouting at his donkey: "You good-for-nothing creature! Now you're milked dry what am I to give the King of Lhoka for his tax?" The king mocked Nyicha Sangpo, the donkey-driver, saying: "Don't you know that men become fools if they eat donkey butter?" to which Nyicha Sangpo replied, "What can we do? We have no more yak or sheep butter left at home so we just have to pay in donkey butter. In fact, the tax we have already sent to Your Majesty is donkey butter!" When he heard this, the King of Lhoka ordered his men to throw out all the "donkey butter," while crafty Nyicho Sangpo took the opportunity to call together all his fellow townspeople. Gathering up all the fresh yak butter the king had cast out, they carried it back to their homes amidst rejoicing.

People could readily identify and sympathise with such true-to-life heroes and situations such as these, which meant that lively tales of this kind were very popular. The clever heroes became representatives of the intelligent and courageous Tibetan people, and offered inspiration and guidance to their lives.

Fairy tales and stories of conquering nature express wishes and fancy in fantastic form. A good example is the story of Tangdong Gyalpo which describes how he mobilised the riverside dwellers to join in the effort to construct thirteen bridges against great natural odds. Thus he made travelling easier as well as protecting the lives and property of monks and laymen alike. Stories of this kind also exist about the two Han princesses Wencheng and Jincheng. These historical personages are endowed with extraordinary powers in the tales. One story records how Princess Wencheng introduced to Tibet the first sheep which were coloured blue, green, yellow, white and black. Another tale describes Princess Jincheng's journey to

Tibet. When she reached a place near Xining, she shattered her magic mirror into pieces, and from these up sprang the Mountain of the Sun and the Moon which blocked her way back home.

One magical tale describes the origins of barley. There was once a prince who with the help of the Mountain God managed to steal some grains of barley from the King of the Underworld, but was turned into a dog as a punishment. Carrying the grains of barley, the dog found his way to a family where he won the love of the daughter of the house and was changed back into a man again. The couple ploughed the land and sowed the seed, and that was how barley first began to be grown. Reflecting man's aspirations to conquer nature, these tales stimulated people's imaginations and inspired them to carry on the struggle against natural forces.

The next type of folk tales are stories of true love and freedom of marriage, which sharply condemn the unfair marriage system of the past and reflect the heartfelt wishes of youth. Marriage between classes is represented in "The Princess and the Blacksmith," while "The Orange Girl" and "The Frog Rider" are about free choice in marriage. Another charming tale, "The Story of Tea and Salt," describes how love sprang up between the son and daughter of two hostile local headmen. Despite their parents' efforts to separate them, the young people swore never to part from one another, and in the end the boy turned into salt and the girl into tea. Even so, the evil parents were unable to keep them apart, for whenever people made butter tea they mixed the salt and tea together.

Animal fables make up the fourth type of folk tale. These tales are about animals with all sorts of human characters and always have a moral. In "the Story of the Partridge," a small and well-intentioned partridge comes to realise the true nature of the fox through a bloody encounter, and later cleverly takes revenge. In Tibetan fables, the larger beasts such as tigers and wolves are portrayed as cruel, domineering, malicious and foolish, while smaller creatures such as hares and lambs are depicted as honest, intelligent and courageous. In these piquant fables, human strengths and failings are vividly portrayed, and they form a source of wisdom and morality for the people to draw upon.

Perhaps the most distinguishing feature of Tibetan folk tales is their amazing variety of form. Among fairy tales, legends and fables, some are direct and hard-hitting, in others the meaning is veiled, while yet others are elaborate metaphors. The strong oral tradition of Tibet has created a rich mixture of song, poetry and recitation, giving Tibetan folk tales their characteristic blend of prose and ballad form. Thus the tales gain in vividness, appeal and variety, while their dramatic content is strengthened. Like folk tales of other nationalities, the language is simple, concise and straightforward, and includes many popular proverbs giving a strong flavour of reality and a fresh beauty bursting with vitality.

The Great Deeds of King Gesar

The jewel of Tibetan secular literature is without question the great ballad-epic "the Great Deeds of King Gesar, Destroyer of Enemies," orally transmitted down the generations and widely known throughout Tibetan-inhabited regions. It tells of the exploits of the king and magical hero Gesar and his prowess in battle as he strives to defend his people. Episodes from the King

Gesar epic can be heard all over Tibet, in the homes of countryfolk, in the yurts of the grasslands, in towns and in remote areas.

With no definitive version as yet set down, the length of the King Gesar epic varies from region to region. Claims as to the number of sections range from thirty to sixty-four, but the most commonly-held opinion seems to be that there are thirty-six sections, with the entire work running to a length of 15,000,000 words in all.

This great popular work tells of fierce battles fought between the ancient kingdoms of Ling and Hur and others, the separatist states which rose up in the four centuries following the fall of the Tubo Dynasty, and gives a clear picture of the tangled warfare during those years of chaos. According to the ballad-epic, Gesar was the incarnation of a Heavenly King sent down to the mortal world to subdue demons, curb the violent, assist the weak and bring peace to all people. Gesar's battles were fought in self-defence or to drive out aggressors and punish those who waged war, and were never directed against the common folk. Instead he opened the storehouses and gave succour to those in need. In stark contrast to the heroic Geser, figures such as the King of Hor and the King of Jang are portrayed as evil characters. The narrative contains more than a hundred characters, all clearly differentiated and painted true to life.

Magic is strongly featured in "King Geser" and the tale contains such fantastic elements as Gesar's talking horse which proffers advice, a crow which finds a wife for the King of Hor, and magic arrows which return to the sender in battle.

Heroic hyperbole and metaphor abound in "King

Gesar." Gesar's horse is described as being as big as a mountain, as swift as the wind, with eyes as large as lakes, back as broad as a desert, tail as long as five hundred ropes*, and a neigh as loud as thunder. This of course reflects on the strength and prowess of its master, King Gesar. A particularly detailed description is given of Gyatsa, King Gesar's uncle. His sword alone merits a seventy-line description, and thus makes a very deep impression on audiences.

The ballad-epic is a treasury of Tibetan vocabulary. Using a combination of alternate prose and poetry, it encompasses a rich variety of language with many verses being sung in the favourite Tibetan ballad style, and peppered with proverbs and lively metaphors.

This great popular literary work not only has a high moral and artistic quality, but also presents a wealth of historical material. As well as battles, the social and political life of the period is chronicled, together with the military organization of warring opponents, and the production relations between slave and owner. Taken altogether, these provide us with a clear understanding of the politics and economy of the time, which is all the more valuable considering the dearth of historical records from the four hundred year period of separatist rule in Tibet.

Information about religious rites, the general mood of society, the marriage system and customs also emerges from the ballad, making it an invaluable wide-ranging social commentary as well as a great work of literature. For example,"King Gesar" shows that at that time monks were confined to purely religious duties and were not involved in politics, which is evi-dence that Buddhism was not especially powerful at the

---

* In ancient Tibet, long distances were measured in ropes.

time as religious-political unification had not yet been achieved. Nomadic tribes form the major social structure against which the ballad is set, which shows that agriculture was still of secondary importance. Tribes provided the basis for military organization and were ruled over by a chieftain who directed production and took command in times of war. This was the underlying system of political organization during this period.

Rich in content, wide-ranging, vivid in narration, and composed in simple yet beautiful language, the ballad-epic "King Gesar" is greatly loved by Tibetans and others the world over. Translations have appeared in Russian, English, French, Hindi and Mongolian. At present many folklorists are engaged in gathering and compiling the ballads circulating among the Tibetan people, and in the near future the complete, definitive version of "The Great Deeds of King Gesar, Destroyer of Enemies" will dazzle the literary world with its brilliance.

16

TIBETAN FOLK SONGS

History and Development

Examples of Tibetan Folk Songs

The Artistry of Tibetan Folk Songs

History and Development

In the course of their development, Tibetan folk songs provide a valuable record of history, social life at various times and social conditions as well as the general development of art and culture in Tibet. Even in the days when the Tibetans had no script folk songs were widespread in the style of oral literature, while after the invention of a writing system together with the consequent acceleration of social and cultural development, folk songs were also enriched by the newly literate.

Ancient documents in Tibetan show that Tibetans often used folk songs to express themselves. According to an account discovered at Dunhuang, at the time of the thirty-first Tubo Tsanpo Takri Nyansik, two ministers of the Sumba people named Wa Yitsal and Nyang Tseng-gu pledged allegiance to the Tubo Tsanpo in this song:

> Yonder o'er this river,
> Yea, yonder o'er the River Tsangpo,
> There is a King, sent from Heaven it seems,
> Who rules over the land.
> He sits well with the people
> As a saddle sits well upon a horse.

The two ministers hid themselves in groves by day and entered the palace of Chingwar Taktse as night fell, and there they offered their vows of allegiance. On seeing this, the people sang:

> Two strong men and two strong steeds,
> Hiding in the groves by the daytime.
> And sneaking into the Chingwar as the night falls,

Wonder who they be, foes or friends?

From this it is clear that from the sixth century at least folk songs were commonly used in place of speech. At the time of Takri Nyansik, (enthroned 610 AD) however there was still no writing system and therefore all folk songs in circulation were oral creations of the people, plain and simple in style, and as yet exhibiting no sophisticated artistry.

But following the introduction of a Tibetan script, great changes began to take place. The emergence of metaphor made folk songs more vivid and artistically enriched. Note the use of analogy and metaphor in this song taken from an account of Tridrug Songtsan (enthroned 676 AD) in *Historical Documents of the Tubos Discovered at Dunhuang.* When the Tsanpo realised that his ministers were plotting to murder him and seize the throne, Tridrug Songtsan sang in his rage:

> The insignificant cockroach
> Feels proud as a bird on the wing.
> It dreams of flying high,
> But, lacking wings, its courage fails.
> The blue sky stretches high above,
> White clouds come rolling by,
>
> Fly up, and you'll not touch the sky,
> Fly down, nor reach the ground below;
> A speck lost in the mists between,
> You'll make a meal for the sparrowhawk.
> In a tiny valley named Cha-bhu,
> A commoner dreams of the kingship.
> He is no other than the son of Gar;
> Fie, even a frog aspires to flight!

---

* Chinese translation by Wang Yao and Chen Jian.

A commoner dreams of the kingship:
Can a river flow up the dale?
Can a boulder roll up the hill?
Nay! Chando has justly observed:
Were the river to flow upstream,
It would ne'er reach the Shampo's summit;
Thus, too, usurpers will meet with failure.
Light a lamp or kindle a fire
On the summit of Mt. Yala Shampo,
But its snows will never melt;
The deep blue waters of the Tsanpo
Flow out to irrigate every field,
But the river will ne'er run dry.

The voluminous "Great Deeds of King Gesar, Destroyer of Enemies" dating from a later period also contains many ballad-forms, and at the end of the fourteenth century the fine lyric poems of Milarepa appeared. Milarepa's lyric poems are written in ballad form. Historical records note that the young Milarepa was fond of folk songs and hence wrote his poems in the style of popular ballads. Even today they are widespread among Tibetans. A comparison of the earlier folk songs from the Dunhuang documents and Milarepa's lyric poems reveals clear changes in the form of the ballad.

Five centuries later, at the beginning of the seventeenth century, Tengchen Rinchen Wangdu brought out his revision of the traditional opera *Prince Norsang*. This revised version drew heavily upon song-form folk songs. These songs differed greatly from the ballads in verse form, syllable structure and wording, and according to written sources many were extant before the seventeenth century. The end of the century saw the creation of a new style - love songs, pioneered by the

Sixth Dalai Lama Tsangyang Gyatso. These had a profound impact on the populace, and have been widely sung and circulated over the past three centuries. Sixty-four of his songs have been identified, although some are now inseparable from genuine folk songs. Written in plain, fresh language very much like the songs of today, they consist of four-line stanzas with six syllables to the line. The popularised love songs of the Dalai Lama have enriched and accelerated the development of the song-form in Tibetan folk songs. Ballads and songs share the same origins, but judging from form and style we can safely claim that songs developed from ballads. Clearer in form, rhythmically more distinct and with more succinct lyrics, songs were easier to sing and memorise and thus gained tremendous popularity.

Traditional Tibetan folk songs were recited or sung, and sometimes accompanied by dance. Throughout their evolution and development, this form has been retained. Characterised by simple musical accompaniment and dance, folk songs should not be confused with elaborate stage dances and their musical accompaniment. Folk songs, including lyric poems, can be classified into two groups - ballad-form and song-form.

There are two kinds of ballad, mountain ballads and nomad ballads. In addition, poetical songs, such as Milarepa's lyric poems, and Buddhist ritual songs like the *tsog-lu* are very ballad-like in structure. Ballads are characterised by their relatively free form. There is no fixed number of lines per stanza, although there are usually between three and ten, but each line has a fixed number of syllables, ranging from six to eleven. Ballads usually follow the rhythmic pattern XXX XX

XXX, and the end of every line or stanza is marked by a regular vocal style with a regular rhythmic beat. Ballads were recorded as early as the eighth century and can be said to be the earliest type of Tibetan song.

Each region has its own type of song, the three major styles being the To, Kham and Ba-thang styles. In addition, songs can be further subdivided into wedding songs, labour songs, round dance songs, archery songs, wandering songs, drinking songs, antiphonal songs, and love songs. In form, songs are divided into four-line stanzas (sometimes six lines, but always an even number), each line containing six syllables divided into three disyllabic groups giving a XX XX XX rhythm.

The names of Tibetan folk songs vary from region to region, and Gansu, Qinghai, Sichuan and Tibet each have their own names. In Tibet itself, while different names reflect different dialects, the content and form of folk songs still fall within the range of ballad and song, and so here we will not pursue the matter further.

Examples of Tibetan Folk Songs

In the feudal-slave society of the past, serfs were required to both pay taxes and perform corvee labour. This system earned the great hatred and resistance of the unfortunate serfs, and their discontent surfaced in the form of biting satire and violent accusations in their songs. The following verses express this very clearly:

> The snow-white *tsampa* of the lords
> Is ground crimson with the blood of serfs;
> The magnificent mansions of the lords
> Are built from the bones of serfs.

> Military tax and horse tax I pay to the county,
> Person tax and land tax I pay to the lord;
> On a scrap of land, no bigger than the palm
>   of my hand,
> Taxes I pay as many as the hairs on my head.

These songs are a direct denunciation of the taxes imposed by the feudal authorities and show that the wealth of the serf-owners was squeezed straight from the poor.

Folk songs also show a spirit of resistance and criticism of the evils of society. For example:

> O Tsering Lhagyal, the vulture,
> Who lives on the slopes of Sheldag Hill,
> Beware when you gulp down the corpses
> Lest the bones catch in your gullet.

> As I till my tiny patch of land,
> Should anyone dare to cross and trace a
>   track,
> Though born a woman was I,
> I must draw my dagger and think of defence.

The moral values of the labouring people are also reflected in a number of folk songs which criticise evildoing and commend merit, while other songs show a longing for a new life and heap praise upon their beautiful native land. Hope shines through these verses:

> The dark clouds in the sky
> Are not stitched in place;
> One day the clouds will part,
> And the sun behind will shine out on all.
> When two hearts unite as one,

Parents can but leave well enough alone;
When three hearts unite as one,
Landlords should leave well enough alone.

With no other outlet in their miserable lives, serfs and slaves poured out all their aspirations and dreams into songs to their beloved and beautiful land:

U is a land of beauty,
Saplings sway to and fro,
The calls of flocks of cuckoos
Sound more melodious than ever.

For centuries feudal serfdom and a theocracy jointly controlled Tibet, and religion remained paramount for five to six hundred years. Although not numerous, several folk songs criticise the rulers' parasitic existence under the pretext of religion. This wry verse expresses it well:

Heavenly Paradise above
Seems far from perfect,
For holy lamas glance down
From time to time.

The Eighteen Layers of Hell below
Can't be as bad as they say,
For sinful noblemen
Rush in one after the other.

A large proportion of folk songs are love songs, which mainly deal with tragedies of parted lovers - a sharp criticism of the yoke of the feudal ethical code which denied freedom of marriage. The songs express the feelings of young lovers fighting for their right to choose their own sweethearts. Romantic tragedies and the fight for freedom within the ruling classes are also chronicled in song; excellent examples are the love songs written by Tsangyang Gyatso, the Sixth Dalai Lama at the end of the seventeenth century. These verses reveal the true feelings of young Tibetans of the time:

> The love between you and me
> Is like a pair of yellow ducks;
> But in this beautiful Lotus Flatland
> There is no freedom to live as one.
>
> The love we share between us
> Is like a torrent deep within a gorge;
> The roaring reaches the ear
> But the sight remains veiled from the eye.

Following the great changes in Tibetan society after the Peaceful Liberation in 1951 and especially after the events of 1959, folk songs too have undergone a transformation. The content and style of the modern folk songs, as songs from this time are called, strikingly reflect the atmosphere of the new period. The new songs are a declaration of a new age. Modern folk songs such as *My Native Land Takes On a New Look, The Big Dipper Shines Over The Plateau, A Dewdrop In My Heart* and *No Ending to My Song of the Heart* are popular with everyone. They are a sign of the changes in people's living conditions and have enriched the repertoire of Tibetan folk songs.

The Artistry of Tibetan Folk Songs

Tibetan folk songs, in common with folk songs of other nationalities, share a popular use of mood, imagery, metaphor and simple language. But Tibetan folk songs are unique in their form of expression and

293

description. Here we will examine five characteristic rhetorical devices commonly employed in the songs.

Figurative expressions are widely used in Tibetan folk songs, adding a vivid touch by describing the nature of one thing in terms of another. For example:

> Blame not the tree for being felled,
> Blame not the bird for being left nestless;
> For the tree has been cut to the root
> By the powerful noble we fear.

Here, "tree" and "bird" act as metaphors for two youngsters in love, hence the "powerful noble's" cutting down of the tree is the cause of their separation.

Tibetan folk songs use things with familiar characteristics to express abstract concepts such as feelings or the inner nature of people. Popular analogies are taken from the natural environment, e.g., flowers, grass, trees, birds, animals, the sun, moon and stars, mountains, rivers and lakes, wind, rain and lightning, and sometimes gods, demons and spirits from the supernatural world. The Tsangpo River, Kampala Pass, Lake Yamdok Tso, and the goddess Tara and Princess Wencheng also often occur in folk songs, and are closely related to the lives of the Tibetans. Vivid analogies make the songs more appealing, easier to remember and thus easier to spread.

More rhetoric devices are applied in Tibetan folk songs by means of "open analogy," "hidden analogy" and "borrowed analogy."

In open analogies the actual object and analogical object are clearly distinguished by the use of formal comparison. For example:

> The life of a maiden
> Is like an early spring blossom;

Before it is offered up at the altar,
It is spoiled by snowflakes.

In a hidden analogy the actual object and analogy both appear but there is no formal comparison. This kind of metaphor has a greater effect on the imagination. For example:

By bringing the game to bay
The hunter shoots innocent beasts;
By bringing the tenants to bay
The noble robs innocent people.

The borrowed analogy consists solely of the analogy used as a substitute for the actual object. For example, in the song *Hope the Clouds Will Gather For Rain* the terms "rain," "mist," "heavy snow" and "willow catkin" all stand for beloved ones and enemies. This device requires effort on the part of the listener to deduce the actual object, and is thus more powerful.

In Tibetan folk songs, such rhetoric device as substitution is used in a way that animate or inanimate objects are substituted for a human subject. This makes for vivid, revealing language. Note its vivid use in these two verses:

If I were a fish in the river,
I'd twist in the same stylish way;
But I'm only a bird in a cage
Unable to soar free with the flock.

The vultures at the sight of a corpse
Forget their rocky mountain eyries,
But as night approaches
They return to the rocky mountains.

Here these striking substitutions express the feeling of the author and deeply affect audiences. In Tibetan folk songs, substitution is customarily used when expressing inner feelings.

Known as "exaggeration ornament" in Tibetan rhetoric, hyperbole is a commonly used device in Tibetan folk songs. Its application should have a solid foundation in fact, when it creates a vivid effect. An example is:

> O you are fairer than a goddess,
> But your gruel is thinner than water;
> You have no need of a mirror,
> For your face is reflected in your gruel.

Where the woman's beauty and the meagreness of her gruel are described using hyperbole. The exaggeration is couched in simple and straightforward language which serves to highlight the device.

Known as "explanatory ornament" in Tibetan rhetoric, using puns as a way to express meaning on two levels, literally and figuratively. Take these verses for example:

> The flavoursome nettles of spring
> Are sought after but elusive;
> The stinging nettles of autumn
> Are everywhere but shunned.

> Think not that the raspberry
> Bears no berry;
> Is not today's white blossom
> Tomorrow's berry?

In the first song the "nettle" also has the meaning of "love." It is a warning to young people not to be too disdainful otherwise the day will come when nobody will want them and their attempts to gain attention will meet with rebuff. In the second verse, the discussion of the raspberry concludes with a philosophical truth: we should be aware of innate capacity for change as well as external appearance. This kind of aphorism offers much food for thought to the audiences.

Language is of vital importance in any discussion of Tibetan folk songs. The characteristics of the language used in these songs can be summarised in two words: simple and clear. Most folk songs are vividly worded, yet simple and straightforward. Avoiding fanciful phrasing and a plethora of facts, the song becomes a lively work of art. Note how these few, simple words sketch a vivid, if rather nauseating, picture:

> A nice fat corpse
> Draws vultures in flocks,
> When only bones remain
> The vultures fly away.

Moulded by Tibetan history, the natural environment and conditions of life, the characteristic language of Tibetan folk songs comes from the hearts of the people, and in the process of oral and written transmission have been honed to perfection. This song was sung by a serf on a corvee errand:

> As the evening twilight fills the sky,
> And the owls come out from rocky mountains,
> How I long for the smoky fire of home,
> With mother waiting by the cosy hearth.

The words describe not only the pitiful scene of the serf on his errand of forced labour but also his misery. Audiences would sympathise not only with the serf's situation but also with his forlorn mother left alone by the fireside. This talent for sketching a scene redolent with meaning in plain and simple words is by no means a rarity among the folk songs of Tibet.

17

MUSIC AND DANCES OF TIBET

Songs and Dances Combined

The Gor-Shae and Gor-Dong Dances

The Drum Dance and the Repa Dance

The Tho-Shae, Le-Shae, and Other Dances

The Land of Snow is known as the "Ocean of Songs and Dances" and indeed singing and dancing are greatly enjoyed by the Tibetans. At holidays and festivals, everyone from toddlers to grannies joins in the dancing, gaily singing hand in hand. When harvest time and the threshing season come round, songs accompany the work and sometimes the labourers even make a circle to dance. Nomads dance round bonfires all through the night without a thought of stopping, while on summer days townsfolk make for the parks with containers of barley beer for a picnic. No picnic is complete without dancing, and the revellers only return home when the day is done. For Tibetans, singing and dancing are not associated with stage performances but are a form of recreation and amusement. Every Tibetan and every Tibetan family loves to sing and dance, and thus the name "Ocean of Songs and Dances" is given.

Song and Dance Combined

Song and dance in Tibet are closely interrelated: there are songs for dances, and dances for songs. Originally there was a clear distinction between the two. Songs were the first to appear, and from them dance gradually emerged with the development of popular art, while songs kept tempo with the dances. Today's terminology of songs and dances, however, can cause confusion. Generally speaking, *lu* and *shae* refer to songs while *dro*, *gor* and *shapdro* denote dances. For example, the former local government of Tibet often held grand ceremonies in which a troupe of singers and dancers were retained to head the procession and enliven the proceedings. Such troupes were known as *dro-pa shae-mu*. *Dro-pa* referred to the dance troupe at the forefront of the procession, while the chorus or *shae-mu* followed the dancers and provided accompaniment. Some claim that *shae* denotes song and dance but this is not strictly accurate. The confusion arises because of the tendency for singing to be accompanied or followed by dancing. However, when *shae* appears in combination it can sometimes refer to dance, as in *gor-shae* or round dance. Tibetans use the term *lu-gar* to refer to both song and dance in an unambiguous way.

The Gor-Shae and Gor-Dong Dances

The *gor-shae* and *gor-dong* are round dances popular in the three major regions of Tibet. In rural parts around Lhasa, Lhoka and Shigatse, where the Tsangpo River flows, the dance is known as *gor-shae*, while in Chamdo and the Tibetan-inhabited regions of Sichuan and Yunnan it has the name *gor-dong*. This kind of round dance is performed by both men and women who form two concentric circles around a bonfire, and holding hands, shoulders touching, sing in alternate choruses of men and women. The dance may continue throughout the night until daybreak. For Tibetans, singing and dancing are a way of relaxing after a hard day's labour, and expressing their feeling for nature. It also provides an opportunity for young people to declare their love for one another. It is clear from watching the *gor-shae* that Tibetan folk songs and dances have their roots in labour. Many of the dance movements come from such collective activities as threshing, house building, levelling a roof or laying flooring. In proof of this, the *gor-shae* always opens with foot-stamping while the dancers all chant "shoo, shoo, shoo" to keep the rhythm of the dance, which never falters despite the fact that there are many participants and no music.

The Drum Dance and the Repa Dance

From the Lhoka region comes a drum dance known as the *drop*. Danced with swift, abrupt movements it calls for highly skilled performance. Dancers in striped costumes stamp backwards and forwards in rhythm, drums at their waists and drumsticks in their hands, twisting their heads as they dance which draws cheers from the audience.

The Chamdo and Kongpo regions and the Tibetan-inhabited areas of Sichuan and Yunnan are home to a bell-and-drum dance. In this energetic dance, the performers circle with flying steps, men beating flat bells while the women drum. At the height of the performance, the men perform pirouettes on one leg while the women beat their drums high above their heads as they twirl. Performers of the *repa* dance, as it is known in Tibet, wander from place to place putting on performances to support themselves. The *repa* dance requires considerable skill and demands a high-spirited, energetic performance, typical of the *dro* style.

Another kind of drum dance is also found in Tibet. Categorised as a group dance, it has lost ground among the people and now appears solely in staged performances. Its dancers are selected from among monks, and its origins go back to the Devil Dances of ancient Bonism. In the dance, double drums are beaten and spells cast to drive out evil spirits. Masks are worn during the religious rituals and often for the dance itself.

The Tho-Shae, Le-Shae and Other Dances

The *tho-shae* or tap dance used to be a group dance with a regular rhythm and simple, unsophisticated movements, but artistically refined and embellished in the course of time, it now displays a number of dance steps and movements. Arms curved above the head in the romantic style, the dancers mainly execute tap steps.

The *le-shae* is a kind of labour song. Everywhere in Tibet a visitor often meets with scenes of people labouring in the fields or on building sites, singing rhythmically in time with their actions. The *le-shae* looks like a work song aimed at synchronising movements. Hands, feet and voice all keep time, coordinating work with singing and dancing. As well as heavy manual labour, lighter work is also combined with songs and dances. Examples include sowing, weeding, reaping, sling-throwing, thread-twisting, spinning, milking and churning.

As vast as the ocean are Tibet's folk songs and dances. Each region has its own variations, and although some appear to be similar they each have the unique characteristics of their own region and nationality. In recent years, after a decade of suppression during the "cultural revolution," efforts have been made to resurrect, keep up and develop the rich and colourful songs and dances of Tibet.

18 ꜱꜱꜱꜱꜱꜱꜱꜱꜱꜱꜱ

TIBETAN OPERA

The Origin of Tibetan Opera

The Sects

The Form of Tibetan Opera

**Eight Traditional Tales
from Tibetan Opera**

The Chinese Consort and the Nepalese Consort

Nangsa Obum

Sukyi Nyima

Dowa Sangmo

Prince Norsang

Padma Obar

Donyo and Dondup

Drimi Kundan

Tibetan opera, known as *a-chi lhamo* (sister goddesses) in Tibetan, is universally popular in Tibet and the Tibetan-inhabited areas of Qinghai, Sichuan and Yunnan. Modern Tibetan opera is a composite of a multitude of arts encompassing text, dance, melodies, masks and costumes, and an orchestral accompaniment for the songs.

The Origin of Tibetan Opera

Tibetan opera is often claimed to have originated from the "religious dance" (formerly known as the Devil Dance in the western world) initiated by Padmasambhava in the Samye Monastery in the eighth century. In fact, these two different performance arts are totally unrelated. In the eighth century during the reign of Trisung Detsan, Padmasambhava was invited to Tibet from the Pure Land (India). An account in the chapter "Dance of the Four Guardian Kings" recorded in Sakyamuni's teachings on the four tantric mysticisms, Padmasambhava performed a religious dance to drive out evil spirits and thus ensure an auspicious inauguration for the newly-completed Samye Monastery. Padmasambhava's biography reads: "At the completion of the translation of sutras in the Samye Monastery, the lotsavas led by the senior lotsava holding the translation, wearing masks and beating drums, formed a line and danced round the Central Palace three times to celebrate the completion of the translation of sutras.'" This was the origin of the religious dance in Tibet which has lasted up to the present.

Tibetan opera, on the other hand, is a composite

---

* Taken from A History of Tibetan Literature compiled by the Institute for Minority Nationalities of Tibet.

performance art in which a story is presented through the medium of song and dance. It is traditionally held that opera was introduced by Thangtong Gyalpo, a fifteenth century yogin of the Kagyupa Sect who had the idea of constructing bridges over every river that flowed in the Land of Snows for the benefit of the people. For three years he racked his brains to think up ways of collecting donations to pay for the project, but met with no success. Then he discovered that among his devoted followers were seven charming sisters skilled at singing and dancing. Thangtong Gyalpo formed them into an opera troupe and composed and directed simple song and dance dramas retelling stories containing Buddhist teachings. The yogin and his troupe travelled all around giving performances and managed to collect donations from the crowds of spectators. This marked the beginning of Tibetan opera. Thangtong Gyalpo is regarded as the founder of Tibetan opera, and the opera itself is known as *a-chi lhamo* after the seven goddess-like sisters who took part in the first opera performances. Naturally, over the centuries Tibetan opera has been enriched, refined and developed by folk artists, and now bears little resemblance to its original form. However, it was probably not until after the seventeenth century that opera became an art in its own right.

Folk opera troupes can be found in every part of Tibet. Performances are frequent in all regions, and may take place in the open air, under awnings or in huge tents, as Tibetan opera makes no use of the proscenium stage, curtains or scenery. People come from up to five kilometres away to watch the show, clustering around the performance area like a living wall. In modern times, with the explosion in amateur and privately organised opera troupes, different opera sects have been given birth and therefore different characteristics and styles formed. Originally, Tibet had the following opera troupes: the Gyalkar Opera Troupe from Rinpung, the Shangpa Opera Troupe from Namling, the Kyormo-lung Opera Troupe from Lhasa, and the Jungpa Opera Troupe from Ngamring. Nowadays amateur opera troupes have become very common, and in some areas almost every region or district has its own opera group. For instance, Medro Gongkar Dzong, located in the suburb of Lhasa, alone has some twenty amateur opera groups.

The Sects

In pre-liberation days, Tibetan opera troupes from all the different regions used to come to Lhasa at the annual Shoton Festival to perform for the Dalai Lama and the local government as a form of corvee. Twelve popular troupes were selected from among the many amateur opera troupes to participate in the festival. These troupes which came to Lhasa in fulfillment of corvee, became the main force among amateur troupes of the different areas, learning from one another and exchanging skills during their sojourn in Lhasa. Nevertheless, their different historical, geographical and linguistic circumstances as well as dissimilar acting styles and artistic attainments meant that each area developed a different Tibetan opera sect having a separate style of its own. Among these sects there was the old White Mask Sect, the new Blue Mask Sect, as well as the Monodrama Sect.

The old White Mask Sect included such troupes as Bingdunpa of Chong-gye in Lhoka, Nangzipa of Tolung Dechen, and Tashi Sholpa of Nedong. The name derived from the white masks worn during performances. The simple melodies and style of acting of this sect meant that it had a limited influence.

The Tung-pa, the Gyalkar-wa, the Kyormulunga and the Shangpa were the four major troupes of the new sect. Their performances began with the actors wearing blue masks, hence they were known as the Blue Mask Sect. The dramatic art of the new sect was more sophisticated and so it gained popularity and gradually replaced the old sect.

The Form of Tibetan Opera

Through actual performance over the centuries, a set style has gradually been formulated for Tibetan opera. Tibetan opera is generally performed in the open while stage performances are rare. Unlike Chinese opera, only simple stage makeup is worn, but masks are a feature of the Tibetan operatic style. The orchestral accompaniment is simple as only two percussion instruments are needed, a drum and a cymbal. As the performance proceeds, a narrator explains the action for the audience in a rhythmic recitation style. Aside from the narrator, spoken parts are very rare and the actors mainly concentrate on singing. Since operas are performed in the open, the actors sing in high, clear voices mostly in extended melodies without words to display the unconstrained vigour of the style. A singer is accompanied by a backstage chorus as well. The melodies of Tibetan opera are generally divided into three main categories: the "long melody" *(gdans rin)* to express gaity, the "sad melody" *(skyo glu)* to express sorrow and the "short melody" *(gdans t'un)* for narration. Through changes of melody the actors express the inner feelings of the characters. Like other opera forms, Tibetan opera uses simple language to narrate the complicated story of the play. Sometimes the plot is related in a spoken prologue by way of introduction. Martial arts, dancing and other skills are also widely employed in Tibetan opera, and singing usually alternates with dancing. Dance movements are varied and include such actions as climbing mountains, boating, flying, going into the sea, riding, fighting and subduing demons, worshipping Lord Buddha and so on.

Tibetan opera exists in both long and short forms, and may take from only a few hours to one or two days to perform. In ancient times a single play would take several days. To lengthen a play, detail can be inserted into the songs and dances, while to make a play shorter, the spoken narration can be cut, and dances made shorter. Long or short, each play is generally performed in three major parts:

1) The Purification of the Hunters:
This serves as a prologue for the main action. The hunters, carrying arrows wrapped in five-coloured silk scarves, appear to purify the stage area and songs asking for blessings are sung. The next scene is entitled "The Welcome of the Elders" or "The Blessing of the Elders." Two elders appear to bless the stage area and greet the audience, after which "The Happy Time of the Goddesses" is performed. Goddesses appear on the scene and perform a graceful dance to express their descent to the mortal world to share happiness with mankind.

2) The Story:
The main body of the play is then performed.

3) The Epilogue:

This marks the ceremonial ending of the play. In the past, opera troupes concluded their performances with a rendering of folk songs and dances and collected money from the audience.

Tales from the Eight Traditional Tibetan Operas

The traditional Tibetan opera repertoire is quite extensive, but in the course of two or three centuries of composition and performance some operas have fallen into disuse while others are still performed today but have undergone extensive revision and refinement. There are eight major plays: *The Chinese Consort and the Nepalese Consort, Nangsa Obum, Sukyi Nyima, Dowa Sangmo, Prince Norsang, Padme Obar, Dongyo and Dondup* and *Drimi Kundan*. Other plays also exist but these eight major operas are performed by most of the opera troupes and they make up the generally acknowledged standard repertoire. A brief outline of each of the plays follows.

The Chinese Consort and the Nepalese Consort

Usually only the part dealing with Princess Wencheng is performed. This is an historical play which tells the story of how Songtsan Gampo, after gaining power over the whole of Tibet, sent his Minister Gar Tongtsan to the Tang Court with an offer of marriage. The Tang Emperor Taizong wanted to test the wisdom of the envoys who had come for the hand of the Princess, and so he set them five tricky tasks. The hand of the Princess was to be given to the prince whose envoy succeeded in performing all five tasks.

The first test was to pass a silk thread through a turquoise pierced with a spiral hole. All the envoys were completely baffled by this problem except for Gar Tongtsan who managed to thread the turquoise by tying the silk thread round an ant. Placing the ant beside the hole in the turquoise, he blew gently on it to make it go in. When the ant emerged at the other end, the turquoise was threaded.

For the second test, each envoy was given one hundred head of sheep and one hundred vessels of wine and told to slaughter the sheep, skin them, finish eating the mutton, finish tanning the sheepskins and finish up the wine all within the space of one day. Of the other envoys, some were drunk before they had finished eating the mutton, while others were exhausted before the tanning was done; and only Gar Tongtsan was able to organize his entourage to sip the wine slowly and tan the sheepskins in between eating and drinking. In this way the task set by the Emperor was finally fulfilled.

The third task was to find out which colt belonged to which mare in a herd of one hundred mares and one hundred colts. Clever Gar Tongtsan separated the colts from the mares overnight and gave the colts only fodder but no water. The next day when the thirsty colts were released, each colt rushed straight to its own mother to suckle. Once again the Tubo envoy had triumphed.

For the fourth task the Tang Emperor brought forth one hundred logs of uniform thickness and bade the envoys determine which end was the top of each log. Gar Tongtsan threw all the logs into the water, and since the root ends were heavier, they sank and the tops emerged from the water. Thus the Tubo envoy was able to clearly distinguish the two ends of each log.

Finally, Tang Taizong sent Princes Wencheng amidst three hundred beautiful maidens all dressed exactly like the Princess, and told the envoys to pick out the real princess. Whoever succeeded was to take her with him. Gar Tongtsan first paid a visit to an old woman who had been in the service of the Princess to find out anything he could know about her appearence and characteristics. The old woman informed him that the Princess had a mole the colour of cinnabar between her eyebrows. Once again the Tubo envoy was successful and picked out the Princess using the information gleaned from the old servant.

Tang Taizong then agreed to give the hand of the Princess to Songtsan Gampo in marriage, and provided many gifts to be taken as her dowry to Tibet.

Nangsa Obum

Once upon a time in Gyantse there lived an aged couple who had remained childless all their lives. However, as their hair turned white, the old woman gave birth to a daughter whom they named Nangsa Obum.

The girl was very beautiful, sweet-tempered and clever, and had the voice of a lark. She was gentle by nature and a good worker, able to turn her hand to every job such as roasting barley, weaving tweed, growing crops and so on. Gradually her fame spread all over Tibet, but everyone who came with an offer of marriage met with a polite refusal.

The day came, however, when the fifteen-year-old Nangsa went to a monastery to see a religious dance.

There she was spotted by Rinang Ponpo Dachen, the headman, who wanted to take her to be his daughter-in-law. Nangsa did not want to marry the headman's son and neither did her parents want to part with her, but because of Rinang Ponpo Dachen's name and fame, they had no alternative but to give way to his request.

And so Nangsa joined Rinang Ponpo Dachen's family. Seven years passed in a twinkling and she gave birth to a son named Lhawu Dharpo. Her respectful manner towards old and young alike and her solicitude for the servants earned her the appreciation of everybody in the family, and the headman himself intended to hand over the keys of his storehouses to her. However, Nangsa's sister-in-law, a nun, had become very jealous of her for in the past it was she who had supervised the family property, and she did not want Nangsa to gain favour and take over her position. The nun spread slanderous rumours and sowed dissension which caused Nangsa a lot of trouble.

When harvest time came round, the family set out for the fields to reap the crop. One day, two wandering monks came to the fields to beg for alms, and Nangsa gave them a few sheaves of barley. Seizing this pretext, the nun gave Nangsa a merciless beating, and accused her in front of Dagpa Samdup, Nangsa's husband, of behaving improperly with two wandering monks, ignoring all advice, giving the nun a good beating, so on and so forth. Dagpa Samdup believed his sister's one-sided statement and without ascertaining the truth of her accusations he beat Nangsa so brutally that he broke three of her ribs and left her on the point of death, so that she had to be carried away by servants.

314

At this time, a yogin named Sakya Gyaltsan, aware of Nangsa's sorrow, transformed himself into a handsome youth and appeared below her window with a monkey at his side. There he recited prayers and taught her to practise meditation to achieve final liberation. Nangsa and her mother were deeply affected by his teaching, and wanted to offer him some alms, either in money or in kind, but since she had no rights to the family possessions all Nangsa could do was to invite the young man up to her room and offer him some of her jewellery. Unfortunately the whole scene was witnessed by Rinang Ponpo Dachen who was spying on his daughter-in-law, and this convinced him that his daughter's accusations were correct. He burst into Nangsa's room and without waiting for a word of explanation from Nangsa, he gave her another beating which finally led her to death.

Rinang Ponpo Dachen and his son ordered men to carry Nangsa's body to the eastern celestial burial ground where it was to be cremated in seven days time. However, since Nangsa's allotted span had not come to an end, the Lord of Death sent her back to the mortal world. When she came back to life, Nangsa decided to become a nun, but the entreaties of her beloved child as well as Rinang Ponpo Dachen and his son persuaded her to reluctantly return to the Dachen family. However, she requested that the family should become Buddhist to which the headman and his son gave their assent.

Not long afterwards, alas, Rinang Ponpo Dachen and his son broke their promise and went so far as to forbid Nangsa to believe in Buddhism, and finally she had no choice but to return to her own home. Some time later, Nangsa once again sought refuge at the hermitage of the yogin Sakya Gyaltsa where she gave herself over to the study of the dharma. When Rinang Ponpo Dachen and his son learned of this, they led a company of men to seek out Nangsa and the yogin and gave them a good beating. Calling upon their supernatural powers, Nangsa and the yogin ascended to Heaven and only in this way did they strike awe into the hearts of Rinang Ponpo Dachen and his son.

Later, the headman and his son became converted to Buddhism under Nangsa's righteous guidance and handed the family authority over to Lhawu Dharpo, Nangsa's son, while they themselves turned to the practice of Buddhism. As manager of the family's property, Lhawu Dharpo shunned evil and practised goodness, and consequently bumper harvests were gathered every year and everybody lived in peace and happiness.

Sukyi Nyima

Once upon a time there was a kingdom called Sangmo Kyilogyal. There, deep within a forest, lived a Brahman. One day, a doe drank of the water from a spring where the Brahman had washed his garment, and some time later gave birth to a beautiful little girl who was named Sukyi Nyima.

The king of Sangmo Kyilogyal was called Dawai Depon and he had two sons, the elder named Dawai Seng-ge and the younger Dawai Shonu. As the king was aged he decided to hand over the throne to his elder son, Dawai Seng-ge. On the coronation day, the king took his son to the imam for the customary ritual. On the way back, the young man was attracted by a bewitching maiden and took her to the palace as his concubine.

Dawai Seng-ge had a hunter who, in chase of his quarry, one day lost his way in the forest and came upon a goddess-like dakini, who gave him some auspicious grass to guide his way home. On returning to the palace, the hunter told the king about his meeting with the beautiful dakini in the forest, whereupon the king expressed a desire to meet her. Sure enough, the king straightaway fell in love with the beautiful maiden and begged the Brahman over and over again for her hand in marriage.

"She is Sukyi Nyima," answered the Brahman. "If you wish to take her as your bride you must first give up your Islamic belief and be converted to Buddhism."

Dawai Seng-ge agreed at once and took his new bride back to his palace.

Sukyi Nyima gained popularity throughout the kingdom, and the king's former five hundred concubines all became jealous of her. With the bewitching maiden Rig-ngan Bhumo (the girl of impure origin) as the ringleader, the concubines laid false charges against Sukyi Nyima. With the help of a sorceress, Rig-ngan Bhumo stole Sukyi Nyima's amulet, a string of pearl prayer beads, and drugged her with an intoxicant. Then the evil pair killed the king's riding elephant, his minister and his younger brother Dawai Shonu, and laid the blame for all this on Sukyi Nyima.

As a consequence, the king sent Sukyi Nyima into exile to a burial place situated amidst a boiling sea of blood. But because Sukyi Nyima was a Buddhist, the guardian deities saved her from death, and in the guise of a wandering storyteller, she travelled from place to place teaching people to give up evil and practise virtue.

One day, Sukyi Nyima came to the capital of the

kingdom of Sangma Kyilogyal to disseminate her teachings. The sorceress, who by then had grown old, listened to the parables told by the wandering story-teller, and overcome with guilt confessed to her every evil deed and returned the stolen amulet, the string of pearl prayer beads. Only then was the truth revealed to Sukyi Nyima. Sukyi Nyima thought of a way to draw the king and his ministers to where the sorceress was making her confession, and in this way they too discov-ered the truth behind the evil deeds committed within the palace in the past. As he listened to the whole story, the king was overcome with repentance. When he realised the wandering storyteller was none other than Sukyi Nyima in disguise, he felt excited, ashamed and glad all at once, and begged her to return to the palace. From then on, the kingdom enjoyed bumper harvests, livestock thrived and the people lived long and happy lives.

Dowa Sangmo

In the kingdom of Mandal-gang there once lived a king named Kala Wangpo who had a queen called Hachang, a she-demon by nature, and furthermore barren. One day, while the king was out hunting in the forest, all of a sudden his hound disappeared. All the king's attendants ran forth in search of the dog and finally found themselves in front of a hut where a Brahman couple lived. The attendants asked the couple to return their dog, but before the Brahmans realised what was going on, the king and his ministers and retinue rushed into the hut in search of the hound. Inside the hut, their attention was caught by a radiantly beautiful girl looking like a goddess. Quite besotted, the king wanted to take the maiden home with him as his bride.

The maiden's name was Dowa Sangmo, and she was the only darling of the aged couple, sent to them by dakinis. At first she considered flying up to the celestial realm to escape from the situation, but the imploring entreaties of the old couple persuaded her to stay where she was even though if she remained in the mortal world she would surely have to go with the king.

Great celebrations took place throughout the kingdom on the day of the bridal party's arrival, and the king announced to the multitudes that from then on they were all to believe in Buddhism. Once in the palace, Dowa Sangmo piously kept up her Buddhist worship. Soon after, she gave birth to a princess named Kuntu Sangmo, and three years later she bore a prince, whom she called Kuntu Legpa.

One day, the wicked queen Hachang's maid servant discovered that Dowa Sangmo had given birth to a son and a daughter when she saw the mother and two children amusing themselves in the garden. She made haste to inform her mistress, the wicked queen, who gnashed her teeth and resolved to eat the trio.

Realising that she was in a precarious situation, Dowa Sangmo flew up to Heaven on the advice of the celestial dakinis, leaving her two babes behind. When the little prince and princess went to see their father, the king shed tears and fainted away.

Hachang then assembled her treacherous ministers and gave the king an intoxicating drug, and then locked him in a dungeon. Hachang next attempted to kill the two children left by Dowa Sangmo by pretending to be sick and claiming that she could only be cured by eating the hearts of two children. She commanded two butchers to kill the royal babes but the butchers were not cruel enough to take the lives of the children. Telling them to stay hidden in safety, the men slaughtered two dogs instead and pretended to Hachang that the hearts were those of the prince and princess.

Some time later, Hachang realised that the two children were still alive, and pretending to be now a goddess and now a demon, the wicked queen ordered two fishermen to throw Kuntu Sangmo and Kuntu Legpa into the sea. Taking pity on the prince and princess, the fishermen set them free and advised them never to return to the kingdom again. But unfortunately the children once more fell into the hands of Hachang's henchmen, and the evil queen again gave orders to two hunters to carry the prince and princess to a cliff and throw them over. The elder of the two hunters was overcome by compassion and set the princess free, but the younger man who was carrying the prince felt no such pity and tossed him over the cliff.

At that very moment, the heavenly Dowa Sangmo transformed herself into a huge garuda and saved her young son, gently setting him down on the beach at the foot of the cliff. Then a parrot came and took the prince to the kingdom of Padma-chen where he was made king.

Begging her way from place to place, the little princess happened to come to the capital of Padma-chen. When people found out who she was, brother and sister were reunited, and from that day on the princess led a happy life with her brother in the kingdom of Padma-chen.

Not long after, this news reached the ears of Hanchang who swore to put an end to the children. Gathering an army from throughout the kingdom, the queen and her troops marched forward to the kingdom of Padma-chen. The new king of Padma-chen, Kuntu Legpa, led the entire army and people of his kingdom in person against Hachang. The wicked queen was eventually crushed to mincemeat, and her mangled corpse was buried under nine layers of earth and a stupa built on top to suppress the she-demon.

Kuntu Legpa then marched on to Mandal-gang and set free his father, King Kala Wangpo, who continued to reign, and Kuntu Legpa returned to his own kingdom of Padma-chen.

Prince Norsang

Long, long ago there were two kingdoms called Rigden of the South and Ngaden of the North. The king of Ngaden of the North and his son were very benevolent, and their kingdom prospered in peace and happiness, while the king of Rigden of the South was cruel and tyrannical. Wanting to bring wealth to his kingdom, he sent a sorcerer to the north to capture the king of the Underworld. However, thanks to the intervention of a hunter, the king of the Underworld escaped his captors and in return he presented the hunter with a precious object which would fulfil any wish. But wealth did not interest the hunter who wanted to secure a beautiful heavenly maiden as his mate. Instead he asked the king of the Underworld to lend him the Precious Lasso and succeeded in lassoing a dakini named Yitok Lhamo whom he wished to marry. Just then a yogin who dwelt in the mountains told the hunter that for a common man to take a dakini as a wife could only bring disaster and misfortune, and advised him to give the dakini to Prince Norsang instead, who was also a heavenly being. The hunter agreed and took the dakini to the prince's palace.

Prince Norsang was overjoyed to have a dakini as a bride, and the couple led a life of great happiness. Alas, Norsang's two thousand and five hundred concubines became jealous of Yitok and schemed to put an end to her. The first step was to get rid of Prince Norsang by sending him into battle. Next, they laid a plot to dispose of Yitok by claiming that the old king had taken ill and that Yitok's heart was the only thing that would cure him.

Aided by her mother-in-law, Yitok Lhamo flew back to her home in the Celestial Realm, and when Norsang returned home triumphant from battle, she was nowhere to be found. Grieving deeply, the prince at once set out to comb the mountains and seas for his beloved dakini.

Guided by the yogin, Prince Norsang underwent many hardships before finally reaching the Celestial Realm where he found his beloved. But Yitok Lhamo's father had changed his mind about giving his daughter to a mortal in marriage. He set many difficult tasks for the prince, including pitting Norsang against his ministers in a contest of arms, but each time Norsang was the victor. Thus Yitok Lhamo and Prince Norsang fulfilled their wish of being reunited, and Yitok Lhamo's father had no alternative but to allow Norsang and Yitok to return to the mortal world with a large dowry.

Not long after, Norsang's father gave up the throne to his son, and under the reign of the new king and queen, the kingdom became happy and prosperous.

Padma Obar

Once upon a time there was a rich king. He had

a lame viceroy who did evil deeds solely to please the king. In the kingdom there was also a merchant who had a wealth of experience in trading. The king was anxious that the merchant might become richer than he, and so the cunning viceroy advised him to send the merchant to sea in quest of the precious Treasure of the Underworld. The merchant could not disobey the king's command so he bade his wife farewell and put out to sea with a crew of five hundred men. The merchant never returned.

Just before the merchant's departure, his wife had given birth to a son who was named Padma Obar. Padma Obar grew up extraordinarily fast, growing as much in one day as other children did in a month, and growing as much in a month as others did in a year. He was also extremely intelligent and his mother was very fond of him. Her one anxiety was that the king might hear of his existence and misfortune befall him. She therefore kept him indoors and made him do his lessons.

Padma Obar was an active youth and disliked staying indoors, so he used to quietly sneak out with other children to gather twigs and kindling. The other children often teased him for not having a father, and so when he returned home Padma Obar would question his mother about the name and whereabouts of his father. His mother, however, would scold him for his naughtiness, give him a slap and pay no heed to his questions. one day, though, while Padma Obar was out on an errand of business, an old woman revealed to him the story of his father, and so the young man resolved to set out in quest of his father.

The lame viceroy discovered what Padma Obar was up to and reported the case to the king. The news made the king anxious again, and he made up his mind to stamp out the source of the trouble by sending Padma Obar to the demon world to fetch two precious objects, the Golden Gong and the Silver Key.

Padma Obar obeyed the royal order and set out for the demon world. After many delays and setbacks, he managed to find the Demon Queen who swallowed him up at one gulp, thinking that she could devour him with ease. But Padma Obar was in fact a heavenly being who had descended to the mortal world. Once inside the belly of the Demon Queen, he caused her such agony that she could stand it no longer, and finally agreed to give him the Golden Gong and the Silver Key. Thanks to the miraculous powers of the precious objects, Padma Obar was now able to return to his own home and be reunited with his mother.

When the news of Padma Obar's return reached the king, he was stunned with amazement and wanted to pay a visit to the demon world himself. Padma Obar agreed to accompany him, and when they reached their destination, the young man pushed the avaricious king off a cliff to become a feast for the demons. Clasping the Golden Gong and Silver Key, Padma Obar then flew back home and took over the kingdom.

Donyo and Dondup

King Pala Dewa and his queen Kunsangma were rewarded with a son whom they named Dondup. From his earliest years Dondup showed himself to be very gifted, and could recite the six-syllable prayer "Om Mani Padme Hum" by the age of five. Unfortunately, his mother, Kunsangma, passed away as a result of a sudden attack of a serious illness, and the following year the king took a woman of low birth named Bomgyal as his bride. In due course the new queen gave birth to a son who was given the name Donyo.

From infancy Donyo and Dondup were inseparable and played together from morn till night. The king loved them dearly. But Bomgyal overheard people speaking highly of Dondup's good nature and declaring that he was sure to succeed to the throne. This made Bomgyal uneasy and she schemed to put an end to Dondup. In face of this, the king could do nothing but send Dondup into exile to a remote and desolate land. When Donyo came to know of this decision, he was determined to accompany his brother by hook or by crook, and so the two brothers set out for the wilderness to the north.

The two princes trudged along sandy beaches and struggled through dense forests until they had eaten all their food. Dondup then gathered wild fruits and fetched water, letting his younger brother eat and drink first. However, things became steadily worse and worse, and Donyo became progressively weaker and weaker, until he finally fainted away from hunger and thirst. Dondup wept for a while and then laying his brother under a sandalwood tree, he continued on his way northwards where he was fortunate enough to come across a hermit who agreed to take him in as a disciple.

Out at play one day, Dondup just for fun told the children of the neighbourhood that he was born in the Dragon Year. Who could ever have guessed what trouble this jest would land him in, for it just so happened that the king of the region was looking for a child born in the Dragon Year to sacrifice to the Lord of the Underworld. Dondup was seized and taken to the royal palace. The king's daughter was very taken with young Dondup and begged her father to let them play together for seven days. But then Dondup had to depart for the palace of the Underworld. On his arrival, the King of the Underworld noting that he was brave and handsome received him with warmth and sent him back to the hermit.

Some time later, Dondup and the hermit happened to come by the king's palace and there Dondup was recognised by the princess who was smitten with both grief and joy. The king gave his daughter's hand in marriage to Dondup and passed on the throne to him. But all this time Dondup had been thinking of his lost brother Donyo. Accompanied by soldiers, the new king set out into the deep forest and eventually managed to find Donyo. Choked with sobs, the two long-lost brothers embraced one another and then returned to the palace. Later they went back to their former kingdom to see their parents. By now advanced in years, King Pala Dewa was delighted to see his sons again, and in the end Donyo succeeded his father while Dondup returned to his own kingdom.

Drimi Kundan

The King of Paldan had one thousand five hundred wives, but only one of them, Kalsang Demo, bore a son who was named Drimi Kundan. As soon as he was born this prince could recite the six-syllable mantra "Om Mani Padme Hum," and later was even able to recite the scriptures in entirety.

One day, the king heard Drimi Kundan say that all men under the sky were pitiful creatures and should be provided with adequate food and shelter. Soon after, the king married Drimi Kundan to Meda Sangmo, the princess of a neighbouring kingdom, who had an upstanding character and was of extraordinary beauty. The young couple loved each other deeply and three sons were born to them. They enjoyed a happy family life together.

One day, while Drimi Kundan and his sons were in the garden, there appeared at the palace gate a group of miserable beggars in rags. Drimi Kundan was filled with compassion at the sight. He wanted to distribute the wealth from the treasury among them, and won the consent of the king.

Just them, a Brahman who had come from a hostile country nearby approached Drimi Kundan ad begged from him the kingdom's most precious treasure as alms. Drimi Kunda had no right to give away the kingdom's most precious treasure, but noticing the stranger was old and feeble and looked so pitiful, he took the treasure by stealth and gave it to the old man.

The king was overwhelmed with anger when he heard about the prince's action, and sent him into exile for twelve years. Accompanied by his wife and three children, Drimi Kundan set off for Mt. Hari. Commoners, ministers and tribal chieftains all came one after another to see him off and showered him with gifts and money, but Drimi Kundan again distributed everything amongst the poor. On his way into exile the prince bestowed all his belongings on beggars and even gave away his children to Brahmans as alms. Finally he and his wife alone reached the wilderness of Mt. Hari.

The twelve years of exile soon passed, and the couple set off back to the kingdom, longing to see their sons and father, the king, once again. On their way they met an old woman who had lost her sight who begged Drimi Kundan to give her his eyes as alms. The prince readily agreed and took out his eyes, leaving himself blind.

When the news of the prince's return reached the palace, the king sent his minister to receive him. The minister was choked with sobs at the sight of Drimi Kundan's miserable condition, but the prince prayed in silence: "To relieve the sorrows of my wife Meda Sangmo and the minister, may the Three Jewels bless me so that I may regain my sight." Sure enough, his eyes recovered their sight and the trio proceeded on their way to the palace. The king of the hostile country who had previously asked for the kingdom's most precious treasure was profoundly moved when he learned the cause of Drimi Kundan's exile. He returned the treasure and expressed deep penitence. People from miles around came to welcome the prince with palms clasped together, and the whole kingdom rejoiced. The old king passed the throne on to Drimi Kundan, and the kingdom prospered while the people lived in contentment.

19

**THE INHABITANTS
OF THE SOUTHERN
BORDER REGIONS**

The Moinba, Lhoba, Tengpa and Sherpa Nationalities

Primitive Socio-Economic Organization

The Language and the Way of Life

Among the Local Ethnic Groups

Costumes
Religion and Beliefs
Marriage and Funerals

A New Way of Life

More than ten nationalities make up the population of 1,890,000 scattered over the 1,200,000 square kilometres of the Tibetan plateau. Besides Tibetans, who account for ninety percent, there are also Hans, Huis, Moinbas, Lhobas, Tengpas and Sherpas. Among them, the Moinbas, Lhobas and Tengpas live in the south-eastern part of the Tibet Autonomous Region, while the Sherpas inhabit the southwest.

Historical evidence in the form of oracle inscriptions from Yin Dynasty ruins and bronze inscriptions of the Zhou Dynasty prove that there were inhabitants on the Qinghai-Tibet plateau in remote antiquity. This history dates back at least four or five thousand years.

After Liberation, Chinese scientists conducted investigations on the Qinghai-Tibet plateau, a virgin land for archeologists and geologists, and found remains of primitive people and evidence of their activities. The first discoveries were made in 1958 in Nyingtri Dzong situated four hundred kilometres east of Lhasa. These remains included a skeleton of a young female which had already lost its ape-man characteristics and had developed into a human. Scientifically determined as belonging to the Mongolian race, palaeoanthropologists named it "Nyingtri Man." Analysis has shown that Nyingtri Man lived at the time of the corresponding Neolithic Age and the entry into the period when metals began to be used in the Central Plains of China. The Karo finds, discovered recently in Chamdo, near the Zachu River are extremely valuable substantial remains of a neolithic village. According to isotope analysis of the stone and bone implements pottery and foundations of houses, etc., excavated so far, the Karo culture flourished 4,600 years ago.

Scientific investigations have confirmed the truth of folk tales explaining the origin of the inhabitants of the Tibetan plateau. One such ancient folk tale comes from the Lhoba people living in Miling and Lhuntse.

Long, long ago, the sky was absolutely empty and the earth bare. Later, the sky and earth got married and the earth became pregnant. But before its birth, the child flowed out as blood, which changed into rain and moistened all the living things on earth. Later, the earth again gave birth to a child which in turn produced two more children named Darao and Dani. The Lhobas believe Darao to be their own ancestor and Dani to be the ancestor of the Tibetans. One day, while Darao and Dani were having a shooting competition, Darao, being the stronger, shot his arrow far away so that it fell deep within the forest. Thereafter, Darao had to live in the forest of Miling while Dani made his home Kongpo.

The Tengpas, living in the deep gorges of Zayul, though not identified as a nationality yet by the government, also, have many age-old tales about their own origins.

One story is told as such:

Way, way back in the mists of time when the world was a vast sea, there lived a golden god called Achani who married a female monkey. He raised a mountain out of the plains, channelled water, cultivated the land and fathered three sons, Tongka, Tongma, and Tongde. This trio are said to be the ancestors of the Hans, Tibetans, and Tengpas.

One day, the elder brother Tongka said to his younger brothers, "We don't need to go anywhere else so let's stay here together forever." But Tongde, the third brother, insisted on going off because he had made up his mind previously to go to the mountains to

sow his fields that very day. When the third brother
returned from the mountains, he found his elder brothers had already taken their leave, and inside the house
all that remained was a dog skin, a bamboo mattress,
and a small quantity of grain. One of the two brothers
had moved to a distant place where golden grain grew,
while the other had settled down in a place not far from
the third brother. Previously they had had a system of
writing but it was taken away by the first and second
brothers. Tongka and Tongma had left a note for the
third brother, but Tongde had eaten it up because he
had been so hungry when he came home. And this is
the reason why the Tengpas do not have a script even
to this day.

The Moinba, Lhoba, Tengpa and Sherpa Nationalities

For more than a thousand years during the course
of development from a primitive society to feudal serfdom, the Tibetans held the dominant position among
the inhabitants of the Tibetan plateau. Right up until
the eve of Liberation, the Tibetan rulers drove these
weaker nationalities, the Moinbas, Lhobas, Tengpas
and Sherpas, deep into the forests, allowing them only
to dwell near the borders of neighbouring countries.

The Moinbas live in Metok, Tsona, and Lhuntse
Dzongs (counties) and in Monyul region located south
of the illegal McMahon Line. The Lhoba nationality live
all over Zayul, Monyul and Miling, the extensive Himalayan regions lying to the south of the Tsangpo River.
The Tengpas live in the Zayul Region in the southeast
of the Tibet Autonomous Region along the courses of
the Ngachu, Zayulchu, Gedochu and Dolegchu Rivers.

This region of high mountains, deep gorges, dense forests and rapid rivers is extraordinarily rich in flora and fauna. The Sherpas live along the Sino-Nepalese border region of Dam, in the Trintang district of Tingkye Dzong, and the Rongshar district of Dingri Dzong. Large numbers also live in the Kingdom of Nepal. "Sherpa" in Tibetan has the meaning of "people of the east," and they believe they originally came from Sichuan and Kham. For the present the Tengpas and Sherpas are not yet acknowledged by the State as separate nationalities.

The Moinbas, Lhobas, Tengpas, and Sherpas all live amid high mountains and deep gorges where one can "walk up to the clouds and down to the rivers," and where people live "just a call away, but a day's walk apart."

Under the yoke of the serf-owners of the old Tibetan society, these national minorities were discriminated against and treated high-handedly. The Moinbas were despised as "miserable wretches" and the Lhobas as "savages" (in old orthography of Tibetan language the term "Lopa" meant "savage," but now the spelling has been changed to "Lhoba" meaning "the people of the south"). The Tengpas and Sherpas were insulted with wames such as "savages with naked arses" or "monkeys that can walk on mountains." The Moinbas living in Lekpo have this folk rhyme:

> Think not of the past, cast memory away,
> Such thoughts bring only grief to mind.
> Treated as beasts of burden were we,
> Bitter water was our only wine.

The folk song above reflects the inner sorrows of the smaller nationalities living in Tibet.

Primitive Socio-Economic Organisation

Isolated from the world, the production methods of the Moinbas, Lhobas, Tengpas and Sherpas remained at the primitive stage of slash-and-burn cultivation and gathering and hunting for a long time. Behind Lhoba New Village in Chongling Hamlet, Miling Dzong, evidence of slash-and-burn cultivation of the past is preserved to this day, and in Zayul, where the Tengpas live in a compact community, when it fails to rain during the sowing season, still maintain their custom of setting the mountains on fire. For centuries, the Moinbas, Lhobas, Tengpas, and Sherpas have opened up land by setting forests on fire; ploughed with primitive sticks, sowed the fields with handfuls of seed, and left the crop to grow if it will until harvest time, when if there is anything to gather, it is a gift from heaven, and if there is nothing to gather, it is the result of cruel fate. The extreme primitiveness of their production methods meant that they had to supplement cultivation with hunting and gathering in order to survive. This system of production and way of living has resulted in their primitive distribution system. The Lhobas still maintain the remnants of the distribution system of the primitive community: they go hunting together and distribute the game equally according to their age-old custom. Even the smallest animal is equally divided with only the skin and head left to the huntsman. The family with the most skins is renowned as having the best hunters. The organisation of labour and system of distribution among the Moinbas, Tengpas and Sherpas have certain similarities to the Lhobas. Primitive production methods naturally led to poverty. Prior to the democratic revolution of Tibet, the majority of their people lived in shacks fashioned from branches and banana leaves and wore clothing made of leaves and wild hemp. This low standard of living meant that the Moinbas, Lhobas, Tengpas, and Sherpas had much less of a private ownership mentality than the Tibetans, and even today when new homes are built, or at marriages or funerals, everyone in the entire village or clan comes together to offer help and support.

The Language and Way of Life Among the Local Ethnic Groups

The Moinbas, Lhobas, Tengpas and Sherpas each have their own language which differs from Tibetan, although they use the Tibetan script for writing all of them. These minority nationalities do not keep records of days, months or years, and are accustomed to keeping accounts by making knots in string or by cutting notches in twigs. In fact, among the elderly hardly any know their exact age.

Living as they do in forests, a hatchet is an indispensable tool for the Moinbas, Lhobas, Tengpas and Sherpas. They use hatchets for building houses, lumbering, cutting down trees, splitting planks, cutting trees into logs, and whittling pieces of wood, and so on. Timber is used for everything: roofs, floors, walls, house posts, of course all requiring the use of a hatchet and the resulting houses are very different from Tibetan mud-brick huts. Even ladders are made of a single tree trunk with notches chopped into it instead of rungs.

The Moinbas, Lhobas, Tengpas, and Sherpas each

have their own kind of tasty food. The Moinbas most appreciate meals of buckwheat bread baked on heated stone slabs flavoured with crushed chilli, while the Lhobas like dried meat, roasted meat, cheese, and buckwheat bread. The staple food of the Tengpas is maize, and they like to smoke and drink, while the Sherpas prefer maize porridge, curry and rice which they eat with their fingers.

Hospitality to guests is a common feature of all these national minorities. Visitors to a Tengpa home must have a drink of their homemade wine, and when Lhobas serve a meal, visitors have to finish it all or else face the disappointment of their hosts. In the past the Lhobas were apt to put poison in other's food, but today these hospitable hosts will take a mouthful or two from the guest's meal as a sign of good intentions and to show that the meal is free from poison.

Costumes

The easiest way of distinguishing these national minorities is by their dress. The Moinbas of Lekpo all wear bright red gowns made of tweed and tiny bright red conical hats with orange borders. Moinba women wear white aprons, and adorn themselves with bracelets, necklaces, and earrings when attired in their best. Old and young alike wear calf skins hanging from their backs as well as embroidered boots reaching almost to the knee. The Moinbas living in Metok dress like Tibetans and the multi-coloured striped apron is a conspicuous sign of a Moinba woman.

Lhoba men and women both wear very simple clothing. A short sleeveless outer tunic and a round hat made of bear skin or bamboo are the major characteristics of a Lhoba man, and he carries a bow and arrows and a sword with him wherever he goes. Lhoba women wear round-necked blouses with fitted sleeves and checked woolen skirts reaching to the knee. Unlike the Moinbas, Lhoba men and women all have long hair with a fringe which they wear loose over their shoulders. All Lhobas appreciate ornaments, and the men wear bamboo earrings and bracelets while the women when attired in their best, wear dozens of bead necklaces with the addition of bracelets, earrings, silver coins, brass bells, iron chains, flints, knives, and shells, weighing about five kilos in all.

Inhabiting the sub-tropical belt of the "rongyul" (deep valleys) of Tibet, the Tengpa men wear sleeveless gowns and short pants, while the women wear short-sleeved blouses which leave the midriff bare and long skirts. Tengpa men and women both wear huge shawls and carry distinctive shoulder bags. The Tengpas have the habit of smoking, and visitors to Tengpa New Village, are greeted by the sight of young girls and aged women, each holding a long pipe with a tobacco bag tied to it swinging to and fro. The Tengpa menfolk wear bamboo hats, while the womenfolk bind their hair into a bun at the back of the head like the hair style of Durmese women. Across their foreheads the women wear silver ornaments as large as the palm of the hand, as well as equally large earrings and strings of beads.

The jackets worn by the hygiene-loving. Sherpas are made of a white tweed called "bedo." Women wear wide trousers called "Galung" with aprons on top. The men wear short pants, and wrap a piece of white tweed called a "kasa" around their waists which is held in place by a sash or "kapu." A dagger is inserted at the waist in front, and this is characteristic of Sherpa menfolk.

Religion and Beliefs

The Moinbas and Sherpas who live thousands of kilometres apart both hold Buddhist beliefs. The famous Tawang Monastery is the major monastery of the Moinbas, and the sixth Dalai Lama, Tsangtang Gyatso, himself was a Manba. The Sherpas have monasteries in Dam and Trintang, and elderly Sherpas make family shrines at home in which they place statues of Sakyamuni.

The Lhobas and Tengpas although far apart, are both animists. Both peoples commonly sacrifice chickens and drive off evil spirits to avoid misfortune. The Lhobas and Tengpas both believe that everything has a soul, and that spirits exist on earth. Whenever there is a marriage or funeral, whenever a house is built, at the sowing season, or when setting out on a journey, a chicken sacrifice is offered as a prognostication of good or evil. Lhoba households generally sacrifice seventy to eighty chickens a year, and ten to twenty chickens may be sacrificed on a single day until an auspicious omen is seen. They believe that everything is directed by spirits and every action has to be preceded with sacrifices to the spirits.

Marriage and Funerals

The Moinbas, Lhobas, Tengpas, and Sherpas generally practise monogamy, but they are all strongly influenced by mercenary marriages. When receiving a Moinba bride, the bridegroom's family must make three presentations of "chang" (Tibetan brew), meat, money and goods, while a price equivalent to three, four, or even more than ten head of zo has to be paid for a Lhoba bride. The Tengpas practice pure mercenary marriage, and they too pay the bride price with cattle or in kind. Buying and selling of brides conforms to the moral precepts of the Tengpas. A married Tengpa woman, without the least embarrassment tells how she was purchased in exchange for cattle, pigs, chickens or meat. The sale of wives has no stigma attached to it among the Tengpas, and when a Tengpa woman is given to a man in marriage, she simply becomes his "property." If the husband dies, the "property" can be inherited by the brothers or close relatives of the deceased husband.

The "kidnap" marriage of the Sherpas is very intriguing. Even though a girl may be willing to marry a young man, she still cannot freely take her departure from home but has to be "kidnapped." In other cases, the parents may be in agreement but the girl is not, or vice versa, and so the only way to solve the problem is by "kidnapping" the girl. Sometimes the parents prearrange the "kidnapping" together with the bridegroom-to-be. The "kidnap" marriage of the Sherpas has become a custom through common practice, and is condoned by society. However, once the girl has been won through "kidnapping," the marriage ceremony still takes place and there is drinking, dancing and entertainment all through the night.

Unlike the Tibetans, the Moinbas, Lhobas, Tengpas, and Sherpas do not practice celestial burial.

The Lhobas bury their dead and Lhoba funerals are very interesting. After being dressed in clean clothes, the body of the deceased is placed at the left behind the door cross-legged in lotus position, wrapped in a cloth, and bound with a rope. Two or three days later, the body is taken to the cemetery where a pit about ten feet deep is dug. The body is untied and straightened and then placed in the pit; a board is placed over the opening and earth is shovelled over it.

Cremation is very popular among the Tengpas and Sherpas. When a Sherpa dies, the body, placed in a coffin, is carried to the crematorium where it is burnt with firewood. Then the ashes are collected and thrown into a river. When a Sherpa infant dies, it is given a celestial burial by being left in a cave on a cliff as an offering for the vultures. The Tengpa way of cremation is more complex: after death the body is placed in a specially built room where the soul is supposed to be living, and in this room the body is kept for one to three days while the family members mourn day and night. After this, firecrackers are let off or gun shots are sounded so as to rouse the soul to consciousness, and then the body is taken out for cremation.

A New Way of Life

Since the liberation of Tibet, under the guidance of the Chinese government's policy of "all nationalities, big and small, are equals," the Moinbas, Lhobas, Tengpas, and Sherpas have all been enjoying a new life. The Tibetans lent them assistance when they moved from the mountains to the plains. furthermore, the government provided them with farm implements and cattle, and sent technicians to supervise land reclamation and cultivation. Clinics and schools have been set up in their new villages. The Moinbas, Lhobas, Tengpas and Sherpas all have young people studying in universities either in inland China or in Lhoba. These people who for generations lived in mountain forests and roamed like vagabonds are now changing their lives, working in peace and contentment and receiving education.

The Moinbas, Lhobas, Tengpas, and Sherpas, who for generations never enjoyed the right to education, now have their own university students, doctors, agricultural specialists, teachers and accountants. These small and weak nationalities who for ages had practised slash-and-burn cultivation have now produced quite a number of tractor drivers and factory technicians. These people who make up one percent of Tibet's total population, are now looking forward to the future, and together with the Tibetans, are contributing their strength to establish a united, rich, and cultured socialist new Tibet.

20 ⊑⊑⊑⊑⊑⊑⊑⊑⊑⊑⊑⊑

APPENDICES

I. Text of the Uncle-Nephew Alliance Tablet

II. A Chronology of Tibetan History

1. The Tsanpo Period
2. The Decentralisation Period
3. The Sakya Dynasty
4. The Pagdu Dynastry
5. The Kamapa Period
6. The Gandan Podrang Period (Dalai Lamas)
7. The Panchen Lamas

III. A Chronology of Chinese History

Text of the Uncle Nephew Alliance Tablet

Emperor Muzong of The Great Tang, an embodiment of human perfection literary and military arts, filial piety and moral integrity, and the Sacred Tsanpo of the Great Tibet Tritsug Detsan, uncle and nephew, have met with agreement to become allied as one. In order to maintain the alliance forever, and so that it may be witnessed and discussed by ecclesiastical and secular communities for generations hence, the treaty is engraved on this stone tablet.

Emperor Muzong and Tritsug Detsan, uncle and nephew, have met with agreement on a wide range of considerations for the present and the future so as to allow all people, within and without, to live in peace and happiness under all conditions. For the sake of eternal goodness, both have agreed to maintain their old friendship and neighbourliness. Both nations, Tibet and Han, should observe their traditional boundary east whereof lies the Great Tang's territory and west whereof is the Great Tibet's territory. Both parties should not treat each other as enemies, should not attack one another, and should not annex one another's territory. In case of suspicion, both parties have the right to question the suspect, but then should send him back provided with clothing and provisions. Having established the present alliance, both nations should inform one another of favourable news. Envoys sent by both parties should take the old route of the past; the horses should be changed at Jiangjungu; to the east of Suirongshan, the Great Tang is responsible for their welfare; to the west of Qingshuixian, the Great Tibet is responsible for their welfare. As the relationship between uncle and nephew has met with improvement, so loyalty and respect should be heightened in a like manner so as to avoid friction, sudden attacks, or hostilities of any sort. Even the frontier guards should be free of suspicion and anxiety, and should live at ease each within their border. May this happiness last from generation to generation, and fine-sounding praise travel like the rays of the sun and the moon. May this noble deed bring peace to the Tibetans in the land of Tibet and happiness to the Hans in the land of the Hans. May the alliance be eternal and immutable. The alliance is sworn in the presence of the Triple Jewels, gods, and the sun and the moon and the stars; it is sworn by the sacrifice of an animal. He who breaks the alliance is a scourge to the Tibetans and Hans and may be condemned. The act of condemnation should not be considered as a nullification of the alliance.

Thus, the ministers of the Tibetans and Hans have taken their oaths and prepared the treaty in detail; the seals of two great Kings have been affixed; the signatory ministers have signed their names; and each will keep a copy of the treaty.

The inscription in Tibetan on the east face of the tablet provides the Tibetan version of the text, which differs somewhat from the Han version. It appears below for comparison:

The Sacred King, Wode Pugyal*, came down to our world in the guise of a man, and became the Great King of Tibet. Amidst great mountains, at the source of great rivers, amidst the unsullied highlands, he descended from Heaven and became the King of mortal beings and established his rule for all ages. With the goodness of the religious Law, he ruled the people; with compassion he ran his internal affairs; and with skilled methods of warfare he subdued external ene-

---

* another name for Nyatri Tsanpo

mies. Thus prospered his rule to the height of fame, and to the eternity of the swastika. Hence, the Mon and Indians to the south, the Taksik[*] to the west, the **Grugu**[**] and **Nemal** to the north all sincerely respected him, believed his words to be honest and everlasting, and heard them with pleasure.

To the east lies the Tang, a kingdom where the sun rises. Unlike Nepal to the south of Tibet, it has as great an administration and culture as Tibet. Formerly, when Emperor Taizong assumed the throne for three and twenty years, the sacred Tsanpo Tri Songtsan and Emperor Taizong, an embodiment of human perfection of the literary and military arts as well as filial piety, became allied as one, and Princess Wencheng, the niece of Emperor Taizong, was given in marriage to Songtsan Gampo in the Zhenguan Year[***]. Later, the Sacred King Tride Tsugtsan and Emperor Zhongzong of the Tang, who is unsurpassed in military art and outstanding in literary cultivation, became allied as one, and Kimshing Kungchu[****] became the Tsanpo's queen in Jinglong Year[*****].

Thus, the two families became related for the second time and the relationship of nephew and uncle came into existence, both lived at ease. At times frontier guards met with clashes, but whenever serious matters arose regarding internal political affairs, each sent a detached force of troops to assist the other. In case of disunity between the two, gifts were exchanged to restore peace. Such was the affection between nephew and uncle. Tride Songtsan, the father of the

---

[*] ancient Persians
[**] present-day Turkestan
[***] 641 AD
[****] Princess Jincheng
[*****] 710

346

Tsanpo, was great in wisdom and talented both in religious and administrative affairs. Owing to his kindness, both within and without the kingdom, friendship flourished with all the neighbouring countries in the eight directions. Extending friendship with the Tangs was more definite for both had become relatives and lived as neighbours, and were eager to become allied as one. Tride Songtsan and Tang Emperor Dezong (779 - 805) held common views to establish a written agreement. They put an end to the enmity of the past and established a new friendship which was maintained throughout Tride Songtsan's lifetime and three generations of Tang uncles'. The two peoples lived free of friction, helping one another, sending envoys and exchanging gifts, but they had not established a written alliance. Instead, old disputes surfaced as suspicions which became obstacles to negotiations, and in consequence the two sides became opposed and threatened by the danger of sending out troops. The Sacred King, Tritsug Detsan, approached the situation with wisdom and insight. Adhering to the religious Law, he treated both sides with equal kindness and made correct predictions. He acted according to the wise thinking of Songtsan Gampo and with Emperor Muzong reached a common view in politics between Tibet and the Tang Dynasty, resulting in a treaty for the happiness of the two peoples for generations.

Thus, at Wanghuisi, in the west of Jingshi Chang'an of the Tang territory, on the tenth day of the tenth month, in the Seventh Kyitak Year of the Great Tibet and the First Changqing Year" of the Great Tang, the treaty was signed on the platform where the oath was

---

* Emperor Dezong, Emperor Shunzong and Emperor Xianzong
" 821

taken. In Tibet, the treaty was signed on the sixth day of the fifth month in the Eighth Kyitak Year of the Great Tibet and the Second Changqing Year of the Great Tang* on the platform where the oath was taken at Dratotsal to the east of the Palace of Lhasa. The treaty was engraved on the stone tablet on the fourteenth day of the second month of the Ninth Kyitak Year of the Great Tibet and the Third Changqing Year of the Great Tang".

This tablet has been examined by the Tang envoy Du Zai, who holds the rank of Master of the Horse. Another tablet with the same inscriptions has been erected at the Tang capital Xi'an.

---

  * 822
  " 823

II. A Chronology of the Tibetan History

1. The Tupan Tsanpos

Name	Reign	Capital
Nyatri Tsanpo	c.400-300 B.C.*	Yalung**
Mutri Tsanpo		
Dingtri Tsanpo		
Sotri Tsanpo		
Mertri Tsanpo		
Dagtri Tsanpo		
Sibtri Tsanpo		
Drigum Tsanpo	c.200 B.C.	
Pude Gungyal		
Esholek		
Desholek		
Tisholek		
Gurulek		
Drongshelek		
Isholek		
Sanam Sinde		
Detul Namshung		
Senol Namde		
Senol Pode		
Denolnam		
Denolpo		
Degyalpo		

* This reffers to the period of the first seven legendary Tsanpos, the exact dates of whose rules has no written historical records.

** Yalung had remained capital of Tibet until Songtsan Ganpo moved his capital to Lhasa.

Name	Reign	Capital
Detintsan		
Gyalto Rilungtsan		
Tritsanam		
Trida Pungtsan		
Trito Jetsan		
Tho-Tho-Ri Nyantsan	c. 300*	
Trinyan Sungtsan		
Drongnyan Deu		
Tagri Nyansik		
Namri Sungtsan		
Songtsan Gampo	629-650	Lhasa**
Gungri Gungtsan	650-655	
Mangsong Mangtsan	655-676	
Dusong Mangpoje	676-704	
Tride Tsugtan	704-755	
Trisung Detsan	755-797	
Muni Tsanpo	797-798	
Mutik Tsanpo	798-804	
Tride Songtsan	804-815	
Triral Pachen	815-841	
Wudum Tsanpo***	841-846	

* Bhuddism is said to have made its first appearance in about 303 a.d. during his rule.
** Lhasa was formally made capital of Tibet by Songtsan Ganpo in 633 and remained capital till the end of the Tupan period.
*** The Tupan Dynasty disintegrated since him and his descendants became rival local rulers (see the following charts of the Decentralization Period).

2. The Decentralization Period

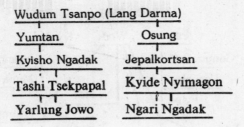

Wudum Tsanpo (Lang Darma)

Yumtan	Osung
Kyisho Ngadak	Jepalkortsan
Tashi Tsekpapal	Kyide Nyimagon
Yarlung Jowo	Ngari Ngadak

A. The Kyisho Ngadak Clan

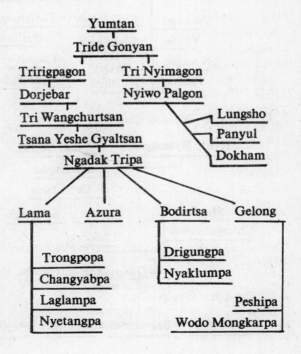

Yumtan

Tride Gonyan

Tririgpagon	Tri Nyimagon
Dorjebar	Nyiwo Palgon

Tri Wangchurtsan

Tsana Yeshe Gyaltsan

Ngadak Tripa

Lungsho
Panyul
Dokham

Lama   Azura   Bodirtsa   Gelong

Trongpopa

Changyabpa

Laglampa

Nyetangpa

Drigungpa

Nyaklumpa

Peshipa

Wodo Mongkarpa

B. The Yarlung Jowo Clan

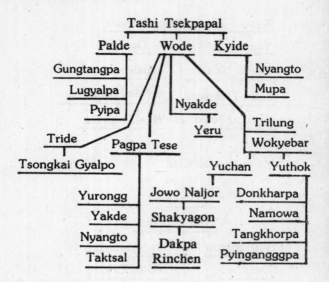

C. The Ngari Ngadak Clan

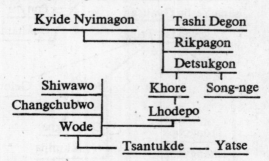

D. The Yatse Gyalpo Clan

Tsanchukde — Bartabmal — Sonamde — Punimal

3. The Sakya Dynasty

Name	Reign	Capital
Pagpa	1235-1280	Sakya*
Rinchen Gyaltsan	1269-1279**	
Dharma Pala	1280-1286	
Rinchen Gyaltsan	1287-1303	
Sangpopal	1304-1323	
Namkhamlek	1324-1342	
Donyo Gyaltsan	1343-1344	
Sonam Gyaltsan	1345-1348	

* Sakya was capital of Tibet during the entire Sakya period.
** He ruled for Pagpa when the latter served in Beijing.

4. The Pagdu Dynasty

Name	Reign	Capital
Changchub Gyaltsan	1354-1371	Sneu-gdong*
Shakya Gyaltsan	1372-1384	
Dakpa Changchub	1385-1390	
Sonam Dakpa	1391-1408	
Dakpa Gyaltsan	1409-1434	
Sang-gye Gyaltsan	1435-1439	
Dakpa Chungne	1440-1468	
Kunka Lekpa	1469-1473	
Rinchen Dorje	1474-1513	
Pyan-nga Ngaki Wangpo	1514-1564	
Ngakwang Tash Dakpa	1565-1578	
Ngakwang Dakpa	1579-1618**	

* It was capital of the 264-year Pagdu Dynasty.
** He was overthrown by Kam Choyang Dorje, who ruled Tibet for a short 24 years.

5. The Dalai Lamas

Generation	Name	Birth	In Position
1st	Gedun Dup	1391	1419-1474
2nd	Gedun Gyatso	1475	1476-1542
3rd	Sonam Gyatso	1543	1544-1588
4th	Yontan Gyatso	158	1603-1616
5th	Lobsang Gyatso	1617	1642-1682
6th	Tsangyang Gyatso	1683	1697-1705
7th	Kalsang Gyatso	1708	1720-1757
8th	Jampal Gyatso	1758	1762-1804
9th	Lungtok Gyatso	1805	1808-1815
10th	Tsultrim Gyatso	1816	1822-1837
11th	Kedup Gyatso	1838	1842-1855
12th	Trinle Gyatso	1856	1860-1875
13th	Thubtan Gyatso	1876	1879-1933
14th	Tenzin Gyatso	1935	1940-

6. The Panchen Lamas

Generation	Name	Birth	Death
1st	Gelek Palsang	1385	1438
2nd	Sonam Choklang	1439	1504
3rd	Ensa Lobsang Dondup	1505	1566
4th	Lobsang Chokyi Gyaltsan	1570	1662
5th	Lobsang Yeshe*	1663	1737
6th	Lobsang Paldan Yeshe	1738	1780
7th	Tenpai Nyima	1782	1853
8th	Tenpai Wangchuk	1854	1882
9th	Chokyi Nyima	1883	1937
10th	Chokyi Gyaltsan	1938	

* The Qing Emperor Kangxi added "Erdeni" to his title, which was adopted by all the following Panchens.

ISBN 7 —80005—072— 6 /Z・012

西 藏 风 土 志

赤烈曲扎 著

旺 多 译

*

新世界出版社出版

北京百万庄路24号

兵器工业出版社印刷厂印刷

中国国际图书贸易总公司发行

（中国国际书店）

北京399信箱

1988年 第一版

编号： （英）17223－279

01050

17 － E － 2352 P